THE OBEDIENCE EXPERIMENTS

A Case Study of Controversy in Social Science

Arthur G. Miller

PRAEGER SPECIAL STUDIES • PRAEGER SCIENTIFIC

New York   •   Westport, Connecticut   •   London

Library of Congress Cataloging-in-Publication Data

Miller, Arthur G., 1940-
  The obedience experiments.

  Bibliography: p.
  Includes index.
  1. Obedience. 2. Obedience—Research.
3. Authority. 4. Authority—Research. I. Title.
HM291.M49 1986   303.3'6   85-25738
ISBN 0-275-92012-7 (alk. paper)

Library of Congress Catalog Card Number: 85-25738
ISBN: 0-275-92012-7

First published in 1986

Praeger Publishers, 521 Fifth Avenue, New York, NY 10175
A division of Greenwood Press, Inc.

Printed in the United States of America

∞™

The paper used in this book complies with the Permanent Paper Standard issued by the National Information Standards Organization (Z39.48-1984).

10 9 8 7 6 5 4 3 2 1

PREFACE

The experiments of Stanley Milgram on obedience to authority have achieved a visibility that is without precedent in the social sciences. Although conducted over twenty years ago, Milgram's research is perhaps the most widely cited program of studies in psychology. The treatment given to these experiments in textbooks is extraordinary in terms of space alone. It is not uncommon for several pages to be allotted to discussion of this research, illustrated with photographs of Milgram's laboratory and of actual episodes of genocide or destructive obedience as these have occurred in our history.

The obedience experiments are not only prominent but controversial. They have been so from their inception. The visibility of the experiments may in fact be a consequence of their controversiality, for they have a sensationalism that is understandably appealing to many writers. It is commonplace now to encounter the terms "classic," "famous," or "controversial" whenever the obedience research is even mentioned. Another term—"notorious"—is also frequently applied, as in this comment by Margaret Eisner (1977) in an article critical of the prevalence of deception in research:

> In discussions of ethical issues, one will find the same pieces of research repeatedly cited as outstanding examples of unethical practices. Included in this category are studies by Milgram . . . which, in spite of their notoriety, do not represent isolated instances of unethical practices, but merely cases in which commonplace experimental practices led to extreme consequences. (P. 233)

My purpose in writing this book has been to assess the impact of the obedience experiments, to gauge the diverse, often impassioned criticisms and debates which have encompassed this research. Why, exactly, are the obedience experiments controversial? What kinds of evidence and argumentation have been used to refute the experiments? Why have so many endorsed Milgram's research with boundless zeal? This book is concerned with questions of this nature. In attempting to answer them, my aim is not primarily to establish the true virtue or infamy of the experiments, but rather to chart the lines of reasoning, the diverse values and priorities, which have been articulated as

v

social science has reacted to the obedience research. Furthermore, I do not consider these reactions to be a closed issue, but rather a process of assimilating research findings into an existing and continuously shifting matrix of conceptual, ethical, and methodological orientations. There are significant disagreements among social scientists regarding the boundaries of ethically acceptable research and the legitimacy of drawing inferences from experimental findings. As will be seen, the obedience research has been at the center of these concerns.

The obedience experiments have been an object of considerable interest to scholars and researchers from a variety of orientations and academic disciplines. In a period of relentless specialization and intellectual provincialism, Milgram's research has been virtually unique in transcending the divisions of academia. Almost everyone in the social sciences and humanities, and in the arts and natural sciences as well, has heard about these experiments and, it seems at times, has expressed an opinion about them. The breadth of interest in Milgram's work has made the task of reviewing its impact a formidable but very meaningful venture.

I have presented in this book a considerable amount of opinion as well as research evidence. The impact of the obedience experiments "exists" in the specific perspectives and analyses that have been articulated by the many researchers and commentators who have been intrigued, and often vexed, by these studies. My choice of citations has been selective, for the number of references to the obedience research—in the *Science Citation Index*, for example—is truly vast. I have used quotations liberally. It is my view that the impact of the obedience experiments has been defined not only in terms of the substance of the reactions but also by their style—their rhetoric, their glowing praise, their veritable disgust. Were I simply to paraphrase the sentiments of others, I think that the essence of the impact of Milgram's research would be diluted. Of course, there is the inevitable risk associated with quoting out of context. I have in fact attempted to provide a context for the many points of view which are, truly, the data base for my analysis. I bear full responsibility for my interpretations and conclusions.

I have not presumed substantial familiarity with the obedience experiments. The early chapters of this book provide a description of the experimental paradigm and basic findings as well as Milgram's interpretation of them. I recommend that the reader become acquainted

with Milgram's own writing (e.g. 1963, 1974) if she or he has not already done so. There are many aspects of his style and perspective
that are difficult to convey but have been, I think, highly significant
in their own right in influencing the many diverse judgments about
his scientific contribution.*

---

*Stanley Milgram died on December 20, 1984, at the age of 51.

CONTENTS

1

INTRODUCTION TO MILGRAM'S RESEARCH ON OBEDIENCE

This article describes a procedure for the study of destructive obedience in the laboratory. It consists of ordering a naive S to administer increasingly more severe punishment to a victim in the context of a learning experiment.

—Stanley Milgram, in the abstract to his 1963 article, "Behavioral Study of Obedience."

In a 1963 issue of the *Journal of Abnormal and Social Psychology*, an article appeared that was destined to have a profound impact on conceptions of human nature.[1] It eventually was to stimulate an extraordinarily large, often impassioned, and diverse array of reactions —not only concerning the topic of the research itself but, in a larger sense, about the role of social science in informing us about ourselves. The writer was a new, unheralded assistant professor at Yale University.[2] The article itself was short—a mere eight pages—with the brief title, "Behavioral Study of Obedience."

This publication was the first announcement of a program of research which has become perhaps the most widely cited and provocative set of experiments in social science. Two of the major journal articles (Milgram, 1963, 1965b) have been reprinted in dozens of anthologies. The research has been the focus of a televised drama (*The Tenth Level*), a CBS *60 Minutes* feature, articles in *Harper's* (Milgram, 1973), *Esquire* (Meyer, 1970), an interview in *Psychology Today* (Tavris, 1974), and a forum on political authority with John Dean (Muson, 1978). Stanley Milgram's 1974 book, *Obedience to Authority*, which contains a complete description of the entire set of

1

experiments, has been translated into several foreign languages. Milgram ranked ninth in a 1978 tabulation of the 200 most frequently cited scholars in social psychology texts (Perlman and Lipsey, 1978), and seventh in a 1984 updating of this ranking (Perlman, 1984), and the obedience research has been cited as one of the most significant contributions to social psychology according to a survey of editors of the leading research journals in this field (Diamond and Morton, 1978).[3] In a tabulation of citations in introductory psychology texts, Perlman (1980) noted that Milgram ranked twelfth among all psychologists, just behind Carl Jung and higher than William James, John B. Watson, Abraham Maslow, or Leon Festinger. To balance the account, the obedience research has also been vilified as being ethically unacceptable (Baumrind, 1985), methodologically flawed (Orne and Holland, 1968), and theoretically uninterpretable (Marcus, 1974).

Why are these experiments so unique? Why have they aroused intense controversy, almost from their inception? How is it that this work retains a freshness, a quality of lasting significance that invariably evokes discussion among students in a host of disciplines? What has extended the impact of these experiments beyond the usual confines of academic archives? In this book, we will attempt to answer these questions. In pursuing them, we will learn not only about obedience to authority but also about the values and objectives of social science in general. The obedience experiments have raised fundamental issues concerning our search for self-understanding, issues pertaining to the proper boundaries or limitations of scientific inquiry. The history of scientific "breakthroughs"—whether one speaks of the discovery of germs, of anesthesia, of a spherical earth, or of nuclear weapons—is replete with controversy, with antagonism directed at the discoverer. This is clearly true regarding the obedience experiments. The heated reactions to Milgram's work (and to Milgram himself) are of importance in their own right and will be a major focus in the chapters to follow. It seems appropriate, however, to begin at the beginning.

A BEHAVIORAL STUDY OF OBEDIENCE—THE 1963 ARTICLE

A brief note on the chronology of the obedience experiments is appropriate at the outset. Milgram conducted the research—actually a very extensive set of experiments involving approximately 1,000 subjects—at Yale University over a three-year period (1960-63). This research program was described, in brief, in a 1965 article by Milgram in *Human Relations*, and in considerable detail in his 1974 book, *Obedience to Authority*.

The first published account of the research, however, was in a 1963 article, "Behavioral Study of Obedience," in the *Journal of Abnormal and Social Psychology*. It is important to describe this first publication in detail for several reasons. First, this article presented the basic paradigm or experimental setting for the experimental analysis of obedience.[4] All of the other experiments, described in subsequent publications, were variations on this basic laboratory arrangement. As we shall see, Milgram's primary intent was to achieve an understanding of the obedience phenomenon by varying a host of relevant parameters; thus, the entire set of experiments was crucial to his purposes. However, the impact of the first publication, the 1963 article, was of such staggering proportions, that it may have, to an extent, defeated Milgram's primary objectives. Once the findings of the 1963 article became known, they stimulated a remarkable tide of reaction, of praise as well as recrimination. Hence, though it constituted but one piece of a complex and much larger puzzle, it was the 1963 publication that became fixed in the mind of the academic community (and other audiences as well) as *the* Milgram experiment.

In considering the 1963 obedience article, another point should be emphasized. The *form* or *style* of a research article can be as influential as matters of substance. Although Milgram's *findings* might at first be viewed as self-evident—few would deny that the data were indeed startling—it was the manner in which Milgram spoke to his observations, the context into which he placed the problem of obedience, and the connotations which were at least implied in his interpretations that made this a very unusual and provocative piece of scholarship.

The Context of Obedience

Milgram's opening sentence places the problem of obedience in a social-psychological context, suggesting that it is a basic feature of human interaction:

> Obedience is as basic an element in the structure of social life as one can point to. Some system of authority is a requirement of all communal living, and it is only the man dwelling in isolation who is not forced to respond, through defiance or submission, to the commands of others. (P. 371)

This perspective in effect "normalizes" obedience, giving it a far less sinister meaning than might be inferred from the very next passage:

> Obedience, as a determinant of behavior, is of particular relevance to our time. It has been reliably established that from 1933-45 millions of innocent persons were systematically slaughtered on command. Gas chambers were built, death camps were guarded, daily quotas of corpses were produced with the same efficiency as the manufacture of appliances. These inhumane policies may have originated in the mind of a single person, but they could only be carried out on a massive scale if a very large number of persons obeyed orders. (P. 371)

Here one sees in Milgram's very first paragraph the association between his experiments and the extermination of Jews and others by the Nazis. Thus, Milgram created an initially unlikely linkage between a ubiquitous feature of social organization on the one hand, and the most horrendous episode of human destructiveness on the other. We shall return frequently to this matter, for it is crucial to an understanding of the impact of the experiments. Milgram's decision to make an explicit reference to the Holocaust at the very outset of his work was clearly to have momentous consequences. From this perspective, it was all too easy to underplay his essentially neutral position on the morality of obedience: "It must not be thought all obedience entails acts of aggression against others. . . . Obedience may be ennobling and educative and refer to acts of charity and kindness, as well as to destruction" (p. 371). With barely a page of introductory material and with a passing reference to previous research on issues related to obedience, such as hypnosis, authoritarianism, and social power, Milgram introduced the general procedure of the research.

The Paradigm of the Obedience Experiments

The 1963 article, "Behavioral Study of Obedience," was as much a methodological presentation as it was a substantive analysis. It described a situational arrangement in a laboratory and how 40 male research subjects behaved in that setting. There were no manipulated variables, no experimental conditions, no theoretically derived hypotheses, and no predictions. Yet, this *was* an experiment in the classic manner, for the research was directed at a question for which there was no available answer: What will people do when ordered by an experimenter to impose electric shocks, in increasing intensities, upon another person?

The experiment was conducted at Yale University. The subjects, recruited by newspaper advertisement and mail solicitation, were 40 men, of varying age (20 to 50) and socioeconomic circumstances (postal clerks, engineers, laborers, high school teachers, etc.). They received $4.50 for their participation. The stated purpose of the study was to examine the effects of punishment on learning. The experimenter went through a list of unknowns regarding punishment and learning, such as the effect of the *amount* of punishment, the *source* of punishment (an older or younger person), and so on. Thus, a highly credible rationale for the ensuing study was presented, one that would justify the subsequent use of electric shocks.

Three individuals participated in the experiment: The experimenter, played by a 31-year-old high school teacher; the learner (or victim), played by a 47-year-old accountant; and the teacher, always destined, by a fixed draw, to be played by the true subject. The role titles of "teacher" and "learner" were used throughout the session. After a short briefing by the experimenter and the role assignments, the learner was placed in an electric chair apparatus, and an elaborate description was given regarding the nature of the task to be learned and the punishment delivery system.

The teacher was instructed to read a series of word pairs to the learner and then to read the first word of a pair and four possible associations. The learner was to indicate which of the four associations had in fact been paired with the first word. The response alternatives consisted of four numbered switches, each of which would light up a corresponding indicator light on the top of the shock generator in front of the teacher. The instructions authorized the teacher to punish the learner for each error of recall by pressing a lever on a shock generator. The teacher thus had the task of (1) administering the word-pair test, (2) deciding whether the response was correct or in error, and (3) administering a punishment for each error. The teacher was also required to announce over an intercom the outcome of each trial, the correct answer if an error had been made, and the amount of shock voltage that would be momentarily forthcoming. The teacher was thus a very busy individual, a factor which, Milgram was later to argue, was an important contributor to his behavior.

The shock generator (see Figure 1.1) consisted of a panel with 30 levers, each accompanying a designated voltage ranging from 15 to 450 volts. Various switches, dials, indicator lights, and meters gave a highly authentic appearance to the generator.[5] A particularly impor-

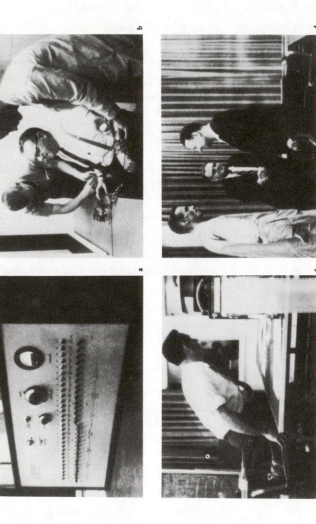

Figure 1.1. Milgram's study of obedience. (a) The shock generator. (b) The teacher watches the learner being strapped into place. (c) An independent subject refuses to continue. (d) After an obedient subject learns he has not really hurt the learner, the two are introduced. The teacher has difficulty looking directly at the learner.

Source: Copyright © 1965 to Stanley Milgram from the film "Obedience," distributed by New York University Film Library. Reprinted by permission.

tant feature (which was later to become a point of controversy) was the verbal labels engraved at various intervals: Slight Shock, Moderate Shock; Strong Shock; Very Strong Shock; Intense Shock; Extreme Intensity Shock; Danger: Severe Shock. The last two shock levers, 435 volts and 450 volts, were marked **XXX**. Every effort was thus made to suggest to subjects that very powerful shocks could be delivered using this formidable apparatus. To convince subjects of the realistic punishment that could be administered, each teacher received a sample shock—more than a tingle—which was described as being 45 volts, that is, position 3 on the generator. Milgram reported that no subject suspected the simulated aspect of the generator.

As will be shown later, considerable controversy arose regarding the precise amount of harm that subjects perceived could be inflicted in this paradigm. It thus is important to note another component of Milgram's procedure. While being strapped into place and having the electrodes attached to his arm, the learner was instructed to inquire about the prospect of being harmed. The experimenter's standard response was, "Although the shocks can be extremely painful, they cause no permanent tissue damage" (p. 373).

The delivery of punishment thus occurred in the context of an interaction between the experimenter (authority), the teacher, and the learner. Two features of this procedure should be emphasized, for they were part of the standard paradigm. First, the teacher was required to increase the voltage level by one switch (15 volts) for each error made by the learner. (On 25 percent of the trials the learner made the "correct" response, to lend a note of credibility to his performance.) Second, in response to questions or hesitation on the part of the teacher, the experimenter answered with one of four increasingly strident prods, to the point that the teacher should continue:

Prod 1—Please continue, or Please go on.
Prod 2—The experiment requires that you continue.
Prod 3—It is absolutely essential that you continue.
Prod 4—You have no other choice, you must go on. (P. 374)

These were made in the sequence shown above, as necessitated by individual reactions on the part of subjects in the teacher role. If the subject refused to continue after Prod Four, the experiment was terminated. There were various inquiries from subjects which received standardized replies, such as a reassurance that no permanent tissue damage would occur, or the statement that "whether the learner likes it or not, you must go on until he has learned all the word pairs correctly" (p. 374), or that the experimenter would assume responsibility for the learner's welfare.

In the experiment described in the 1963 publication, the physical setting involved the teacher and learner in adjacent rooms, with the experimenter in the same room as the teacher. If the subject (teacher) continued to shock the learner to the 300-volt level (the twentieth lever), feedback from the learner was supplied by his pounding on the wall. This was clearly audible to the teacher. After this point, the learner's responses no longer appeared on the indicator light. This non-response was, according to the experimenter, to be treated as an error, with the shock series being continued as it had been to this point.

A Comment on the "Prods"

The prods used by the experimenter can justifiably be regarded as one of the most central methodological elements in this paradigm. They constitute the operationalization of authority. While any experimenter would be expected to encourage his or her subject to continue, whatever the task or behavior might be, Milgram's experiment is unique in using verbal commands which blatantly contradict the subject's wishes. The element of authority seems to occur most vividly at Prod Three—*It is absolutely essential that you continue*. This assertion is qualitatively more emphatic than the two earlier prods (*Please continue. . . . The experiment requires that you continue*). The final prod—*You have no other choice, you must go on*—is, factually, a clear falsehood. These last two prods, examined out of context, would seem to detract from the credibility of the experiment. The fact that such verbal utterances, without clear substantive meaning, appear to have strongly influenced subjects to shock (in their own minds) a protesting individual is, of course, one of the most intriguing findings of the study.[6] As we will see, however, not every analyst of the obedience research has endorsed this view of what transpired in Milgram's laboratory.

Responses to Authority

The primary measure was the maximum shock administered to the learner, ranging, in principle, from 0 to 450 volts (that is, from pressing no lever to pressing the thirtieth lever). Although individual differences in following orders were clearly evident (not as much in this first experiment as in later variations), Milgram's orientation always focused upon the *ultimate* behavior:

A subject who breaks off the experiment at any point prior to administering the thirtieth shock level is termed a *defiant* subject. One who complies with experimental commands fully, and proceeds to administer all shock levels commanded, is termed an *obedient* subject. (P. 374)

This categorical designation—obedience versus defiance—has an appealing simplicity, and facilitates a comparison of different procedural variations on the subjects' performance. However, there is the suggestion in such a dichotomy that all acts of defiance are similar, whether occurring at the 30-volt or 435-volt level. There is also the fact that there were noticeable individual differences in a number of the experiments. This issue will be considered in later chapters. It is an important issue, if for no other reason than that people tend to *believe* that individual personality factors are the crucial determinants of how far people will go in Milgram's paradigm.

The 65 Percent Obedience Result

Forty subjects participated in the experiment described in the 1963 publication. Of these, 26 pressed the 450-volt switch. This result —an obedience rate of 65 percent—is the major finding of the study. It has become, certainly, the best-known result of the entire obedience research project, despite the fact that in a number of Milgram's experiments the obedience rate dropped to zero. Thus, the 65 percent obedience result has become, in effect, a baseline finding against which other findings, including people's intuitive perceptions (see Chapter Two), are compared.

It is interesting to speculate what the consequences might have been had the first published account emphasized the programmatic nature of the obedience research project. Milgram, himself, was later to express some reservations concerning the manner in which his findings were assimilated by the public (Milgram, 1979—preface to French edition). Yet, given that the basic data from all of the experiments were available prior to the 1963 article, it was Milgram's decision to write as the initial presentation an article which featured the striking 65 percent obedience result. It is this finding, that is, of a startling, unexpected majority obeying to the maximum, that people tend to remember, above anything else, about the obedience research.

Table 1.1 presents the results as displayed in the 1963 publication. This was the format Milgram used to present the results of all of the experiments in the series. It represents an analogue of the shock generator, with the data entries showing the number of individual

Table 1.1. Distribution of Breakoff Points

Verbal designation and voltage indication	Number of subjects for whom this was maximum shock
Slight Shock	
15	0
30	0
45	0
60	0
Moderate Shock	
75	0
90	0
105	0
120	0
Strong Shock	
135	0
150	0
165	0
180	0
Very Strong Shock	
195	0
210	0
225	0
240	0
Intense Shock	
255	0
270	0
285	0
300	5
Extreme Intensity Shock	
315	4
330	2
345	1
360	1
Danger: Severe Shock	
375	1
390	0
405	0
420	0
XXX	
435	0
450	26

Source: From Milgram, S., Copyright © 1963 by the American Psychological Association. Reprinted by permission.

subjects who proceeded to various stages in the sequence of shock switches. Thus, 300 volts was the lowest point at which subjects refused to continue—Recall that this was the point at which the learner pounded on the wall in protest. In this first experiment, of course, the key entry is the "bottom line"—26 subjects at the 450-volt level.

Arousal and Tension

In addition to the subjects' willingness to shock the learner, expressions of emotional conflict and tension were an important result, with extremely significant consequences in terms of the reception given to the obedience experiments by the academic community. Had Milgram simply reported, in the abstract, the presence of tension or agitation in many of the subjects in their role as teacher, the reaction of readers might have been more restrained. Consider, however, the manner in which Milgram spoke to the arousal seen in his laboratory:

> In a large number of cases the degree of tension reached extremes that are rarely seen in sociopsychological laboratory studies. Subjects were observed to sweat, tremble, stutter, bite their lips, groan, and dig their fingernails into their flesh. These were characteristic rather than exceptional responses to the experiment. . . . On one occasion we observed a seizure so violently convulsive that it was necessary to call a halt to the experiment. . . .

> After the maximum shocks had been delivered . . . many obedient subjects heaved sighs of relief, mopped their brows, rubbed their fingers over their eyes, or nervously fumbled cigarettes. . . .

> At one point he pushed his fist into his forehead and muttered: "Oh God, let's stop it." And yet he continued to respond to every word of the experimenter, and obeyed to the end. (Pp. 375-377)

Milgram's narrative accounts of the stress experienced by his subjects are vivid, some might say even gruesome. There is no attempt to "go easy" on the reader. The most chilling terms are used. Here, for example, is a passage that has been quoted in numerous sources (such as textbooks), where the obedience research is described: "I observed a mature and initially poised businessman enter the laboratory smiling and confident. Within 20 minutes he was reduced to a twitching, stuttering wreck, who was rapidly approaching a point of nervous collapse" (p. 377).

There is little doubt that this depiction of human conflict and agony is fascinating for many readers. Milgram was highly adept at creating images of the stress and torment experienced by many of his subjects. The writing style itself added a kind of "clinical" perspective to what otherwise might have been a more traditional social-psychological research report. There clearly was nothing traditional about this 1963 article.

However, the most significant and lasting consequence of the tension and arousal reported by Milgram was a concern with the *ethics* of the obedience experiments. As will be discussed in Chapter Five, the 1963 obedience article, more than any other piece of research in social science, may have stimulated a renaissance of concern with research ethics, specifically the right of an experimenter to subject human beings to the kind of strain and conflict noted above.

The initial reaction was an essay by Diana Baumrind published in a 1964 issue of the *American Psychologist*. The large readership of this journal was thus sensitized to a number of problematic aspects regarding the ethics of Milgram's paradigm. Baumrind's extremely impassioned arguments against the obedience study may have had the unintended effect of alerting thousands of psychologists (as well as other social scientists, graduate students, and professionals) to the very existence of the study. Milgram's sharp rebuttal appeared five months later in the same journal. The extensive concern with a variety of ethical issues in social research that occurred in the decade of the 1970s and continues unabated to the present was, without question, stimulated by the Baumrind-Milgram debate, an interchange which is cited in virtually every serious discussion of ethical issues in human research.

The symptoms of tension and conflict displayed by Milgram's subjects also have substantive implications regarding the nature of obedience to authority. Many subjects appeared willing to obey the experimenter despite having strong misgivings about doing so. That is, there was little obvious correlation between a subject's feelings about what he was doing and what he in fact did: "One might suppose that a subject would simply break off or continue as his conscience dictated. Yet, this is very far from what happened" (p. 377).

This disjunction between a subject's emotional reaction and his or her behavior was counterintuitive. It spoke to the extraordinary power of authority. Because the subjects were a sample of presumably adjusted individuals, the high obedience rate accompanied by strong indications of negative emotion suggested that "good people" could be induced to perform immoral actions against a protesting victim simply because of the force of the authority represented by the experimenter. Thus, it was not that naturally sadistic types somehow found their way into a research project which gave them license to inflict pain, but rather it was the structure of the context itself which seemed capable of inducing such acts in most people. Referring to the Holocaust, Milgram addressed the situational focus that was to be a continuous feature of his analysis: "Facts of recent history and observation in daily life suggest that for many persons obedience may be a deeply ingrained behavior tendency, indeed, a prepotent impulse overriding training in ethics, sympathy, and moral conduct" (p. 371).

WHAT DO PEOPLE EXPECT TO OCCUR IN THE MILGRAM PARADIGM?

Fourteen Yale psychology majors, provided with a detailed description of the obedience setting, were asked to predict how 100 hypothetical subjects would perform. The average estimate of maximum obedience (that is, to the 450-volt level) was 1.2 percent—a dramatic underestimation of the 65 percent figure obtained by Milgram in the actual experiment.

The problem of what people expect to occur in this paradigm is an interesting one. The marked underestimation noted above suggests that people have naive, erroneous intuitions about such behavior. The informational value of the obedience research itself is often claimed by contrasting the "expected" rate of obedience with what actually occurred. But why do people underestimate obedience to authority? And, what kind of impressions do observers form about people who obey or defy the experimenter? These questions, of interest in their own right, are fundamental to an understanding of the general impact of the obedience research. There are also a number of research articles and commentaries addressing these issues. We shall consider them further in Chapter Two.

MILGRAM'S INTERPRETATION OF HIS FINDINGS—1963

Milgram's theoretical interpretation is found in two main sources, one being the "discussion" section of the 1963 article (and similar accounts given in subsequent journal articles), the other located in the closing chapters of his 1974 book. These two presentations are quite different. We will note here some central features of his earlier analysis, and consider more thoroughly his 1974 conceptualization in Chapter Eight.

As stated earlier, Milgram opened his first article with a brief statement on the problem of obedience and proceeded directly to a description of his procedure and findings. There was no concise theoretical formulation or hypothesis stated in the introduction to his article. After describing his results, Milgram offered a diverse set of perspectives on the meaning of his data. There was no mention of personality dynamics that might be operative in his paradigm. Rather, his approach was strictly contextual and phenomenological. Milgram isolated a variety of features of the setting, the roles involved, the perceptions likely to be generated, and the conflicting sources of information present in the experiment.

One theme emphasized by Milgram is the *legitimacy* of the entire enterprise. The university setting, the scientific importance of the problem being studied (punishment and learning), and the apparent competence of the personnel conducting the research all serve to define what occurs in the experiment as proper, as reasonable and acceptable. Initially, at least, the instructions regarding possible harm to the learner are reassuring. As we will note later, the issue of legitimacy was to be examined in subsequent research.

Another element is the subject's commitment or sense of obligation to the experimenter. This perception is perhaps more germane at the beginning of the subject's participation, but Milgram suggests that there is a norm which dictates that people complete a task for which they have volunteered. Subjects are also likely to see the learner, who (in their view) has also been randomly assigned to his role, as operating under similar circumstances.

In addition to the relatively clearly defined factors of legitimacy and commitment, there is presumably a measure of ambiguity. Subjects are being cast into a situation which they have never encountered. They are thus vulnerable to influences of all kinds, and, of course, they in fact receive a very pointed and unambiguous directive from the experimenter, namely to shock the learner. But they also receive, ultimately, clear signals from the learner. Here, Milgram points to the idea of the no-win conflict situation faced by the subject: "The subject is placed in a position in which he must respond to the competing demands of two persons: the experimenter and the victim. The conflict must be resolved by meeting the demands of one or the other; satisfaction of the victim and the experimenter are mutually exclusive" (p. 378).

This is the central psychological dynamic—the subject's wish (1) not to harm the learner and (2) not to disobey a legitimate authority. The *rapidity* with which events occur in the experiment, and the complexity of the subject's task are other relevant contextual factors.

Although not mentioned in the 1963 paper, another important feature is the sequential nature of the subject's responses—one shock level higher for each error made by the learner. The subject becomes involved in an escalation of harm, the nature of which is likely to be totally unforeseen at the start of the experiment.

Thus, it is a combination of features which defines the experimental setting and, according to Milgram, works toward the eventual outcome of extreme obedience. Because Milgram did not articulate a formal theory nor state precise hypotheses or predictions, it is obviously difficult to evaluate his theoretical interpretation. But it is nevertheless important to make such an assessment. We will be in a better position to do so after considering the wealth of additional research and critical commentary that soon was to follow the 1963 obedience article. At this point, however, it is appropriate to go back to the beginning, and to trace the important lines of research and thinking which led to the undertaking of the obedience research.

THE ORIGINS OF THE OBEDIENCE EXPERIMENTS

It is customary to inquire about the origins of works of science (or art) which ultimately achieve celebrity status. One examines previous research and the life circumstances of the scientist in order to learn what inspired the work and helped to give it its essential form. Milgram's work was not, of course, the groundbreaking of interest in social pressure. An early study by Jerome Frank (1944), for example, had demonstrated the unexpected power of the experimenter to induce subjects to eat huge quantities of soda crackers. Frank, in an imaginative set of studies, varied the conditions (for example, using force versus persuasion) and observed powerful effects on his subjects' resistance to eating the crackers. Milgram was aware of an impressive analysis of social power by French and Raven (1959). These investigators conceptualized authority into various dimensions, such as legitimacy, reward power, coercive power, expert power, and so on, and performed laboratory experiments to examine the relative impact of different bases of social influence (see French, Morrison, and Levinger, 1960). The tasks involved were relatively benign, such as sorting computer cards or making paper cutouts. Perhaps the earliest but extremely consequential study of social influence was that of Muzafer Sherif, on the "autokinetic phenomenon" (1936). Sherif demonstrated powerful effects of the opinions of others on the judgments made by individuals regarding the apparent motion of a point of light in a darkened laboratory. The magnitude and perseverance of the influence shown in Sherif's experiments serve to establish his research, even to this day, as a classic in the history of social psychology. Although it involved considerable deception, Sherif's experiment used a relatively innocuous response, namely, making a verbal judgment regarding the movement of a dot of light.

All of the works noted above (and others as well, such as Max Weber's sociological analysis of authority) were well known to Milgram (see 1961b). However, the obedience experiments reflect most directly Milgram's close association with the eminent social psychologist, Solomon Asch. Asch's research on conformity, in which subjects were shown to make glaring errors on an unambiguous line-estimation problem as a result of the pressure exerted by the judgments of other individuals, had attained substantial visibility both within and outside of academic circles. Although Asch had distinguished himself with contributions in other areas—for example, his pioneering analysis of personality impression formation (1946)—his experimental investigation of group pressure became an almost immediate classic. It was featured in a 1955 issue of *Scientific American* and soon was to appear in countless anthologies and textbooks, as it does to the present time.

Milgram was Asch's teaching assistant when Asch visited Harvard in 1958, and worked for him at the Institute for Advanced Study in Princeton in 1959 and 1960 (Evans, 1980). Milgram has acknowledged that Asch was his most important intellectual influence, that he was "certainly the most impressive social psychologist I have known" (Tavris, 1974, p. 77).

Not surprisingly, then, the obedience experiments were to bear, in certain respects, a striking resemblance to Asch's studies of conformity. Not only was the technological approach or design of the research similar—for example, the idea of using a basic paradigm with numerous parametric variations—but if one examines Asch's 1956 monograph on conformity, one will notice similarities in the manner in which Milgram presents his data and conceptualizes his findings. Both investigators, for instance, tended to minimize extended theoretical derivations and hypotheses, and to frame their interpretations in terms of an extensive listing of factors which could plausibly be critical determinants of their findings.

While it would be presumptuous to assert that Milgram's personal identification with the Jewish people was a major factor in the development of the obedience research, it is not an issue to be totally dismissed. In principle, all people may share an outrage at the atrocities of Nazi Germany and wish to understand the causes of the Holocaust, but it is undeniable that Jews have a very heightened sensitivity in this regard. Milgram spoke to this issue: "The laboratory paradigm merely gave scientific expression to a more general concern about authority, a concern forced upon members of my generation, in particular upon Jews such as myself, by the atrocities of World War II" (1977a, p. 92). In this context, Raven and Rubin (1983, p. 421) have noted the temporal proximity of Milgram's experiments to the trial of Adolf Eichmann in Jerusalem in 1961.

It is difficult, of course, to gauge in retrospect the precise linkages between the obedience research and the Holocaust. As noted earlier, Milgram made this reference at the very opening of his first publication; thus it was not simply a stance taken once the research had become popular. It should be noted, more generally, that social psychology as a discipline was profoundly affected by the events of World War II. In writing about the history of social psychology, Jones (1985) notes the importance of the social and political zeitgeist:

> The study of attitude change received enormous impetus from concerns during the Second World War with propaganda, military morale, and the potential integration of ethnic minorities into established military units. Authoritarian personality research obviously grew out of the Nazi experience as did, in a quite different way, Milgram's later research on obedience. (P. 55)

Because the association between the Holocaust and the obedience experiments is so compelling to many students of this research, the fact that Milgram himself acknowledged this factor as motivating his original interest should be recognized. It should also be pointed out that Milgram's position could be viewed as an important source of bias in the subsequent interpretation of his findings. We shall consider this issue in more detail in subsequent chapters.

THE DERIVATION OF THE OBEDIENCE RESEARCH
FROM ASCH'S CONFORMITY PARADIGM

As noted, Milgram worked with Asch during the latter phase of his graduate training. His doctoral dissertation involved a cross-cultural investigation of conformity in Norway and France (Milgram, 1961a). Milgram was thus very familiar with Asch's approach to the experimental analysis of social influence. Not unexpectedly, perhaps, there

was a close historical relationship between Asch's conformity procedure and the paradigm developed by Milgram to investigate obedience.

Milgram states that the feature of the Asch paradigm with which
he was initially most concerned was the task itself, that is, the line-
estimation problem in which the subject was required to match a test
line to one of three comparison lines.[7] Milgram was interested in
modifying the nature of this task in order to make the experiment
more humanly significant:

> It seemed to me that if, instead of having a group exerting pressure on
> judgments about lines, the group could somehow induce something more
> significant from the person, then that might be a step in giving a greater
> face significance to the behavior induced by the group. Could a group, I
> asked myself, induce a person to act with severity against another per-
> son? (Evans, 1980, p. 188)

Milgram envisioned a replication of the Asch procedure in which
each of a group of subjects would have a shock generator. Instead of
estimating the lengths of lines, each subject, in turn, would administer
a shock to another person (for a "good" reason, such as for erring on
a problem). The group (accomplices of the experimenter) would, by
prearrangement, administer increasingly severe shocks. The primary
question would be the degree to which the real subject would conform to the group.

It should be noted here that an important feature of the Asch
paradigm was the control condition, in which subjects were administered the line-estimation task without the preceding judgments of
other (apparent) subjects. This had shown that subjects made virtually
no errors in the absence of group pressure. In Milgram's hypothetical
modification, however, the possibility of a control condition was not
immediately apparent, because it was not obvious what the inducement would be for a solitary individual to administer shocks in increasing intensities to another person. (In the Asch technique, the
inducement for the control subjects was simply the desire to perform
the line judgment task correctly.)

Milgram then expressed that specific moment in which the idea
of studying obedience seemed to emerge from his previous concern
with conformity:

> What would be the force that would get him to increase the shocks?
> And then the thought occurred that the experimenter would have to
> tell him to give higher and higher shocks. Just how far will a person go
> when an experimenter instructs him to give increasingly severe shocks?

Immediately I knew that that was the problem I would investigate. It was a very excited moment for me, because I realized that although it was a very simple question, it would admit itself to measurement, precise investigation. One could see the variables to be studied, with dependent measure being how far a person would go in administering shocks. (Evans, 1980, p. 189)

2

INTUITIVE ACCOUNTS OF OBEDIENCE: THE ROLE OF BELIEFS AND EXPECTATIONS

As 'intuitive' psychologists, we seem too often to be nativists, or proponents of individual differences, and too seldom S-R behaviorists. We too readily infer broad personal dispositions and expect consistency in behavior or outcomes across widely disparate situations and contexts. We jump to hasty conclusions upon witnessing the behavior of our peers, overlooking the impact of relevant environmental forces and constraints.

—Lee Ross and Craig Anderson (1982)

The reactions elicited by any program of research depend substantially on the reader's answer to this question: "What do I know, now that I have read this study, that I did not know before?" Of course, a common-sense finding can, in principle, be of considerable value, just as a bizarre result can be meaningless. But it is a fact of academic life that researchers want their results to be viewed as informative and, if possible, counterintuitive. The extreme popularity of research on cognitive dissonance theory in the 1960s and 1970s, for example, was undoubtedly sustained by the continuous derivation of nonintuitive predictions and the abundance of surprising findings.[1] On this matter of common sense or intuition, the obedience experiments constitute evidence of the most dramatic kind. Nobody expected what in fact occurred.

It is important to examine how people intuitively think about the obedience experiments, to inquire about their perceptions of the experiment, their impressions of the kind of people who obey or defy the experimenter, their beliefs about their own likely performance in this paradigm. If the obedience research is in fact the remarkably challenging and substantively vital work that many claim it to be, it is important to discover precisely what this research is informing us about—what it is teaching us that is *new*, that differs from our "natural" way of considering such things. To accomplish this understanding, it is necessary to subject the question of intuitive accounts of obedience to careful analysis. This will also set the stage for our later treatment of several of the major controversies which came to surround the obedience research, controversies which are based, fundamentally, on how Milgram's research has been perceived by other social scientists.

In his 1974 book, *Obedience to Authority: An Experimental View*, Milgram devotes an early chapter to the issue of "expected behavior." He treats the matter in an empirical rather than strictly speculative manner:

> The respondents consist of an audience that has come to hear a lecture on the topic of obedience to authority. The experiment is described in detail without, however, disclosing the results in any way. The audience is provided with a schematic diagram of the shock generator, showing verbal and voltage designations. Each respondent is asked to reflect on the experiment, then privately to record how he himself would perform in it. (P. 27)

Three groups were examined—39 psychiatrists at the Yale University School of Medicine, 31 college students, and 40 middle-class adults. The average shock levels which these groups predicted as their own maximum, out of a possible 30, were 8.2, 9.4, and 9.2, respectively. This contrasts with 27.0, the actually observed result in Experiment 1, described in Chapter One. *Every individual in these groups indicated that he or she would break off prior to the 450-volt level,* that is, that they would at some point defy the experimenter.

People were also asked to predict how others would behave. Groups of psychiatrists, graduate students, faculty, and middle-class adults were asked how far each of "one hundred Americans of diverse ages and occupations" would go on the shock generator. The psychiatrists predicted, on average, that less than 50 percent would still be obedient at the tenth level (150 volts), that less than 4 percent would reach the twentieth level, and that less than .1 percent would administer the maximum shock level. These predictions, which were confirmed in the judgments of the other groups, contrast sharply with the figure of 65 percent which represented the number of fully obedient subjects in the first experiment.

WHY DO PEOPLE UNDERESTIMATE OBEDIENCE?

Milgram's interpretation of the pronounced underestimation of obedience is that people are basing their predictions on the assumption that it is the *personality* of the individual which determines his or her response to the experimenter's commands: "They focus on the character of the autonomous individual rather than on the situation in which he finds himself. With this view, they are likely to expect few subjects to go along with the experimenter's orders" (p. 31). People thus presume that the vast majority of subjects are kind and empathic, and that these dispositions will prevail, that the subject will resolve the conflict presented in this experiment in favor of the victim. Clearly people seem, in their estimations, to agree that defying the experimenter is the "right thing to do." On the assumption that most people, including themselves, are good, that is, are inclined to do the right thing, it is logical to predict defiance and low shock levels. But this kind of answer begs another question. Why do people think about the obedience situation this way? Why are they not immediately oriented to the power of the experimenter and to the vulnerability of the subject once placed in the role of "teacher?"

The Fundamental Attribution Error

Developments in the area of social perception and cognition bear on this important issue. Lee Ross (1977), in a highly influential analysis, has discussed the general tendency for people to explain the actions of others in personal rather than situational terms. It may involve more than a mere preference. Ross defines this tendency in terms of a *bias* to perceive the actions of others as reflecting personal or characterological traits, even when there are powerful situational forces operating on the individual.

There are several factors contributing to this bias, or fundamental attribution error, as Ross terms it. One issue concerns the salience of the actor as the observer's focus of attention. Research on these matters indicates that people often attribute causal significance to those aspects in the social field to which they are particularly attentive (Taylor and Fiske, 1978). In the Milgram paradigm, as one views the general arrangement, the person in the teacher role is a particularly dominant image. The major question, at all times, is: What is he or she going to do? It is thus difficult to avoid investing this person with a primary causal role in terms of what ultimately transpires. This is not to say that the experimenter's prods or the learner's protests are invisible, but rather to emphasize the salient position occupied by the teacher.

Jones has suggested that the inclination to see the actions of others as reflecting personality traits may also result from our general need to predict their behavior, to anticipate what others will do (Jones and Nisbett, 1971; Jones, 1979). Thus, attributing dispositional qualities to others may serve as a kind of illusion of control. Even if we are not sure what they in fact are like—and even if there are no traits that in fact describe people accurately in all circumstances—it makes sense, from a functional point of view, to *believe* that what people do is a reflection of their "inner nature." Jellison and Green (1981) have discussed this in terms of our adherence to a cultural "norm of internality," that in addition to covert or perceptual factors, there are external or public inducements to make internal (that is, personal) attributions. Holding others "responsible" for their actions, good or bad, obviously is one such inducement.

Research in the field of attribution theory testifies to the prevalence of the observer bias noted above. Experiments on the problem of "attitude attribution," for example, have shown that observers will infer that an essay writer believes in the position of his or her essay (such as a "pro" statement on the issue of abortion) *even when that position has been randomly assigned to the writer by an experimenter* (see, Jones, 1979; Miller and Rorer, 1982). In these studies, the essay itself bears no necessary relationship to the true attitude of the writer, yet observers appear to think otherwise. Making an analogy to the obedience paradigm, one might say that the subjects fail to appreciate the implications of the experimenter's "orders" to compose an essay on a particular side of an issue, and instead tend to perceive the writer as responsible—"you wrote it, you must believe it."

Ross, Amabile, and Steinmetz (1977) have also examined the observer bias phenomenon in a structured role context. They asked two subjects to play a quiz game. One subject was assigned, by random draw, to be the questioner, and to compose ten questions to which he or she knew the answer, which would be difficult but not impossible for the other student to answer. The questions were to be of the kind that one might find in an encyclopedia, on any of countless topics, such as history, sports, the arts, geography, etc. The other student, randomly designated as the contestant, attempted to answer these questions. The quiz, by design, was intended to be difficult and to give the questioner a decided advantage. This proved to be true, as the typical contestant achieved a success rate of less than 40 percent.

The key measure was a rating of the "general knowledgeability" of both participants. These ratings were made by both questioner and contestant, as well as by an individual who observed the quiz game but did not participate. The major finding was the unusually high rating given to the questioner by both the contestant and the observer. The questioner was perceived as significantly more knowledgeable than the average Stanford freshman.[2]

Thus, even when it had been made clear at the start that the advantage bestowed upon the questioner was *completely situational in origin*, that is, by the experimenter's flip of a coin regarding who would be questioner or contestant, the judgments seemed to focus upon the unique brilliance of the questioner. He or she knew the answers to questions, which the contestant, in general, did not. The conditions were such that anyone in the role of questioner would have performed in a similarly advantaged way, yet the impressions about the questioner were not at a typical or average value but at a considerably more positive level.

These experiments indicate that there is a pervasive tendency to infer personal qualities (such as attitudes, abilities, traits) from the behavior of others and to underestimate, at times very markedly, the situational pressures which are actually influencing that behavior. With respect to the obedience paradigm, therefore, people are likely to focus on the actions of the "teacher" and to infer that qualities of the person in this role are critical, not for reasons which are unique to problems of obedience or to Milgram's specific procedure, but for reasons which pertain to how people perceive others *in general*.

As noted above, Milgram (1974) has suggested that people underestimate the degree of obedience generated in this experiment because they assume that "people are by and large decent and do not readily hurt the innocent" (p. 31). However, the attribution research suggests that people are likely to underplay the significance of external social pressure even when their need to judge others, or themselves, as virtuous is essentially irrelevant. In other words, Milgram's predictors may underestimate the level of harmful obedience not because they refuse to acknowledge that people are capable of evil or social destructiveness, but because they fail to recognize the power of social circumstances to pressure otherwise good people into performing such actions.

That people are not aware of the powerful situational pressures in the obedience paradigm has been shown in a study by Martin Safer (1980). College students were first shown the film, "Obedience"[3] (Milgram, 1965a). This film, while showing individual differences in subjects' willingness to obey orders as well as situational variations in rates of obedience, features an extended portrayal of one subject who, with considerable agitation, proceeds to the final 450-volt level. The students were then read a description of Milgram's control condition (1974, pp. 70-72). This condition is virtually identical to that of the baseline study described in Chapter One with one critical exception—the subject is free to choose the shock level which will be administered to the learner for each of his 30 errors. Thus, there are no orders from the experimenter, no prodding or pressure. As will be noted in Chapter Three, Milgram found a very reduced amount of punishment in this condition, with the average maximum shock level less than 6. Only one subject pressed the 450-volt switch.

Safer's major question was simple: What would be the effect of the film on his students' predictions of the behavior of Milgram's control subjects? Would they learn Milgram's major thesis, that people are surprisingly responsive to the experimenter's authority? If so, they should have predicted very low rates of shocking, recognizing that without the experimenter's presence, subjects would not be inclined to punish the learner. Safer included another group of subjects who were not shown the obedience film in order to make the necessary comparison.

His results were unexpected. Those "sophisticated" students who had seen the film estimated that Milgram's control subjects would shock at a significantly *higher* level than did students in the no-film group. The students who had seen the film appear to have missed its central argument:

> Apparently, they fail to understand a key point of Milgram's experiments, the extent to which situational factors rather than individual character determine behavior. The students still attribute the behavior of subjects in the movie primarily to their character, rather than to the experimental situation. Hence, the students apparently concluded that most people are evil rather than decent, and if given the opportunity, would harm a stranger. Thus the students make the same type of fundamental attribution error as the people in Milgram's audiences, but with the difference that knowing about the research and having seen the movie, the students now overestimate rather than underestimate the "aggressive character" of the subjects. (P. 208)

Safer's students thus appear to have focused upon that feature of the obedience film which was most intuitively convincing or salient— the act of shocking the learner—rather than the more subtle but crucial point that the act was a reflection of the "teacher's" responsiveness to orders from an experimenter.

Bierbrauer (1979) investigated the perception of obedience by having subjects observe a "live" re-enactment of Milgram's baseline experiment (1963) in which a subject obeyed to the 450-volt level. In the first part of the study, Bierbrauer's major interest was whether the judgments of his observers would be influenced by a delay manipulation. Specifically, he hypothesized that subjects would be more likely to acknowledge the situational dynamics in the obedience paradigm if they were given some time to reflect on what they had observed, rather than asked to make their judgments immediately. Three conditions were used: no delay (subjects filled out attribution items immediately); a distracted delay (subjects played some games for 30 minutes prior to filling out items); and undistracted delay (subjects were asked to think about the obedience scenario just witnessed for 30 minutes prior to filling out items).

As Bierbrauer had predicted, subjects in the undistracted-delay condition (compared to the other two conditions) estimated that people generally would administer higher average voltages and would be less likely to defy the experimenter at various stages in the shock sequence. However, the delay manipulation had no effect on subjects' trait impressions of the teacher, and when asked how many people would be defiant at the 450-level, the anticipated percentages ranged from 82 percent (undistracted delay) to 90 percent. Recall that Milgram observed a defiance rate of 35 percent.

Bierbrauer concluded that while the delay technique had the anticipated effect of creating more situational awareness, the tendency to personalize the act of shocking was still prevalent:

> Subjects who spent 30 minutes in active contemplation of what they had witnessed, appear able to identify to a greater degree the situational forces operating upon the teacher's behavior in the Milgram situation, compared with observers who had no time to consider the event witnessed or who were prevented from doing so. However, this greater awareness of situational forces did not affect the extent to which they were willing to decrease the amount of traits or dispositions of the teacher whose behavior was subject to such situational forces. (P. 76)

In a second part of his investigation, Bierbrauer examined the judgments of subjects who were placed in either the role of *actor* or that of *observer*. Two subjects came to the laboratory and, by a coin flip, were assigned to their roles. Actors actually role-played the part of the teacher in a re-enactment of the obedience study.[4] Observers simply watched. Bierbrauer's major hypothesis, based on a conceptual analysis of the divergent perspectives of actors and observers by Jones and Nisbett (1971), was that actors should be particularly cognizant of the situational pressures inherent in Milgram's experiment.

A variety of perceptual judgments obtained from both observer and actor subjects, following the role-played obedience experiment, provided *no* support for the hypothesized effect of the actor-observer perspective. Subjects who had the advantage of being in the situation itself, were no more inclined to predict relatively high voltage levels on the part of hypothetical persons in the teacher role, nor were they immune from inferring unique personality traits when asked to describe the original teacher whose role they had just played.

Bierbrauer suggests several reasons for the priority given to personal or internalized attributions in the obedience paradigm. First, there is evidence that when the action being observed is harmful or deviant, and involves important or dramatic consequences, there is a tendency for observers to assign more responsibility to the actor (Walster, 1966). This may reflect a heightened need to distance oneself from the threatening implications of the observed action by blaming the actor. Bierbrauer also suggests that previous conceptualizations of personal and situational forces may have been somewhat naive. That is, people do not necessarily think in terms of two major types of causes, personal and situational, which must add up to 100 percent. Thus, one's perception of situational forces may be increased *without a simultaneous decrease in one's belief in personal causation.* Bierbrauer's conclusions are pessimistic:

> While social scientists are accumulating evidence that human behavior and even human nature are products of man's environment and the prevailing social and historical conditions, the naive man remains essentially unmoved by these facts. He continues to believe that the inner qualities of his fellows ultimately reveal themselves; that only good men do good and merit praise and that only evil men do evil and deserve punishment. It is only rare writers like Hannah Arendt (1963), when commenting on Adolf Eichmann, who see conformity and compliance as the product of unexceptional men and disobedience to such pressure as rare heroism rather than common decency. (P. 82)

Miller et al. (1974) investigated "expectations about obedience" in a study of social perception. College students were first presented with a detailed account of the obedience paradigm, taken directly from Milgram's 1963 article. Subjects were then shown slides of the photographs of 24 students. These photographs had been previously rated on physical attractiveness, and three levels of attractiveness were represented for both males and females. Told that normative data were needed for a later study, subjects were asked to record for each slide the maximum shock they thought the person would have administered had he or she been the teacher in the obedience experiment. Subjects were then asked to predict their own behavior.

Males were predicted to administer higher shock values (264 volts) than females (188 volts), and highly attractive persons were expected to shock less than moderately attractive or unattractive persons. All of these predictions were far below the actual average shock value of 375 volts obtained in the study reported in 1963. Subjects thus used physical attributes of the persons they were judging—sex[5] and attractiveness—as a basis for predicting their degree of obedience. The significant effect of the sex of the photograph indicated that subjects were employing a gender-based stereotype, that women would be less likely to harm the learner than would men. Similarly, the attractiveness effect confirms previous findings indicating a stereotype for this variable, namely, that people associate highly attractive persons with a variety of socially desirable personality traits and behaviors (Berscheid and Walster, 1974).

The *self-predictions* of male and female students differed dramatically, with males predicting higher shock levels (242 volts) than did females (75 volts). Thus, whether judging others or themselves, subjects underestimated the level of obedience shown in the actual baseline experiment, and an extraneous variable, namely sex, was viewed as a meaningful clue upon which to base one's estimate. This utilization of a stereotype is further support for the general proposition that people think about obedience, at least in this context, as a function of personal qualities of the individual.

What impressions are formed when one observes an obedient or defiant subject? Miller et al. (1974) examined this issue in another study in which subjects were first given a detailed description of the obedience paradigm (but not the results observed by Milgram). Subjects were then shown a photograph of a college student who had allegedly participated in the experiment. They were told that this individual had proceeded to either 90 volts (low obedience), 240 volts (moderate obedience), or 450 volts (high obedience). Subjects were asked to record their impressions of the personality of this individual on a series of judgment scales, such as weak-strong, warm-cold, likable-not likable.

The results were clear. The impressions were strongly related to the shock level—extremely positive for the 90-volt teacher, moderate for the 240-volt teacher, and strongly negative for the 450-volt teacher. Miller et al. also included a condition in which some of the subjects were informed about the results of the baseline experiment (that 65 percent obeyed to 450 volts). It was suggested, on the basis of the "consensus principle" of attribution theory (Kelley, 1973), that subjects would not base their impressions so markedly on the shock level of the person they were rating *if they were informed ahead of time that considerable degrees of obedience were in fact the norm in this setting.* That is, knowing that a given action is typical should prevent one from inferring unique personality attributes. Regardless of these considerations, however, subjects continued to base their impressions solely on the shock level of the "teacher"—favorable perceptions for disobedience, highly unfavorable for obedience.

The final segment of the Miller et al. investigation asked subjects to indicate their impression of the "degree of aggressiveness," involved in the act of shocking the learner (1 for no aggressiveness, 10 for extreme aggressiveness) and to explain, in their own words, their rating. These explanations were coded into one of three categories: *Internal* —a response indicating that the person administering the shock was aggressive or actively responsible for his behavior. Illustrative of this category were a number of subjects who emphasized that the teacher did have a choice not to shock despite the urging of the experimenter. *Internal-external*—a response suggesting that the act of shocking was related to both internal and external forces. An illustration here was the view that only shocks at the higher voltage levels implied true aggressiveness. *External*—a response indicating that the primary force was external to the person pressing the shock levers. Explanations of this type focused on the idea that the teacher was following orders, that there was no intent to harm the learner, and that the act of shocking was part of the rules of the experiment.

Several judgments related closely to the subject's manner of explaining the act of shocking.[6] Those emphasizing its *externality* rated the shocking as relatively low in aggressiveness (3.2), whereas those in the other categories rated it higher (*internal-external*, 5.0; *internal*, 8.2). Those in the *external* category also rated the act of shocking as having less generalizability to other acts of harming than did subjects in the other categories, and indicated that they themselves would have gone further on the shock generator in response to the experimenter's orders. Thus, a given subject's particular account of the act was logically related to other judgments and perceptions.

However, the subjects' explanations of the act of shocking did *not* relate to their trait perceptions of the person in the teacher role. Regardless of their causal perception (internal, external, internal-external), subjects attributed positive traits to the 90-volt teacher and increasingly unfavorable traits to the 240-volt and 450-volt teachers. While it might have been expected that persons with an external view would have been less inclined to base their impressions on the particular shock level (90, 240, or 450), there was no evidence of this result in the impression data.

Thus, there may be important differences between making judgments about abstract behaviors and forming impressions of individuals based on their actions. That is, it might be relatively easy for many individuals to attribute external causality to the *concept* of shocking someone upon command (55 percent of the explanations were in fact categorized as "external"), but when this is redressed into a 450-volt act by a real person, facilitated by a photograph of the individual, one is inclined to attribute traits which seem correspondent with the specific action taken by this person.

Nisbett and Ross (1980) have described how people are strongly influenced in their perceptions by the *vividness* of what they observe, by the most salient or memorable images which characterize certain actions or events. The impact of this feature of a behavior may well override other, more logically compelling aspects. In the obedience paradigm, the act of shocking another human being is an extremely vivid event for most observers, a fact readily demonstrated when showing the filmed account to any audience. The research reviewed in this section, by Safer, Bierbrauer, and Miller et al., points to the extraordinary "pull" that the act of shocking has for a personalized or internal perception. Thus, for reasons that are fundamental to the way in which people tend to perceive others in general, the major *social-psychological* perspective—which is at the heart of Milgram's theoretical orientation—is exceedingly difficult to convey. This issue, of how the obedience in this paradigm is perceived, will be shown later to be critical in terms of the generalizations or extrapolations that have been made from Milgram's findings.

A Different Perspective on the Underestimation of Obedience

John Sabini and Maury Silver (1983) have analyzed the "underestimation effect" in Milgram's paradigm. They argue that people underestimate obedience because they assume *more* rather than less situational control. Noting that Milgram in fact observed a considerable amount of variability—65 percent going to 450 volts, but 35 percent breaking off at earlier stages (with even more variability in subsequent experimental variations)—Sabini and Silver suggest that personality factors did play a significant role in subjects' behavior. In their view, the fact that people expect no one to obey to 450 volts is evidence that they *are* taking the situation into account:

> We suggest that observers predict subjects in the Milgram experiment will break off because they expect everyone . . . to see that he/she should. And we suggest that observers assume that everyone . . . will see this morally relevant aspect of the situation, and respond to it appropriately. (P. 149)

Thus, observers (predictors) are in effect saying, "In the kind of situation you have described, I think just about everyone would disobey." Sabini and Silver feel that this kind of thinking, in presuming a minimum of individual variability (dispositional causality), reflects an exaggerated emphasis on the situation.

Sabini and Silver agree that behavior in the Milgram paradigm is in fact heavily controlled by situational factors, but not in the sense that everyone behaves similarly (they don't):

> Behavior in the Milgram experiment is externally controlled, not just, or even, in Ross's sense—everybody does the same thing—but in the stronger sense that something about the nature of the situation subverts subjects' ability to do what they want to do. Behavior in a post office is situationally controlled in Ross's sense—people do the typical things there, but in the Milgram experiment, unlike the post office, people do things they couldn't imagine themselves doing there. (P. 151)

In my view, part of Sabini and Silver's challenge is largely semantic. That is, to say that people expect everyone to disobey in the Milgram experiment because they view (erroneously) the behavior in *situational terms* could readily be transformed into the idea that observers believe that people are internally disposed to follow their humane instincts on behalf of the protesting learner in such a setting. The real value of Sabini and Silver's argument is that it raises an issue too easily ignored, namely why people are so surprised at Milgram's results. Their "surprise" is perhaps not convincingly accounted for, whether one speaks in terms of personal or situational determination. Sabini and Silver, however, make the following contribution:

> In the Milgram experiment people act irrationally—not in the sense that they fail to pursue the ends *we* think they ought, but in the sense that

they fail to pursue the ends *they* would pick for themselves were they not in the situation. . .It is this irrational deviation from their own desires that surprises us and makes us want to say the subjects are controlled externally, by the situation. The subjects' behavior in its irrationality resembles the compelled quality of an addict's behavior. (P. 151)

Thus, people's underestimation of obedience to authority cannot, according to Sabini and Silver, be clearly explained in terms of an attribution error, at least in terms of Ross's (1977) and others' interpretation of the "fundamental attribution error"—that is, that people believe that behavior is determined by unique personality traits of the actors. Rather, obedience is underestimated because observers do not understand authority itself and what it can make people do.

The analysis by Sabini and Silver is provocative because it deals with an issue that has not been well handled to this point by traditional views of personal versus situational causality, namely the "irrationality" component in the behavior of Milgram's subjects. Their example of the post office is particularly useful—here behavior is, of course, almost completely situational (everybody behaving in a generally similar way, such as standing in line, dropping letters in slots, and so on) but yet so extraordinarily different from the kind of situational influence seen in the obedience experiment. Curiously, however, Sabini and Silver do not deal with what might, in some respects, be viewed as the ultimate in terms of proof of situational control, namely that the behavior of the typical subject varies radically with procedural variations in the paradigm itself.

In addition, their view of personal causality seems restricted to individual differences or unique personality disposition. While this may reflect the fact that they are challenging Ross (1977) who adopts this view, it should also be recognized that people hold to varying conceptions of human nature. That is, I may believe that most people are kind and compassionate—with rare exceptions, suppose I believe that all people are of this nature. This, I feel, would reflect a personal-causality orientation, even though it pertains to my belief about "people in general" rather than individual differences.[7] If I based my estimations of obedience on this presumption, it would reflect a fundamental attribution error in the sense in which this phenomenon has been defined earlier. In other words, I would be basing my prediction on my beliefs about what people are like, rather than on my understanding of their responsiveness to social influence.

The Role of the Step-by-Step Increase in Shock Levels

The experimenter's instructions to increase the shock level by one 15-volt unit for each error made by the learner is a relatively subtle but potentially crucial feature of Milgram's paradigm, with implications concerning the underestimation of obedience. From Milgram's account of the origin of his paradigm, it is apparent that the concept of a step-by-step increase in punishment was an early decision:

> I transformed Asch's experiment into one in which the group would administer increasingly higher levels of shock to a person, and the question would be to what degree an individual would follow along with the group. That's not yet the obedience experiment, but it's a mental step in that direction. (Evans, 1980, pp. 188-89)

Thus, it was never an issue of whether or not an individual would inflict, at the start, a severely punishing shock to another, but rather, the question concerned the degree to which a person would *gradually escalate* his level of punishment under social pressure.

In the research on "expected obedience" described earlier, people were asked how far they would go in the shock sequence. In the actual experiment, however, the issue is different in that subjects are never asked to go farther than 15 volts from their current position. For observers who are making predictions or estimations of obedience, it may be difficult to visualize, in the abstract, the progressive aspect of the shock series. They are not likely to focus upon the fact that in actuality, no shock level is ever administered that is more than 15 volts from the subject's previous level. From this perspective, it might be of interest to ask subjects a slightly different question: "Given that you had administered shock level number 1, what is the likelihood that you would also obey instructions to administer level 2?" and so on. It is not surprising, in terms of the evidence reviewed in this chapter, that people deny that they would shock as high as 300 volts. One wonders, however, what their response would be if they knew that they had indeed administered the 285-volt level and then were asked about going just 15 volts higher.

Steven Gilbert (1981) has analyzed the role of the gradated shock series in terms of its effect on the actual rates of obedience obtained by Milgram. He points, convincingly, to its importance:

> The gradated shock method . . . avoids a single, explicit confrontation of values. Instead, the subject is carefully shaped into obedience. Indeed, the first step—delivering a small shock after a foolish mistake by the

learner—may not feel particularly repugnant to subjects, because the implications of the act are unclear to them. As they press the first switch, they may not anticipate that the learner will do badly enough to require many more shocks, or that one shock will seem to "occasion" the next, or that delivering a few shocks will feel so much like publically declaring acquiescence to the requirements of the experiment, or that such an apparent declaration will feel so personally binding . . . . (Pp. 691-92)

Gilbert makes several thoughtful observations regarding the psychological effects of the gradated shock procedure. He relates this feature to the so-called "foot in the door" phenomenon, the idea that once a person agrees to a relatively trivial request, he or she is more likely to agree to a much more demanding request at a later time. Freedman and Fraser (1966) demonstrated this effect in a well-known experiment in which people who had first agreed to a routine request (such as to sign a petition advocating a "drive carefully" campaign) subsequently allowed the researchers to place a very large sign on their front lawn for an extended period of time. Another group who had not first performed the small-scale request were far less likely to agree to the lawn sign. Although there is evidence that this effect is complex and not always highly generalizable (Beaman et al., 1983), there are sufficient replications to suggest that it is a reliable phenomenon (Snyder and Cunningham, 1975; Zuckerman et al., 1979).

As Gilbert points out, a request to administer an intense shock of 450 volts is analogous to the large sign request in the Freedman and Fraser study—very few people would be expected to perform such an act or estimate that others (or themselves) would perform such acts. However, the same act is considerably more likely to occur if the individual has agreed to perform similar acts, previously, on a smaller scale. The most compelling theoretical account of the foot-in-the-door effect is that a change in self-perception occurs as a result of the initial small-scale behavior. This facilitates subsequent compliance with the larger, more demanding request, because such action is then more consistent with the individual's self-perception as "the kind of person who agrees to do such things." We will observe a similar focus on self-perception in Milgram's theoretical account (1974) of obedience.

Gilbert also observes that the gradated nature of the shocks prevents the subject from experiencing a qualitative change in his or her behavior. The subject, in effect, is entrapped or seduced as each lever is only 15 volts higher than the preceeding one, and the experimenter is programmed to respond in a similarly methodical manner at every choice point for the subject.

We have noted earlier that the data regarding "expected behavior" serve as an important context or baseline against which to compare the behavior observed in the authentic situation itself. It is crucial, therefore, to recognize what factors are responsible for the underestimation of obedience. Clearly one such factor is the tendency for people to focus more on the personal qualities of the "teacher" and less on the influence wielded by the authority, discussed under the rubric of "the fundamental attribution error." Another factor, not as well documented but of potential significance, is the step-by-step schedule of shocks. The "psychology of escalation" may escape the attention of those trying to predict behavior in this paradigm and, as a result, they may fall far short in their estimations.

A Note on Role Playing

In response to the ethical controversy surrounding the obedience experiments and, more generally, all research involving deception, a number of social scientists have advocated role playing as an alternative methodology. One type of role playing is to describe the experimental procedure to subjects and ask them what they would do if they were a subject. This should be familiar in that it was the strategy used by Milgram, and by Miller et al., to investigate what people expect to occur in the obedience paradigm. The findings reviewed in this chapter, of course, would offer dismal prospects for role playing to serve as an effective alternative methodology.[8] This is not, however, the conclusion reached by a number of investigators who have advocated rather different role-playing techniques. We shall review their research in Chapter Six.

CONCLUSIONS

Milgram, in addressing the discrepancy between people's expectations and the actual incidence of obedience, noted:

> The expectations then come to have the character of an illusion, and we must ask whether such an illusion is a chance expression of ignorance or performs some definite function in social life. (1974, p. 27)

From research on the fundamental attribution error, and other findings reviewed in this chapter, it would seem that the underestimation of obedience—hardly a "chance expression of ignorance"—is now reasonably well understood.

One basic determinant is the observer's tendency to focus on the behaving actor and to pay less attention to situational forces. A related issue is the sheer usefulness of believing that the behavior (for instance of the teacher) is primarily shaped by one's character. This allows the observer to understand what is normal or acceptable and what is not, and to predict how others at least *should* behave. It is also clear that the act of shocking the learner at high voltages is viewed in extremely negative terms. It is thus conceivable that the low level of predicted obedience reflects an element of social-desirability bias—people do not wish to acknowledge, to researchers at least, that they would use the higher voltage switches. Perhaps for some individuals there is an awareness that they would be tempted to obey to the end, but to admit this in the presence of a research psychologist would not be acceptable.

As noted earlier, the impact of the findings concerning "expected obedience" has been considerable. Evidence which hints at a sharp disparity between what people say and what they do is unsettling. It conveys a basic lack of understanding or control in one's social universe. If one cannot imagine how one would behave in a defined circumstance, one could be particularly vulnerable to whatever forces are operative in such a setting. It is as if one worked in a hospital but did not have the necessary immunization against a host of common but potentially lethal diseases. How can one be vigilant and resistant against malevolent authority if one does not have an appreciation for the degree to which people are susceptible to such influence?

Finally, the evidence concerning "expected obedience" enhances the value of Milgram's research. If people have such strong but erroneous ideas about obedience, it becomes mandatory to set the record straight by showing what the truth is concerning such behavior.

3

THE OBEDIENCE EXPERIMENTS: THEME AND VARIATIONS

The crux of the study is to vary systematically the factors believed to alter the degree of obedience to the experimental commands, to learn under what conditions submission to authority is most probable, and under what conditions defiance is brought to the fore.

—Stanley Milgram (1965)

In his 1974 book, Milgram describes the results of 18 experiments. The first experiment, described in Chapter One, established the paradigm, and the remaining 17 experiments consist of variations on this theme. Before describing the central features of these experiments and their effect on obedience to authority, several preliminary issues are in order.

THE TIME OF THE RESEARCH

Although the first complete account of the research program appeared in Milgram's 1974 book, the experiments were conducted at Yale University between 1960 and 1963. Two of the experiments were described individually in major research journals, Experiment 1 in the 1963 *Journal of Abnormal and Social Psychology*, and Experiment 17 in the 1965 *Journal of Personality and Social Psychology*. A review of several of the experiments also appeared in a 1965 issue of *Human Relations* and a 1967 issue of *Patterns of Prejudice*. During this period, the obedience experiments had become extremely controversial. Numerous published criticisms as well as endorsements had appeared, for example, the symposium on the experiments that was featured in the 1968 *International Journal of Psychiatry*.[1] Milgram's position, then, when writing the 1974 book, was that of a controversial though generally highly acclaimed social scientist who not only was reviewing his findings but was understandably preoccupied with the diverse, often sharply objecting commentaries his research had stimulated.

THE SUBJECTS

Milgram's subjects were adults in the area of New Haven, Connecticut. All were males, except in one experiment which used females in the role of teacher (see discussion of Experiment 8 to follow). By design, each of the experiments used a similarly balanced distribution of subjects according to age (most in their thirties and forties), and socioeconomic class (mostly blue-collar and white-collar, with a smaller number of professionals). Milgram noted that this kind of sample reduced the likelihood that subjects would know about the experiment before participating and created a more representative or heterogeneous group of subjects than would be available in the typical college "subject pool."

Milgram's subjects were *volunteers*, who had been recruited by newspaper advertisement (see Figure 3.1) and by direct mail solicitation announcing that $4 (plus $.50 for carfare) would be paid for a one-hour participation in a study of memory and learning.[2] Diverse answers were given when subjects were asked why they had volunteered—curiosity about experiments being the most frequent, with other rationales including money, an interest in memory, and self-understanding.

PROJECT PERSONNEL

Milgram describes in detail the individuals who played the roles of experimenter and learner (1974, pp. 16 and 58-59). The filmed version of the obedience experiment (Milgram, 1965a) is of considerable value in portraying the main "team." (A second team was also involved in some of the variations—see Experiment 6.) The particular role of the experimenter—specifically the script which the experimenter enacted—has become a matter of considerable controversy (Mixon, 1977; Orne and Holland, 1968). Milgram invested the experimenter with the look of authority: "The role of experimenter was played by a thirty-one-year-old high school teacher of biology. Throughout the experiment, his manner was impassive and his appearance somewhat stern" (p. 16).

Public Announcement

WE WILL PAY YOU $4.00 FOR ONE HOUR OF YOUR TIME

Persons Needed for a Study of Memory

*We will pay five hundred New Haven men to help us complete a scientific study of memory and learning. The study is being done at Yale University.

*Each person who participates will be paid $4.00 (plus 50c carfare) for approximately 1 hour's time. We need you for only one hour: there are no further obligations. You may choose the time you would like to come (evenings, weekdays, or weekends).

*No special training, education, or experience is needed. We want:

Factory workers	Businessmen	Construction workers
City employees	Clerks	Salespeople
Laborers	Professional people	White-collar workers
Barbers	Telephone workers	Others

All persons must be between the ages of 20 and 50. High school and college students cannot be used.

*If you meet these qualifications, fill out the coupon below and mail it now to Professor Stanley Milgram, Department of Psychology, Yale University, New Haven. You will be notified later of the specific time and place of the study. We reserve the right to decline any application.

*You will be paid $4.00 (plus 50c carfare) as soon as you arrive at the laboratory.

- -

TO:
PROF. STANLEY MILGRAM, DEPARTMENT OF PSYCHOLOGY, YALE UNIVERSITY, NEW HAVEN, CONN. I want to take part in this study of memory and learning. I am between the ages of 20 and 50. I will be paid $4.00 (plus 50c carfare) if I participate.

NAME (Please Print). . . . .

ADDRESS . . . .

TELEPHONE NO. . . . . Best time to call you . . . .

AGE . . . . OCCUPATION . . . . SEX . . . . . .
CAN YOU COME:

WEEKDAYS . . . . EVENINGS . . . . . . WEEKENDS . . . .

Figure 3.1.

Source: From *Obedience to Authority*: *An Experimental View*, by Stanley Milgram, Copyright © 1974 by Stanley Milgram. Reprinted by permission.

It was the "impassiveness" which was to become a source of criticism. Several commentators raised the possibility that the credibility of the experiment was jeopardized by the presence of a passive experimenter in the face of a screaming person demanding to be released. This issue will be considered in Chapter Six.

The role of learner (also described as "victim" by Milgram) was played by a forty-seven-year-old accountant who had been trained for the role. In certain experimental variations, particularly those in which the learner was in direct physical proximity to the naive subject (teacher), it was obviously crucial that the learner perform in a standard and totally believable manner.

PILOT RESEARCH

Pilot studies, completed in 1960, were described in Milgram's research proposal to the National Science Foundation (January, 1961).[3] The purpose of the pilot studies was to establish a viable paradigm within which to examine the obedience process and to obtain preliminary data concerning the reaction of subjects to the experimental setting.

What is of unique importance regarding the pilot research was the actual behavioral responses of these early subjects:

> At first no vocal feedback was used from the victim. It was thought that the verbal and voltage designations on the control panel would create sufficient pressure to curtail the subject's obedience. However, this was not the case. In the absence of protests from the learner, virtually all subjects, once commanded, went blithely to the end of the board, seemingly indifferent to the verbal designations ("Extreme Shock" and "Danger: Severe Shock"). This deprived us of an adequate basis for scaling obedient tendencies. A force had to be introduced that would strengthen the subject's resistance to the experimenter's commands, and reveal individual differences in terms of a distribution of break-off points. (Milgram, 1965b, p. 61)

Thus, Milgram had designed, originally, a procedure that produced a disconcerting lack of subject variability, namely total obedience! It was to be only the first of a number of unexpected findings. Milgram does not make reference to the possibility that the extreme acquiescence on the part of the pilot subjects indicated that they doubted the reality of the shocks, a thesis that was to be advanced by later critics (see Chapter Six). Milgram reports that pilot subjects frequently averted their eyes from the person they were shocking, "often turning their heads in an awkward and conspicuous manner" (1961b, p. 11). This avoidance response suggested that the immediacy of the victim with respect to the teacher would be a relevant dimension to investigate, and it is this problem which was addressed in the first four of the obedience experiments.

CLOSENESS OF THE VICTIM: EXPERIMENTS 1 THROUGH 4

Milgram describes the results of four experiments in which the variable of interest was the spatial distance between the persons occupying the teacher and learner roles (1974, Chapter Four). The first experiment—that featured in the 1963 publication and described in Chapter One—was entitled *Remote*. The learner was situated in a different room and there was no use of vocal protests. At the 300-volt level, the learner pounded on the wall, a sound easily heard by the teacher. This protest stopped at the 315-volt level. As indicated previously, the results of this initial experiment were provocative in terms of the unexpectedly high incidence of total obedience—26 of 40 subjects—and the extraordinarily intense displays of tension and conflict in many subjects.

Vocal protests were introduced in Experiment 2, entitled *Voice-Feedback*. It is not clear, precisely, when these protests were introduced, although a description of Experiment 5 (which was very similar to Experiment 2) indicated that the learner's first protest, described as "Ugh!" by Milgram, occurred at the 75-volt level. Thus subjects heard the first protest from the learner when pressing the fifth shock lever. The protests (all of which were "emitted" in standard form by means of a tape recording) became increasingly strident and are described as "agonized screams" at the higher voltage levels.

Experiment 3, entitled *Proximity*, involved placing the learner in the same room with the teacher and seated a few feet from him. The protests were (apparently) on the same schedule as in Experiment 2, but, of course, were acted out in a live manner as the learner was visible as well as audible to the teacher.

Experiment 4, entitled *Touch-Proximity*, was similar to Experiment 3 but here, the subject was under the impression that the learner could only receive a shock by placing his hand directly on a shock plate. The learner was, according to plan, willing to do this on his own through the tenth level (150 volts), at which point he demanded to be released and refused to place his hand on the plate. The experimenter then ordered the teacher to place the learner's hand on the plate. Thus, obedience, in this experiment, required physical contact at or beyond the 150-volt level. It is not clear as to the precise degree of force involved or how much exertion was prompted by the learner's unwillingness to be shocked. The "drama" of this particular study was undoubtedly high, and the talents required by the personnel to conduct it in a controlled "routine" manner were, to say the least, severely tested.[4] Actually there was a precedent for this variation. Frank (1944), in the "cracker-eating" study mentioned in Chapter One, included a procedure in which the experimenter "tried physically to force S to eat, either by pushing the cracker into his mouth or by trying to push S's hand with the cracker in it to his mouth" (Frank, p. 43).

Many of the details of the paradigm, described in Chapter One, need not be repeated here. Of course, a feature present in each of the experiments described above (and most of the others as well) and of the utmost significance, was the systematic use of increasingly authoritative prods by the experimenter.

Results

The results of Experiments 1 through 4 are shown in Table 3.1. Obedience, assessed in terms of the average maximum shock level, as well as the percentage of subjects obeying to the 450-volt level, was reduced as the proximity between teacher and learner increased. Milgram does not provide statistical analyses of these data. It is unlikely that there is a statistically significant difference between Experiments 1 and 2, although there are some comparisons that would likely prove to be significant.

An examination of the data tables in Milgram's book reveals an interesting pattern. As noted above, beginning with Experiment 2, the learner initiated vocal protests upon receiving the fifth shock level, that is, 75 volts. However, it was at the tenth level that the learner specifically asked to be released. The data indicate that this was a highly significant event for many subjects. In Experiment 2, 5 (of the total of 40) subjects defied the experimenter at this point; in Experiment 3, 10 subjects defied at this point, and in Experiment 4, 16 subjects broke off. The learner's protests became increasingly vehement after the initial plea for release, and additional subjects broke off at various subsequent points in the sequence of shocks. The fact that a sizable minority of subjects broke off at that particular moment when the learner made his first explicit request to be released is important

Table 3.1. Maximum Shocks Administered in Experiments 1, 2, 3, and 4

Shock level	Verbal designation and voltage level	Experiment 1 Remote (n = 40)	Experiment 2 Voice-Feedback (n = 40)	Experiment 3 Proximity (n = 40)	Experiment 4 Touch-Proximity (n = 40)
	Slight Shock				
1	15				
2	30				
3	45				
4	60				
	Moderate Shock				
5	75				
6	90				
7	105			1	
8	120				
	Strong Shock				
9	135		1		1
10	150		5	10	16
11	165		1		
12	180		1	2	3
	Very Strong Shock				
13	195				
14	210				1
15	225			1	1
16	240				
	Intense Shock				
17	255				1
18	270			1	
19	285		1		1
20	300	5 *	1	5	1
	Extreme Intensity Shock				
21	315	4	3	3	2
22	330	2			
23	345	1	1		1
24	360	1	1		
	Danger: Severe Shock				
25	375	1		1	
26	390				
27	405				
28	420				
	XXX				
29	435				
30	450	26	25	16	12
	Mean maximum shock level	27.0	24.53	20.80	17.88
	Percentage obedient subjects	65.0%	62.5%	40.0%	30.0%

*Indicates that in Experiment 1, five subjects administered a maximum shock of 300 volts.

Source: Table 2, page 35, from *Obedience to Authority: An Experimental View* by Stanley Milgram, Copyright © 1974 by Stanley Milgram. Reprinted by permission.

in suggesting that the paradigm was in fact highly believeable, that is, that subjects were convinced of the learner's suffering.

Theoretical Interpretation

Characteristic of Milgram's general theoretical style is the listing of a number of potentially relevant psychological dynamics. Here are excerpts from his 1974 book regarding the data from Experiments 1 through 4:

> *Empathic cues.* "In the Remote and . . . Voice-Feedback conditions, the victim's suffering possesses an abstract, remote quality for the subject. . . . Diminishing obedience . . . would be explained by the enrichment of empathic cues in the successive experimental conditions" (pp. 36-38).

> *Denial and narrowing of the cognitive field.* "The Remote condition allows a narrowing of the cognitive field so that the victim is put out of mind. When the victim is close it is more difficult to exclude him from thought. . . . One subject . . . said, 'It's funny how you really begin to forget that there's a guy out there, even though you can hear him'" (p. 38).

> *Reciprocal fields.* "Possibly, it is easier to harm a person when he is unable to observe our actions than when he can see what we are doing. His surveillance of the action directed against him may give rise to shame or guilt, which may then serve to curtail the action" (pp. 38-39).

> *Experienced unity of act.* "In the Remote conditions it is more difficult for the subject to see a connection between his actions and their consequences for the victim. . . . The two events are in correlation, yet they lack a compelling unity" (p. 39).

> *Incipient group-formation.* "When the victim is placed close to the subject, it becomes easier to form an alliance with him against the experimenter. . . . Thus, the changing set of spatial relations leads to a potentially shifting set of alliances over the several experimental conditions" (pp. 39-40).

> *Acquired behavior disposition.* " . . . we may learn not to harm others simply by not harming them in everyday life. Yet this learning occurs in a context of proximal relations with others and may not be generalized to situations in which the others are physically remote from us" (p. 40).

Milgram clearly was not attempting to test, and hence possibly to falsify, a specific theoretical basis for the proximity effects. Rather, his primary concern was to *demonstrate* explicitly that obedience varies with changes in the dimension of proximity, and then to identify those factors which may have produced the effect. His theoretical orientation appears to have reflected a basically Lewinian field-theory position. He consistently expresses an interest in the linkage between psychological processes and physical or structural aspects of the situation:

> We move about; our spatial relations shift from one situation to the next, and the fact that we are near or remote may have a powerful effect on the psychological processes that mediate our behavior toward others. (P. 40)

Milgram's theoretical accounts were, of course, post hoc. He seemed to have an intuitive "feel" for what would be an interesting or relevant experimental variation. Thus, he would first perform the experiment and *then* concern himself with formally accounting for the result. Given that there was virtually no previous systematic research on obedience, it was understandable that Milgram's focus was essentially in a context of discovery or exploration rather than confirming or disconfirming specific hypotheses. But it is also likely that he simply followed his own best instincts regarding the style of his theorizing. Because his style did not conform to the classic hypothesis-testing format of much of social-psychological research in the 1960s, it was inevitable that Milgram would assume, for some at least, the status of a "maverick."

It should be noted, however, that in the concluding chapters of his 1974 book, Milgram attempts a more systematic theoretical statement. Rather than explaining each experimental result by listing a variety of psychological dynamics, he develops a set of general concepts that pertained more globally to the process of obedience. We will examine this theoretical analysis in Chapter Eight.

Milgram's conclusions regarding Experiments 1 through 4 bear emphasis here, because they set an interpretive perspective for the entire set of 18 experiments. He first indicates that the general degree of obedience in the four studies was unexpectedly high (approximately 50 percent). He then speaks rather explicitly to a *moral failure* on the part of the subjects:

> Subjects have learned from childhood that it is a fundamental breach of moral conduct to hurt another person against his will. Yet, almost half of the subjects abandon this tenet in following the instructions of an authority who has no special powers to enforce his commands. . . . It is clear from the remarks and behavior of many participants that in punishing the victim they were often acting against their own values. . . . Yet many followed the experimental commands. (P. 41)

This interpretation is highly significant. It allowed Milgram, and countless others who have accepted its premise, to generalize from the experiments to other instances of moral failing in the context of destructive obedience, the Nazi regime being the most striking such illustration. Not everyone accepted Milgram's interpretation, however. Reservations were based primarily on methodological issues, that because of the manner in which the experiments were conducted, it was implausible to draw conclusions regarding a moral failure on the part of the subjects. This debate will be discussed more thoroughly in Chapter Six. The commentary, noted above, also represented a value judgment on Milgram's part. It could be inferred that he personally disapproved of the behavior of his subjects—a stance which left him open to charges of being biased, unethical, and lacking proper scientific objectivity. There is little doubt that Milgram's interpretation, facilitated by his literary style, captivated many readers. As will become apparent, however, it produced its share of alienation as well.

Another major issue raised by Milgram at this point concerns the emotional strain experienced by many of his subjects. As noted in Chapter One, the symptoms of conflict and anxiety were described vividly in the 1963 journal publication, and the filmed account (1965a) of the experiments also indicated the strong arousal created in this paradigm. In his 1974 book, Milgram presents self-report data, obtained during post-experimental interviews, which attest to moderate to extreme levels of tension experienced by most of the subjects.

This evidence is important in several respects. First, it is used by Milgram as testimony to the realism of the experiment, reflecting the strength of the dilemma presented to subjects. Second, it points to *conflict* as the basic psychological state induced in subjects. However, because the degree of tension did *not* predict who would or would not obey to the maximum level, the findings point to the power of authority to override the dictates of conscience. Were it simply a matter of reacting to one's emotional experience, most subjects would have broken off relatively early. But this did not occur:

In the present situation even where tension is extreme, many subjects are unable to perform the response that will bring about relief.... Every evidence of extreme tension is at the same time an indication of the strength of the forces that keep the subject in the situation. (P. 43)

FURTHER VARIATIONS AND CONTROLS: EXPERIMENTS 5 THROUGH 11

Following the proximity experiments, Milgram presents the results of seven additional experiments. Each of these can be viewed as a variation on the procedure used in Experiment 2: the teacher and learner are in separate rooms, but the learner's protests are audible. As a set, these seven experiments speak to the reliability of the basic findings and, in several instances, serve as control conditions to rule out the relevance of certain potentially important causal factors. We will describe each experiment briefly, and then comment on their collective impact.

Experiment 5: A New Baseline Condition

The key feature of Experiment 5 is the learner's statement regarding a previous heart problem. As the learner is being "wired into place," the experimenter inquires about any questions or problems. The learner then states: "When I was at the West Haven V.A. Hospital, a few years ago, they detected a slight heart condition. Nothing serious, but are these shocks dangerous?" (p. 56). The experimenter replies that although painful, the shocks cause no permanent tissue damage. The verbal protests, on tape recording, include reference to the heart condition at three points (150, 195, and 330 volts). Experiment 5 also involved moving the laboratory to the basement, a less elegant setting than the Yale Interaction Laboratory where the earlier studies had been run. All subsequent experiments were conducted in this new location, and included reference to the learner's previous heart problem.

The reason for including the "heart problem" was to provide an additional basis for disobedience: "Perhaps this new element would provide additional justification for disobeying and make such a course of action seem even more compelling and necessary" (p. 55). After the 330-volt level was reached—that is, the twenty-second of the 30 possible shock levers—there were no further protests or responses of any kind from the learner. In the minds of some subjects, at least, the learner could have either been unconscious or dead.

Given these considerations, the results of Experiment 5 are more interesting than might be inferred from the simple title of the study (A New Base Line). Twenty-six of the 40 subjects (65 percent) proceeded to the maximum shock level, essentially duplicating the results of Experiments 1 and 2. (As in previous variations, the tenth level prompted a noticeable amount of disobedience, with six subjects breaking off after this shock point.)

Experiment 6: Change of Personnel

To increase the efficiency of the study, Milgram reports that a second team was set up to run the paradigm. The individuals playing the role of experimenter and learner were very different in physical appearance—a "milder-looking" experimenter, a "rougher-looking" victim. The maximum obedience rate, once again, was high—50 percent—leading Milgram to conclude that the "personal characteristics of the experimenter and victim were not of overriding importance" (p. 59).

It should be noted, however, that while Experiment 6 attests to the basic reliability of the findings—that is, in replicating the results of Experiment 5—it does not rule out the possibility that systematic differences in the nature of the individuals occupying the experimenter and learner roles could in fact be of major significance. In his original research proposal to The National Science Foundation (NSF), Milgram included, as a point of future inquiry, an investigation of the effect of "propaganda against the victim." To my knowledge, he did not conduct an experiment on this problem. One would be interested, for example, in the effect of using a member of a minority group as the learner, or someone reduced in social status by means of stigmatizing information.[5] Variations on these issues would be particularly meaningful in relating the obedience research to the Holocaust.

Experiment 7: Closeness of Authority

To this point, the experimenter was always seated a few feet from the subject (or "teacher"). In Experiment 7, after giving initial instructions, the experimenter left the laboratory and gave his orders by telephone. The results were dramatic. Obedience was reduced to a third of previous levels—only 22.5 percent went to 450 volts. Milgram observes that several subjects "cheated" by administering lower shock levels than they were ordered to give, another illustration of the power of authority, "although these subjects acted in a way that clearly undermined the avowed purposes of the experiment, they found it easier to handle the conflict in this manner than to precipitate an open break with authority" (p. 62).

The basic result of Experiment 7 is conceptualized in terms of the psychological impact of spatial relationships: Not having to confront the experimenter face to face, subjects found it easier to resist his influence. Thus, the physical presence and surveillance of the authority were of vital significance, further indicating that subjects were being instructed to do something that they fundamentally did not want to do.

Experiment 8: Women as Subjects

In this experiment, women served as subjects in the role of teacher. The experimental procedures were those of the new baseline condition, used in Experiment 5. The results were virtually identical to those of the parallel experiment with male subjects—65 percent reaching 450 volts, and an average maximum shock level of 24.7 (compared with 24.6 in Experiment 5). Milgram indicates that there were many "specifically feminine styles in handling the conflict. In postexperimental interviews women, far more frequently than men, related their experience to problems of rearing children" (p. 63).

The results of this experiment contrast sharply with the expectations that people seem to hold regarding the behavior of women. As mentioned in the previous chapter, Miller et al. (1974) observed that college subjects expected women to shock far less than men, and that the self-predictions of women were extraordinarily low. Milgram's findings are therefore instructive when compared to beliefs that people hold, beliefs which, as noted earlier, seem based on a dispositional interpretation of behavior in this setting. Milgram also suggests that the research literature on conformity might actually have predicted the opposite result, namely, that women would be more subservient to the experimenter's instructions than would men. Of course, the data do not confirm such a prediction. A number of other obedience experiments have also examined the performances of women (such as Hofling et al., 1966; Kilham and Mann, 1974; Sheridan and King, 1972). We shall examine their findings in Chapter Four.

Experiment 9: The Victim's Limited Contract

In this variation, Milgram introduced a further "testing of the limits." Just as Experiment 5 had ordered the subject to administer shocks to a person with a known heart condition, Experiment 9 involved an agreement beforehand among all parties—experimenter, teacher, learner—that the learner would be released whenever he so desired, "I'll agree to be in it, but only on condition that you let me out when I say so; that's the only condition" (p. 64). The teacher readily agreed and, as Milgram describes it, "the experimenter grunts in a mildly positive manner" (p. 64). At the tenth level, the learner protested and demanded to be released in accordance with the contract. The experimenter disregarded the protest and ordered more shocks, as in the usual procedure.

Sixteen of the forty subjects (40 percent) obeyed to the 450-volt level. Although stating that a quarter of those who defied the experimenter explicitly mentioned the contractual agreement, Milgram's major conclusion is that the results point to the essential *weakness* of the contractual agreement. The real force in the situation is the experimenter: "Subjects were aware of the injustice being done to the victim, but they allowed the experimenter to handle the issue as he saw fit" (p. 66).

This variation is unique in presenting to subjects what might constitute counternormative behavior on the part of the experimenter. Milgram himself suggested this in noting that "an element of betrayal and patent injustice was thus introduced" (p. 65). The experimenter, in this variation, would seem to have lost considerable credibility or authenticity and subjects would have had every reason to think that "something's strange here—experimenters aren't supposed to act this way."

From this perspective, the relatively high rate of obedience suggests the power of authority even under conditions which might ordinarily be viewed as de-legitimizing. For many individuals, the power of authority proves to be greater than their verbal commitment to a prior agreement. Milgram also suggests that these results rule out the possibility that subjects obey because they feel that the victim, too, has voluntarily made an agreement to participate and "stick it out." This experiment made *explicit* the fact that the learner was being shocked against his will, yet obedience, though somewhat reduced, was nevertheless relatively high.

Experiment 10: Institutional Context

Milgram indicates that in post-experimental interviews, many subjects indicated that they would not have shocked the learner had the experiments been conducted at a different location than Yale University. Milgram is *not* saying that the trust and integrity evoked in a university environment gave subjects reason to doubt that they were punishing the learner (others *have* made this claim, as will be noted in Chapter 6). Rather, he is arguing that social influence is often inextricably bound to specific social contexts:

> On request, we expose our throats to a man with a razor blade in the barbershop, but would not do so in a shoe store; in the latter setting we willingly follow the clerk's request to stand in our stockinged feet, but resist the command in a bank. . . . *One must always question the relationship of obedience to a person's sense of the context in which he is operating.* (P. 68)

To explore the extent of its dependence upon the university context, the obedience paradigm was moved to an office building—not overly impressive in its location or furnishings—in the downtown area of Bridgeport, Connecticut, and conducted under the auspices of "Research Associates of Bridgeport."

The results indicated only a slight (not statistically significant) reduction in the percentage of fully obedient subjects—48 percent as compared to 65 percent obtained in the corresponding variation at Yale (Experiment 5). Levels of tension in subjects, as well as estimates of pain felt by the learner, were similar to those seen at Yale.

The aura of Yale University was not, therefore, a necessary precondition for the obtained levels of obedience in this paradigm. The crucial factor may have been what was *common* at Bridgeport and at Yale, namely the subjects' belief that a legitimate and significant enterprise was at issue—scientific research. Differences in social reputation or image were, it seems, apparently trivial.

Experiment 11: Subjects Free to Choose Shock Level

Thus far the experiments have shared a basic procedure, the presence of an experimenter who insists that the subject administer increasingly severe shocks. The question remains as to what subjects would do without such pressure. This is the classic "control" question in research on social influence, since one may learn significant things about the nature of influence by observing what occurs in its absence. Accordingly, Milgram used the baseline procedure of Experiment 5 with the exception that the subject was free to select any shock lever in each of the 30 instances in which the learner made an error.

Subjects were clearly unwilling to use high shock levels. Thirty-eight of the 40 subjects used levels ranging from 15 to 150 volts. Only one individual pressed the 450-volt switch. For purposes of comparison, a meaningful index is the average maximum shock level. For Experiment 11, this value was 5.5 (out of a possible 30). For Experiments 1 through 10 combined, the value was 22.2.

Milgram utilized this particular variation to examine the possibility that subjects would have a propensity to inflict strong shocks on their own:

> It is not enough to say that the situation provided a setting in which it was acceptable for the subject to hurt another person. This setting remained the same in the present experiment, and, by and large, subjects were not inclined to have the victim suffer. (P. 72)

Thus, "autonomously generated aggression" is removed as a major explanation of the subjects' behavior. The dispositional component in the action of shocking the victim, particularly at levels beyond the initial indication of discomfort, is shown to be minimal. What remains is Milgram's central thesis, "the transformation of behavior that comes about through obedience to orders" (p. 72).

Summary of Experiments 5 through 11

Obedience is a highly reliable outcome of this paradigm. Circumstances which might at first be thought as necessary to produce the high rate of total obedience—the university setting—or likely to reduce obedience sharply—a prior agreement to release the learner—are shown to have negligible effects. Changes in personnel, including the gender of the subject, or physical aspects of the laboratory are similarly inconsequential. The only variation shown to be effective in modifying the subjects' behavior is one which explicitly involved the role of authority itself: a markedly reduced pattern of obedience when the experimenter is physically removed from the laboratory.

As alluded to earlier, a pattern of potential significance characterized the break-off point for many subjects. Prior to level 10—the point at which the learner indicated a prior history of a heart problem—there was a virtual absence of disobedience. Of the 240 subjects participating in Experiments 5 through 10, only ten (4.1 percent) broke off prior to this level. However, in these six experiments, 35 subjects (14.6 percent) broke off after pressing the tenth lever (150 volts). No other single shock level produced even this minor sort of "consensus of defiance" on the part of subjects as a group.

Thus, approximately one seventh of the subjects were able to muster the resources to defy the experimenter's orders at the tenth level. If one interprets this pattern of *disobedience* as indicating that subjects generally are convinced of the increasingly dire situation facing the learner, then these findings only add to the dramatic quality of the results pertaining to obedience itself: In Experiments 5 through 10, 116 subjects (48 percent) followed instructions to the thirtieth and final shock level.

ROLE PERMUTATIONS: EXPERIMENTS 12 THROUGH 16

Milgram next describes five experiments that were designed to distinguish between three elements in his research paradigm: position, status, and action. *Position* refers to the site of action—is one ordering, administering, or receiving the shocks? *Status* refers to the person's power or prestige level in the hierarchy—is the person an experimenter or an "ordinary man?" *Action* refers to the specific directive —is the order one of administering shocks or of ceasing to deliver the shocks?

In the previous experiments, these factors have been constant— that is, an experimenter (high status) orders (position) the teacher (low status) to administer (action) shocks to the learner (low status). Milgram viewed this arrangement as presenting a certain ambiguity in interpreting the observed behavior. One cannot, for example, be certain that it is authority per se which is responsible—subjects might be equally obedient to a peer or to instructions from a computer. Would authority be effective if the order were to *stop* administering the shocks? Would subjects be obedient if the learner were a person of *high* social status?

These and related questions were examined in a series of imaginative variations. In each, twenty subjects (in contrast to the 40 used in the previous experiments) were used. A number of departures from the basic procedure will be apparent as the individual experiments are briefly discussed.

Experiment 12: Learner Demands to be Shocked

This variation was a reversal of the usual procedure. The learner demanded that the shocks continue, but the experimenter ordered, at the 150-volt level, that they be stopped. The learner's protests, in this instance, were based on a variety of motives—a challenge to his manliness, his commitment to do the job. As before, the learner's demands were in conflict with the experimenter's orders, but here, the linkage between position and action was reversed.

The results of this experiment are unequivocal, as each of the 20 subjects followed the experimenter's instructions to stop after the 150-volt shock was delivered. The learner's pleas that the punishment be continued were ignored. Thus, obedience to authority was demonstrated, but in the direction of the cessation of harming, rather than its escalation. For Milgram, the learner's wish to be shocked has essentially no impact within the larger context of the experiment. It is the experimenter's definition of the situation which is pivotal, not that of the learner, "It is not the substance of the command but its source in authority that is of decisive importance" (p. 92).

Experiment 13: An Ordinary Man Gives Orders

To what degree would subjects follow the instructions if these were issued by a peer instead of by the experimenter? Milgram tested this question by the use of an elaborately staged scenario in which three subjects (two of them accomplices of the experimenter) arrived at the laboratory. One accomplice was assigned the role of victim (by means of the fixed draw). The second accomplice was required to record times from a clock on the experimenter's desk. The naive subject was asked to read word pairs and administer shocks to the learner. There was at this point no mention of the specific shock levels to be administered. A prearranged phone call was the cue for the experimenter to leave the laboratory. He left, saying that the two subjects should proceed without him and that the learner's performance would be automatically recorded.

Upon the experimenter's departure, the accomplice suggested that the shocks be increased one step for each error, and took an insistent position on this. Thus, a "common man" (to use Milgram's phrase) assumed the role of authority and issued the usual orders.

Four of the 20 subjects (20 percent) obeyed to the 450-volt level. As in previous variations, a substantial number (7 subjects, or 35 percent) broke off after the tenth level. Milgram interprets the result as a "sharp drop in compliance." With all basic factors held constant, a removal of the authority inherent in the experimenter's status resulted in approximately one-third of the baseline degree of maximum obedience. Of course, given that the experimenter had essentially turned the management of the study over to the subjects, it was likely that a modicum of "derived authority" was still present in the confederate's enactment of the role. A study by Mantell (1971), to be described in Chapter Four, also bears on this issue of "peer authority."

Experiment 13a: The Subject as Bystander

In Experiment 13, 16 subjects refused at some point to follow the other accomplice's instructions to administer shocks. The script called for the accomplice himself to assume the role of shocking the learner and to assign the defiant subject the task of recording the shock durations. Having been relieved of their role in shocking the learner, how did subjects now respond to their more passive duties?

Milgram reports that virtually everyone protested the accomplice's action, with five subjects making an effort to physically restrain him from shocking the learner. Milgram notes the active, discourteous manner of these subjects, in contrast to the polite deference typically shown to the experimenter. Nevertheless, 11 of the 16 subjects (69 percent) allowed the accomplice to proceed to the 450-volt level. The initial defiance of these subjects thus did not extend to a more explicit intervention in behalf of the pleading victim, a result again suggesting that the experimenter, though physically absent, was not without at least residual authority.

Experiment 14: Authority as Victim—An Ordinary Man Commanding

In this variation, Milgram was concerned with the status of the person *receiving* the shocks. He created a scenario in which the experimenter played the role of learner and received shocks for making errors, accomplished by having the confederate (the learner) indicate that he was afraid of shocks and would continue only if someone else would perform the learner's role first. The experimenter agreed, and the usual procedure was then activated with the confederate (serving as experimenter) ordering the subject to administer increasingly severe shocks to the experimenter. At the 150-volt level, the experimenter demanded that he be released, but the confederate, playing the standard role of authority, ordered that the shock series be carried out to its proper conclusion.

The results again document the impact of status. Each of the 20 subjects obeyed the experimenter at precisely the point at which he first demanded that they stop—the orders of the confederate were ignored. Milgram describes a typical response in this experiment:

> Many subjects explained their prompt response on humane grounds, not recognizing the authority aspect of the situation. Apparently it is more gratifying for the subjects to see their action as stemming from personal kindness than to acknowledge that they were simply following the boss's orders. When asked what they would do if a common man

were being shocked, these subjects vehemently denied that they would continue beyond the point where the victim protests. (Pp. 103-4)

Thus, as noted in the previous chapter, people have an almost reflex-like tendency to explain the behavior observed in these experiments in personal or characterological terms.

Summary of Experiments 12 through 14

We have seen in these experiments a peer of the subject ordering that shocks be administered to himself (Experiment 12); to another subject (Experiment 13); and to a protesting experimenter (Experiment 14). In each instance, obedience was either totally absent or sharply reduced. Milgram concludes, from these data, that there is no evidence that subjects have aggressive or sadistic motives which are unleashed by the opportunity to inflict punishment. The participants appear to focus almost exclusively on *who is giving them instructions*: a legitimate authority is obeyed, whether the instructions are to shock or to stop shocking, even if the authority is placed temporarily in a low-status role. A peer is relatively uninfluential, regardless of what he asks from the subject, even if he is placed temporarily in a high-status role.

Experiment 15: Two Authorities—Contradictory Commands

Milgram posed the question of what would happen if authority itself was in conflict. In this variation, the subject, as usual, was ordered to shock the learner, but the experiment was conducted by two experimenters. Initially in perfect accord, they took opposing positions regarding the continuation of the study at the critical 150-volt level. As described by Milgram, the script entailed the typical insistent posture on the part of one experimenter, with the second continuously undercutting him.

The results were clear. Of the 20 subjects involved, 18 broke off at precisely the moment where the experimenters began to argue. One subject had withdrawn 15 volts prior to this point, and one continued one shock level beyond it. Once again, subjects did not take advantage of the opportunity to shock the learner. The inertia in all of the experiments appears, rather, to be in the direction of not shocking the learner. In the present experiment, a legitimate authority admonishing the subject to stop prevailed over an experimenter urging him to continue: "Once the signal emanating from the higher level was 'contaminated,' the coherence of the hierarchical system was destroyed, along with its efficacy in regulating behavior" (p. 107).

Experiment 16: Two Authorities—One as Victim

In the previous experiment, the two authority figures occupied the same position relative to that of the subject, that of high status. What might occur if the two experimenters were once again to disagree regarding the administration of shocks, but one of these individuals was temporarily placed in the learner role? The structure of this experiment was similar to that of Experiment 14, in which the experimenter played the learner's role, but in this instance there was another experimenter in the role of authority. Milgram was interested in which facet would prevail—the *power vested in the role itself*, in which case one would expect the experimenter (in the learner's position) to be shocked as if he were an ordinary peer, or the *position in the hierarchy*, in which case the pleas of the "victimized" experimenter might, in contrast to those from the usual learner, be more influential.

A scenario was arranged in which one of the two subjects "failed to appear," making it necessary (from the real subject's point of view) to have one of the two experimenters play the role of learner. A rigged draw was employed to decide which experimenter would play the learner and which the experimenter. The experimenter-as-victim performed in the usual manner, pleading at the 150-volt level to be released. The experimenter-as-authority, again according to the script, insisted that increasingly intense punishments be inflicted.

The results indicated obedience to the experimenter in the position of authority. Thirteen subjects (65 percent) obeyed to the 450-volt level, a result identical with that of the base line (Experiment 5). Once again, a substantial minority broke off at the 150-volt level. The majority, however, were influenced more by the experimenter-in-authority. Milgram suggests that despite the unusual circumstances, subjects were able to re-establish a meaningful sense of hierarchy or social structure, so that obedience was relatively intact here, as compared with Experiment 15, in which "there was no clearly discernible higher authority, and consequently no means to determine what line of action to follow" (p. 111). Thus, all of the role-permutation variations—Experiments 12 to 16—are testimony to Milgram's emphasis upon the concept of a hierarchical social structure.

GROUP EFFECTS: EXPERIMENTS 17 AND 18

In the variations described up to this point, the subject, in the role of teacher, is alone. He is without allies or pressures from peers—from others at his or her level in the hierarchy. It was inevitable, given Milgram's close association with Solomon Asch (discussed in Chapter One), that he would investigate the role of group dynamics within the obedience framework.

From a conceptual point of view, Milgram was intrigued with the differences between *obedience*—the central problem of his own work —and *conformity*, the process which had received extraordinarily sophisticated analysis by Asch (and which had been the focus of his own Ph.D. dissertation). He points to four distinctions: (1) Obedience involves a hierarchical structure, while conformity involves influence from peers, that is, from those at a similar level of status. (2) Obedience involves performing an act that is required rather than modeled, while conformity involves imitation. (3) Obedience is explicit—little subtlety is involved in being given orders—while conformity has a greater element of "implicitness" in the type of pressure exerted. (4) People readily acknowledge the source of their obedience, namely, the authority figure, while they generally deny that they have conformed to peers. Thus, two phenomena that are readily thought of as being similar (how easy it is to simply use the terms interchangeably) are quite distinct in their psychological foundations.

Experiment 17: Two Peers Rebel

This experiment, which was also featured in an earlier publication (Milgram, 1965c), involved what might be termed "conforming to disobedience." Four (apparent) subjects appeared for an experiment on the effects of "collective teaching and punishment" on memory and learning. Only one of the individuals was a true subject. A rigged draw produced the learner and three teachers. Teachers 1 and 2, who were confederates of the experimenter, were given the duties of administering the test and recording the learner's responses; the real subject, Teacher 3, actually pressed the shock levers (see Figure 3.2).

What would the subject do if the other "teachers" disobeyed the experimenter? This was the central issue. The experiment placed the subject in another dilemma: what to do when receiving orders from the experimenter but witnessing, simultaneously, the defiance of two peers. The script for this variation called for Teacher 1 to withdraw at the tenth level (150 volts), and for Teacher 2 to disobey at the fourteenth level (210 volts).

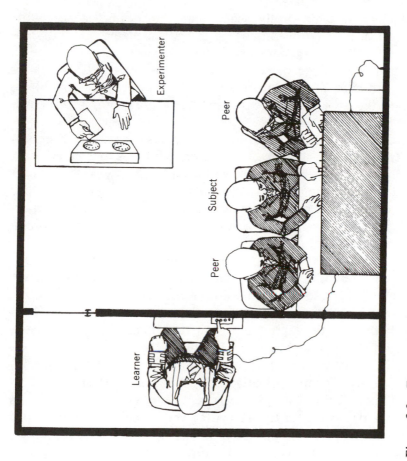

Figure 3.2. Two peers rebel.

The defiant "peers" were an extremely powerful influence. Only four subjects (10 percent) followed instructions to the 450-volt level. Four broke off at the point of the first act of defiance; 23 broke off after the second. Milgram views this result as particularly significant: "The effects of peer rebellion are very impressive in undercutting the experimenter's authority. Indeed, of the score of experimental variations completed in this study, none was so effective . . . as the manipulation reported here" (p. 118).

Milgram, characteristically, scanned an array of plausible accounts for the effect of peer rebellion. One suggests that the peers (or confederates) provided a model of successful defiance. They presented a vivid example of a specific behavioral choice, a response which resulted in no harmful consequences, and which obviously could have weakened the impact of the experimenter's threatening prods (such as "you have no other choice").

Once having defied the authority, the peers became in effect part of the true subject's audience. They were witnesses to his continued obedience, a factor which may have increased the psychological cost involved in remaining in this setting. Their acts of disobedience also may have removed some of the awkwardness or sense of embarrassment experienced by subjects as they considered their own possibilities of withdrawing.

Milgram also tested the proposition that group pressure might work in the opposite direction and facilitate harmful obedience.[6] An experiment was conducted using a procedure similar to that of Experiment 17, the exception being that the two peers were completely faithful to the experimenter's instructions. The naive subject, once again, had the primary responsibility for pressing the shock levers. The peers reinforced the experimenter's instructions and criticized any signs of imminent defiance on the part of the subject.

Here the effect of the peers was negligible. Twenty-nine subjects (72.5 percent) obeyed to the 450-volt level, a result not significantly greater than the baseline figure of 65 percent. Milgram's interpretation emphasizes the predominance of the authority wielded by the experimenter. Peer pressure in this variation overlaps with the influence of the experimenter, but does not seem to contribute beyond it. In effect, there were no subjects who would have been able to defy the experimenter but remained in the situation solely because of the additional influence exerted by the peers.

Experiment 18: A Peer Administers Shocks

In the final variation, Milgram placed the naive subject in the role of a bystander who was formally engaged in subsidiary acts while another subject (a confederate) actually pressed the levers. This peer was completely obedient. The question raised here was the degree to which subjects would intervene on behalf of the victim when their role in delivering the shocks was only a very indirect one. This variation resembles Experiment 13a in which the subject also observed another subject shocking the learner. In that variation, however, the subject was faced with a peer who "spontaneously" had adopted an authoritative manner and suggested that the subject administer shocks to the learner. As noted, most subjects refused to obey this individual. In Experiment 18, however, the subject and his partner (confederate) were placed in essentially the same middle position in the hierarchy —teacher and helper. How would subjects react to the obedience of someone else?

Thirty-seven subjects (93 percent) remained in their subsidiary role and took no action in terms of leaving the scene or rescuing the learner. Milgram suggests that one's willingness to be a party to the consequences of destructive obedience is increased if one is psychologically removed from *immediate* responsibility:

> Any competent manager of a destructive bureaucratic system can arrange his personnel so that only the most callous and obtuse are directly involved in violence. The greater part of the personnel can consist of men and women who, by virtue of their distance from the actual acts of brutality, will feel little strain in their performance of supportive functions. They will feel doubly absolved from responsibility. First, legitimate authority has given full warrant for their actions. Second, they have not themselves committed brutal physical acts. (P. 122)

A study by Kilham and Mann (1974), to be described in the next chapter, has pursued the "chain of command" issue raised here by Milgram.

Group Pressure and Action Against a Person

Milgram performed an additional experiment which, though involving the basic paradigm, did not deal with obedience but rather, conformity.[7] He introduces this experiment by noting that Asch's conformity paradigm involved a verbal response (to the line estimation task). Milgram had questioned whether a similar conformity effect would be observed when the response involved a concrete act with irrevocable consequences. It is in this context that he also raised the subject of studying behavior of greater significance (harming a person) as compared to the performance of laboratory tasks with little intrinsic interest.

Four adult subjects arrived and, by random draw, were assigned the roles of teacher (1, 2, or 3) and learner. The experimenter's instructions gave the three teachers the duty of punishing the learner for errors as in the usual procedure, but with this very crucial restriction:

> Now the amount of punishment given on any trial is decided by the teachers themselves. Each of you will suggest a shock level. And the shock actually administered will be the lowest level suggested by any of the three teachers. (1964, p. 138)

To impose the element of group pressure, the arrangement was that two of the teachers would recommend that the shocks be increased by one step for each error. The naive subject was in a position to control the maximum shock level regardless of the advice given by the other teachers (confederates). This experiment is, of course, similar to Experiment 11, in which the subject was free to select the amount of punishment—neither that experiment nor the present variation involved commands from the experimenter.

The results indicated a pronounced effect of the peers' recommended shock levels. By the thirtieth trial, at which point the other "teachers" were advocating that 450 volts be delivered, the average subject was pressing the fourteenth lever (210 volts). The corresponding shock level for the control condition—in Experiment 11—was approximately the fourth lever. Only two subjects administered shocks beyond the tenth level in Experiment 11, as compared to 27 in the present group-pressure investigation.

Thus, subjects will indeed conform to the action suggested by two peers, results which confirm and extend those reported by Asch. Milgram observes that the experimenter does in fact play at least a subtle role in the group-pressure scenario, specifically in sanctioning the use of severe shocks. Thus, his presence and instructions that *any* shock level might be administered are factors that cannot be dismissed completely when accounting for the effects of peer suggestion.

TENTATIVE CONCLUSIONS

The remaining chapters will be concerned with a detailed analysis of reactions to the obedience experiments from a number of perspectives. At this point, however, it is appropriate to draw some tentative conclusions bearing on Milgram's research.

Figure 3.3 summarizes the entire set of experimental variations in terms of the index given highest priority by Milgram, the percentage of subjects obeying to the final 450-volt level. Variations in the specific setting in terms of status, position, and peer influence were often associated with marked changes in the degree of obedience. Other differences—in gender, personnel, locale—turned out not to matter. It is clear, after examining Figure 3.3, that Milgram's central thesis regarding the situational dynamics of obedience receives very considerable support.

One cannot fail to be impressed with the sheer scope of Milgram's research effort. Approximately 1,000 individuals participated in the obedience research program, including the pilot studies, the main set of 18 variations, and several additional conditions reported in journal publications. These individuals were, in virtually all instances, observed on an individual basis![8] It is perhaps unmatched in the social sciences for a single investigator to obtain this kind of extensive data from one paradigm, within the relatively brief time frame (three years) in which the experiments took place. Whatever reservations the reader might have concerning one or another aspect of Milgram's procedures or interpretations, there is, at least, an abundance of empirical evidence. One is thus not likely to be uncertain as to the reliability of his results —at least within his own laboratory—or to have the kind of doubts that often accompany a typical one-shot study, as would be the case if we had been given access only to the 1963 publication.

Milgram was dealing with a unique problem. It is fortunate indeed that he provided such a wealth of data obtained in the systematic design and variations of the obedience paradigm. The strategy of constructing a basic experimental setting and proceeding with numerous methodological variations has an appealing simplicity and elegance. It allows one to grasp quite readily the central ideas, despite the voluminous details. An examination of Milgram's 1974 book will also illustrate an interesting format for presenting the extraordinary amount of statistical data. For each variation, Milgram tabulated the number of individuals proceeding to each of the 30 shock levels (see, for example, Table 1.1 in Chapter One). The entire set of studies is described in terms of such break-off points. One is thus able to visually scan the tables and draw, quite easily, conclusions about a variety of relevant findings, such as the average shock level attained, the percentage of totally obedient subjects, the degree to which individual subjects varied in a particular setting, and so on.[9]

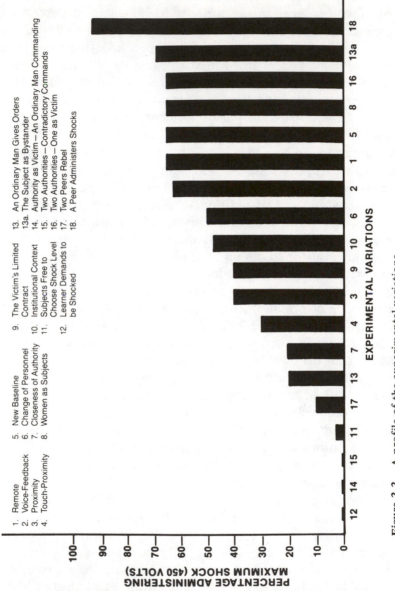

Figure 3.3. A profile of the experimental variations.

Source: Adapted from *Obedience to Authority: An Experimental View* by Stanley Milgram, Copyright © 1974 by Stanley Milgram.

A comment on style seems also in order. Milgram's articulateness, his novel use of metaphor and analogy, the sheer boldness and directness of his presentation—these are, in my view, significant in terms of the impact of his work. This is not to say that these stylistic features have always won support for his position or interpretation, but it is undeniable that Milgram's expressive gifts are part of this story. It is almost as if his goals, at times, were those of a playwright or film director, as much as of a social scientist. People have always been intrigued by this work. It is fair to say, I think, that Milgram's skill as a communicator of ideas has contributed in an important way to the fascination and consternation that his work evokes in so many of its readers.

PLAN OF THE REMAINING CHAPTERS

There are four major types of reactions which have been stimulated by the obedience experiments. The first consists of research on the *substance of obedience*—by investigators other than Milgram himself—and will be the focus of the next chapter. A second concerns the *ethical controversy* that was initiated by Baumrind's (1964) critical essay, and which will be the theme of Chapter Five. A third reaction deals with the *methodological criticisms* of the obedience research—issues concerning the manner in which the experiments were conducted and corresponding difficulties in interpreting their meaning. This area will be considered in Chapter Six. A final reaction concerns the *generalizations* that have been made on the basis of the obedience experiments, specifically to the Holocaust and other socio-political instances of genocide and harmful obedience. This issue, of the "lessons of the obedience experiments," will be examined in Chapter Seven.

Although there is a sufficient coherence in the research literature to justify each of these four categories of reaction or impact, I should point out that it is occasionally somewhat arbitrary whether a particular source has been identified as primarily of one type or another. In actuality, there is often considerable overlap. For instance, a particular essay dealing with the ethics of the obedience research might also provide insightful ideas concerning the political meaning of the research. A methodologically oriented study might have significant implications for generalizations to be made from the laboratory to other settings.

After examining the complex, often vexing issues raised in the four chapters listed above, the reader should be in an informed position to evaluate Milgram's 1974 theoretical position on the nature of obedience to authority. This will be the focus of Chapter Eight, which will also survey the reviews given to Milgram's 1974 book, *Obedience to Authority*. An overall appraisal of the obedience experiments will be the object of the Epilogue.

4

EXTENSIONS AND REPLICATIONS
IN OTHER LABORATORIES

When new views emerge, it is important to test them. It is also important to continue to test rather well-accepted views under new and differing conditions. If questions are never raised, then possibly false views are never challenged. It is a hallmark of science that no views remain immune to challenge.

Selltiz, Wrightsman, and Cook
(1976).

There are important reasons for reviewing research on obedience that has been performed specifically by investigators other than Milgram. First, in science there is a traditional homage given to replication. The most basic requirement of a scientific experiment is that another investigator should obtain similar results if he or she replicates the procedure of the original. Independent verification is informative on a number of grounds, one being the implication that the findings are not dependent upon a particular investigator's biases or influence. Milgram and his research team may, for example, have had expectations about the likely outcome in one or more of their experimental variations. Their subjects' behaviors may have, to a degree, been shaped by these anticipations. Of course, a similar bias could exist in other laboratories, given the same basic methodology. Nevertheless, there is a meaningful increment in the reliability of a scientific phenomenon if it can be observed by other investigators—and particularly in settings which differ in substantively interesting ways from that used by the original researcher. Demonstrating harmful obedience in a setting *other than a psychological laboratory* would, according to this line of reasoning, be a highly informative result.

The existence of a body of literature on a research problem also speaks to the vitality of the topic itself, suggesting that it is provocative, that it has stimulated fresh ideas and novel interpretations. These considerations are particularly germane to the obedience problem, because Milgram, quite justifiably, could have been viewed as having had "the last word" on the subject. For a number of years following his initial publications (1963, 1964, 1965a, 1965b, 1965c), this in fact seemed to be the case. There were no major empirical investigations of obedience to authority until the early 1970s. There is now, however, a reasonably large *research* literature on this issue, and the number of essays and commentaries on Milgram's work is truly extraordinary.

We will examine a number of the major investigations of obedience. Our focus is not upon details of procedure or fine-grained analyses of the results, although information on these matters will be reviewed at least briefly. Rather, attention will be directed at the significance of the research in terms of building upon Milgram's initial development of the obedience concept.

OBEDIENCE IN GERMANY

David Mantell (1971) conducted one of the first major replications of the obedience paradigm. In introducing his investigation, Mantell does not address himself to a specific theoretical issue, but refers to *political or cultural factors* that might be relevant to obedience:

> Those of us . . . who have wondered whether violence and destructiveness are the exclusive property of particular nations at particular times will perhaps be interested to read about the potential for violence in a nation which has been relatively peaceful and quiet for the past 25 years. During the summer of 1970, the Milgram experiment was repeated in Munich, West Germany. (P. 102)

Mantell not only replicated Milgram's original procedure, but he included a novel modeling condition, and also made a number of insightful comments on the obedience paradigm itself. First, however, let us examine his experiment.

Three conditions were involved.[1] A *baseline* condition consisted essentially of a replication of Milgram's original (1963) experiment. A second condition, termed *modeling delegitimization*, was identical to the baseline, with the exception that the subject was first "allowed" to watch an enactment of the obedience study before participating himself. This enactment was a staged scenario in which the teacher, after administering the fourteenth shock, refused to continue. He challenged the authority of the experimenter, and it eventually became apparent that the experiment was not supervised, that the experimenter was not a member of the Max Planck Institute. The person in the teacher role then left, at which time the experimenter returned and proceeded, as usual, with instructions to the (real) subject and the confederate who would play the learner's role. A third condition, *self-decision*, was similar to Milgram's control variation (Experiment 11), with subjects free to decide how much, if any, punishment to administer to the learner.

Results

The three conditions of this experiment produced markedly different behaviors. As in Milgram's control variation, subjects in the *self-decision* group resisted harming the learner—only 2 (7 percent) pressed all 30 shock levers, and 80 percent did not exceed the twenty-fourth lever. Obedience was, however, very extensive in the *baseline* group, with 85 percent of the subjects administering the maximum shock. In the *modeling delegitimization* condition, fifty-two percent[2] of the subjects obeyed instructions to the 450-volt level. Of those defying the experimenter at some point, the majority did so at relatively high levels.

An intensive post-experimental interview was held with each subject. Mantell reports that a pronounced majority of subjects was convinced that the experiment was genuine. Only 6 of the 101 subjects indicated that they would have been willing to play the role of learner (apparently the subjects at this point had not yet been told that the shocks were not actually delivered). Many subjects claimed that in view of the total lack of a response by the learner toward the end of the shock series, they thought that he might have been dead or, at least, unconscious.

Interpretation

Mantell takes a rather grim position on the basis of his findings. As with Milgram, Mantell presents the classic *social-psychological* point of view:

> It would seem that nearly everyone is willing to commit acts of aggression against other people. The differences which appear in their behavior

have less to do with whether they will hurt others or not, but rather under what conditions. The conditions are the primary issue. Why, how much, and with what consequences are secondary concerns. (P. 110)

Mantell concludes his paper with an interesting commentary on the paradigm itself. In one sense, it is a methodological criticism, but in another, it represents a strong inference regarding the validity of the observed behavior:

All the experimental variations share several disturbing features, which make the results they achieved all the more difficult to understand. Every experiment was basically preposterous. While one might expect a person to agree that the study of the effects of punishment on learning is worthwhile, the entire experimental procedure from beginning to end could make no sense at all, even to the layman. A person is strapped to a chair and immobilized and is explicitly told that he is going to be exposed to extremely painful electric shocks. . . . This experiment becomes more incredulous and senseless the further it is carried. It disqualifies and delegitimizes itself. It can only show how much pain one person will impose on another. . . . And yet, the subjects carry on. . . . That is at once the beauty and tragedy of this experiment. It proves that the most banal and superficial of rationales is perhaps not even necessary, but surely is enough to produce destructive behavior in human beings. We thought we had learned this from our history books; perhaps now we have learned it in the laboratory. (Pp. 110-11)

Mantell also raised a number of issues which he considered worthy of further research—a number of these had been addressed in Milgram's own research program but were not accessible at the time of Mantell's investigation. The important problem of the "assignment of responsibility," however, is an issue that Mantell himself addressed in a subsequent publication (Mantell and Panzarella, 1976). We will examine this study in Chapter Eight, since it pertains more directly to Milgram's (1974) theoretical model.

Mantell's experiment is important in several respects. It was one of the first published replications of the obedience experiment, and it included a new situational variation—the modeling-delegitimization condition.[3] The location of the study in Germany also provided a cultural extension of the paradigm. It is unlikely that many readers could fail to visualize images of the Third Reich and the Holocaust given this particular setting. The results were consistent with Milgram's findings, both in terms of the generally high rate of obedience, and of the relevance of paradigm variations in controlling the specific level of obedience. Finally, like Milgram, Mantell took a strongly political and moralistic interpretation of the findings.

INCREASING BUREAUCRATIC COMPLEXITY
IN THE OBEDIENCE PARADIGM

Central to Milgram's (1974) view of obedience is the idea of a *hierarchical social structure*. Obedience to authority rests on the simple fact that people occupy roles of varying power or status—that there are rules or expectations which define appropriate behaviors in one or another position in the hierarchy. There are also different psychological sets or frames of reference that may be associated with different positions in a hierarchical social structure.

In many organizations, such as the military or government, there are complex chains of command. It is rare for the highest authority to issue orders *directly* to the person carrying them out. Rather there is a delegation of responsibility to a subordinate who, in turn, instructs another individual to perform a specified duty or task. Historically, this functional aspect of organizations or bureaucracies has been recognized as of considerable importance. The key role played by Adolf Eichmann in the Nazi extermination policy is usually interpreted as an illustration of the middle-level bureaucrat, one who does not define orders or establish policy but who is assigned the role of managing the execution of such directives.

Kilham and Mann (1974) were interested in the degree to which a person would obey orders from an experimenter when he or she was not required to administer shocks directly to the learner, but, rather, was given the job of relaying the orders to another person who actually pressed the switches. Their hypothesis was that, "the individual in the transmitter role, because he is one step removed from the act, is more obedient to destructive commands than the subject in the executant role" (p. 697).

The execution of this experiment followed the basic obedience paradigm, specifically that of the "voice-feedback" variation (Experiment 2), but with the inclusion of the role of transmitter. The person in this position monitored the learner's responses and announced to the teacher—termed "executant" by Kilham and Mann—whether or not they were correct. The transmitter also indicated the particular voltage to be administered, based on preliminary instructions from the experimenter. Other features, for example the tape-recorded protests and the prods used by the experimenter, were similar to the procedure used by Milgram. The transmitter was thus a functionary, a kind of "extra" who performed most of the duties typically performed by the teacher, with one crucial exception—he did not actually press the shock levers.

Kilham and Mann used three conditions. The naive subject (recruited from students at the University of Sydney, Australia) was randomly assigned to either the *transmitter* role, the *executant* (teacher) role, or a *control* condition. When the subject was in the role of executant, the person acting as transmitter (confederate of experimenter) kept pressing for increasingly severe shocks. When the subject was in the transmitter role, the person acting as executant (confederate) followed the transmitter's instructions. Control subjects were assigned to either the transmitter or executant roles but were told to administer as much or as little shock as they wished, as in the control groups used by Mantell as well as Milgram. The learner, in all instances, was a confederate of the experimenter. Finally, the experiment was replicated for each sex. The physical arrangement of the laboratory is shown in Figure 4.1.

Results

The results of this study are summarized in Table 4.1. The hypothesis that the transmitter condition would facilitate obedience was clearly supported. In terms of both average shock level and percentage of obedience to the 450-volt level, transmitters were significantly more obedient than executants. Transmitters, when they defied the experimenter, did so at a considerably later phase in the shock series

Table 4.1. Mean Obedience Level and Percentage of Subjects Fully Obedient for Experimental and Control Conditions

Condition*	Mean level of obedience (0-30)	% fully obedient
Male transmitter	28.30	68
Female transmitter	27.50	40
Male executant	23.00	40
Female executant	17.80	16
Control (male and female combined)	3.12	0

*n = 25 for each condition.

Source: From Kilham and Mann, Copyright © 1974 by the American Psychological Association. Reprinted by permission.

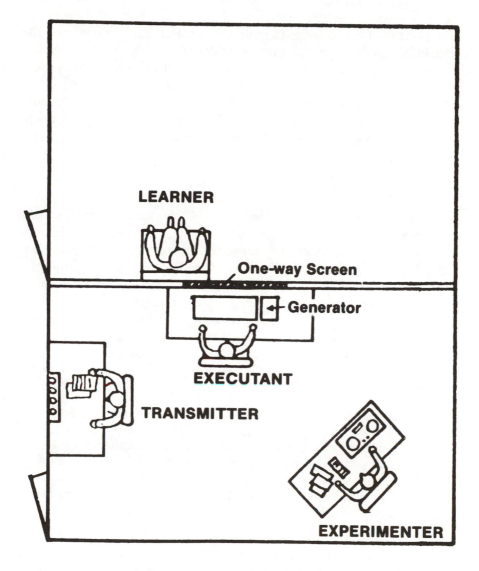

Figure 4.1. General layout of laboratory showing seating arrangement for experimenter, transmitter, executant, and learner.

Source: From Kilham and Mann, Copyright © 1974 by the American Psychological Association. Reprinted by permission.

than did executants. At level 20, more than 90 percent of the transmitters were still obedient. Less than 50 percent of the executants were obedient at this point.

Control subjects were, as in previous research, inclined to use the minimum amount of punishment. Kilham and Mann also note that males were more obedient than females, a difference that was more substantial in the executant condition. This cannot be taken as clear evidence that males are generally more obedient, however. Because males were being asked to shock a *male learner*, whereas females were punishing a *female learner*, the results could just as likely reflect a greater resistance to harming women than men.

Interpretation

Most impressive is the ingenuity of Kilham and Mann in creating a microcosm of a bureaucracy. They relate this study to Milgram's Experiment 18, in which the subject occupied a bystander role vis-a-vis a totally obedient peer. This condition was not precisely that of a transmitter, but it also involved the subject in a subsidiary role, a position that was tolerable to 90 percent of the participants who observed another person shocking the learner to the 450-volt level. Kilham and Mann's transmitters were less obedient, but their role was far more explicit and central to the operation of the experiment.

Kilham and Mann explain the transmitter role in terms of *responsibility*:

> In real organizations the transmitter role is often regarded as a minor one that entails little or no responsibility. The transmitter's function may be merely that of a medium, a cog in the machine who does nothing more than shuffle papers or move them from one tray to another. Perhaps it is one of the characteristic effects of the role that with the passage of time, individuals who act as transmitters often begin to respond as machines, dehumanizing themselves and others. (P. 701)

A similar theme is expressed by Hannah Arendt in her influential and highly controversial analysis of Adolf Eichmann. In *Eichmann in Jerusalem* (1963), Arendt does not exculpate Eichmann, but she recognizes the plausibility of the transmitter function as a defense:

> In its judgment the court naturally conceded that such a crime could be committed only by a giant bureaucracy using the resources of government. But insofar as it remains a crime—and that, of course, is the premise for a trial—all the cogs in the machinery, no matter how insignificant, are in court forthwith transformed back into perpetrators, that is to say, into human beings. (P. 289)

Thus, Kilham and Mann's transmitters may have felt exonerated because of their role—they weren't ordering the shocks, nor were they delivering them—but in Arendt's view, this hardly provided a *moral justification* for their actions.

Notice that subjects in the role of executant (that is, teacher) were less obedient. The average for male and female subjects was 28 percent, compared to Milgram's result of 65 percent. Kilham and Mann speculate that this may have reflected socio-cultural dynamics:

> The zeitgeist in Australia in 1971 was different from the climate in the United States 10 years earlier when Milgram conducted his studies. A decade of campus unrest and antiwar demonstrations would have made some difference in student attitudes toward authority. . . . There may also be national differences in obedience ideology that contribute to a predisposition to obey or defy authority, as suggested by studies comparing Australian and United States reactions to the Calley trial verdict and to the problem of following military orders (Mann, 1973). (P. 702)[4]

It is difficult to establish, with certainty, this kind of rationale. However, its cross-cultural perspective illustrates another aspect of the impact of Milgram's obedience research on social science. For further investigations of obedience with a cross-cultural theme but also including a unique subject population, we turn to two studies conducted in Jordan.

OBEDIENCE IN CHILDREN

Shanab and Yahya (1977) conducted an obedience experiment in Amman, Jordan, using 192 female and male students enrolled in public schools. Their stated purpose was "to extend Milgram's original work on obedience to a new culture and age group" (p. 531). They predicted that females would be more obedient than males (based on a study by Sheridan and King, 1972, which had observed a sex difference in obedience—this will be described in Chapter Six), not noting, however, Milgram's own failure to find such an effect (Experiment 8). They also anticipated that older children would be more obedient than younger children, on the assumption that obedience is a learned social response.

The basic obedience paradigm was used with the following changes. A female played the role of experimenter—the only instance, to my knowledge, in which this has occurred. The shock generator consisted of only 20 levers. Verbal protests from the learner, who was in an adjoining room, were "live," that is, not standardized on tape. For male subjects, male confederates, ages 11 to 15, played the role of learner; for females, one female confederate, aged 15, was used. Subjects were at one of three median ages: 7.5, 10.15, and 14.5 yrs. Subjects were assigned to the experimental condition, that is, the obedience paradigm, or to a control condition in which they were free to stop giving shocks at any time. If they did choose to administer shocks, however, they, also, were asked to increase the voltage by one unit for each successive response.

Results

Shanab and Yahya observed a striking confirmation of Milgram's baseline result. Seventy-three percent of their subjects obeyed instructions to the final shock level on the generator. Only 16 percent of the control subjects proceeded to this final level. *Obedience was not related to either the sex or age level of the subjects.* The investigators reported that female subjects were more likely to manifest relatively extreme symptoms of emotional tension (nervous laughter, lip biting, trembling, etc.) than males, but this response pattern was quite pervasive. There was also a tendency for older subjects to express less intense emotional arousal.

Interpretation

This experiment provides important evidence with respect to the validity of Milgram's initial results. The overall level of obedience is itself noteworthy, but more interesting, perhaps, is the *failure* to confirm hypotheses based on the age and sex of the child in the role of teacher. Once again, individual differences (in age and gender) which are presumed to relate to obedience are shown to be without significance. The fact that approximately 25 percent of the children in this study were able to disengage themselves from the experimenter's authority might well be viewed as an achievement in itself, a triumph of conscience! It would be of no minor interest to observe defiance in a 7-year-old child. Readers who have seen the film, *Obedience*, will remember the great drama that was occasioned by defiance, the crisis of conscience which seemed to be the necessary precursor to disobedience. One wonders if defiance in young children involved a similar scenario of conflict, embarrassment, and ultimate persistence.

This investigation, by itself, contributes relatively little in terms of a theoretical advance in our understanding of obedience. Nevertheless, the fact that the results clearly corroborate those of Milgram, given marked differences in so many particular details of the procedure, is significant. The likelihood of young children being suspicious of the experimental setting—of the reality of the learner's pain, for example—would seem to be extremely remote. Thus, from a methodological point of view, this investigation is highly informative.

Shanab and Yahya (1978) also performed an obedience experiment using students at the University of Jordan as their subjects. The procedure was similar to Milgram's baseline experiment (1963). Male as well as female subjects were used, each paired with a same-sex partner (confederate) in the role of learner. The experimenter was female. Other minor departures from Milgram's paradigm included the use of 20 (rather than 30) steps on the shock generator, and the use of three rather than four increasingly insistent prods (Milgram's Prod Three was omitted). The learner was positioned in an adjoining room, with the door ajar so that the subject would be able to hear the learner. The schedule of protests included pounding on the wall at the fourteenth shock level and a painful scream at the sixteenth level, after which the learner was completely silent.

Subjects in the experimental group were instructed to increase the shock level for each error on the memory task. Subjects in the control group were free to shock or not shock, as they chose, at any time during the experiment. If they did shock the learner, however, each succeeding shock had to be one step higher than the preceding one. As with Milgram's procedure, all subjects were told that the shocks would not cause any tissue damage.

The results were clear. Of the experimental group, 62.5 percent delivered the complete series of 20 shocks. Of the control group, only 12.5 percent reached the final shock level. The sex of the subject was not a significant factor, either in terms of obedience to the final shock level or average maximum shock level. Unfortunately, the investigators did not outline in any detail the expression of conflict or tension in their subjects, a behavioral outcome with importance in its own right. The authors noted, "All subjects were fully debriefed at the conclusion of the experiment. No subject appeared to be affected adversely throughout the experiment" (p. 268). Thus, it is unclear whether subjects generally did not manifest the agitation reported by Milgram or whether their emotional responses were simply not viewed as "adverse" reactions by the investigators.

Shanab and Yahya interpreted their findings as a powerful testimony to the reliability of Milgram's basic finding, specifically to the cross-cultural generality of destructive obedience. The absence of sex differences supports a similar finding of Milgram (1974) and of their own study with children (Shanab and Yahya, 1977), but differs from research showing greater obedience in males (Kilham and Mann, 1974) as well as in females (Sheridan and King, 1972).

OBEDIENCE WITH ONE'S SELF AS VICTIM

John Martin and his colleagues (1976) were interested in "how far [subjects] would be prepared to carry out an experimental task clearly and explicitly described as being potentially harmful to themselves" (p. 346). The background to this investigation was the general finding that experimental subjects are willing to comply with requests to perform acts which are noxious, tedious, and perhaps dangerous (Orne, 1962). Milgram's work was cited briefly in their introduction. The implication was that any sizable amount of obedience whose outcome might involve personal injury would be testimony to the extraordinary influence of behavioral researchers, a kind of "testing of the limits."

Their procedure was quite unique. The stated purpose was to identify individuals who possessed a rare ability to hear ultra-high-frequency sounds. Forty-two male school children, aged 13 to 14, were asked if they wished to participate. They were first told that the test involved each subject's administering to his own ears a signal which could vary from 0 (20,000 cycles per second, with no danger) to 10 (70,000 cycles per second, with maximum danger). Subjects were told that no danger existed for people who possessed the hearing trait, but that only about 5 percent did in fact have such an ability.

The apparatus involved a variety of electrical gadgetry, the key feature being a dial, labeled 0 to 10, and an accompanying chart listing the frequencies and associated danger levels. For example, level 4 was described as 40,000 c.p.s.—Danger Condition 2—12 percent possible hearing loss. Level 8 was presented as 60,000 c.p.s.—Extreme High Danger Level—50 percent hearing loss has been reported at this level. Level 10, at 70,000 c.p.s. was not labeled. Martin et al. thus employed a graded series of potentially damaging stimulus levels, analogous to the shock generator used in the obedience paradigm. The primary measure was the dial setting of each subject. Before describing these results, I should mention several features that make this experiment substantially different from the usual obedience study:

1. Subjects were told by their regular teacher that another scientist would speak to them about the sound experiment. Thus, to a degree at least, one of the authority figures was the subject's own teacher.

2. The voluntary aspect of the subject's participation was emphasized at several points. No prods were used to elicit higher frequency settings.
3. No sound actually passed through the headphones. In effect, this experiment asked subjects to indicate how great a *risk* they were willing to take regarding their own hearing loss, with the entire rationale being framed in terms of the subject's response to the authority of the investigator. It should be noted that the investigators demonstrated considerable concern for the subject's welfare both during the experiment and in post-experimental interviews.

Results

The results, according to Martin et al., were indicative of considerable compliance; whether this should be viewed as "obedience" will be considered below. Ninety-five percent of all subjects turned the dial to at least level 6 (high danger: 20 percent possible hearing loss), and *53.9 percent proceeded to the maximum level*. Reactions of tension and anxiety were prevalent, as in Milgram's subjects:

> El observed considerable concern in many Ss. He was frequently asked such questions as "Will we go deaf?" "Whose fault is it if we go deaf?" "Is it bad to go in there with a headache?" "If you go deaf, can you sue the bloke?" These concerns were fairly characteristic of the group of Ss as a whole. . . . Several Ss expressed concern about "what happens if you don't go in?" Despite the reminder "you don't have to participate if you don't want to" given by El (the teacher), one anxious-looking S nevertheless remarked, "Oh hell! I'm next," and without further hesitation proceeded to the experiment. (P. 351)

In responding to post-experimental questionnaires, subjects invariably expressed a belief in the stated purpose of the study. Approximately half of the subjects mentioned "trust in the office and authority of the experimenter" as a basis for their participation. A large number indicated that they agreed to participate out of curiosity—"to see if I could hear the sound."

Interpretation

The authors clearly view their data as related to Milgram's obedience experiments, in the sense that their subjects committed themselves to a course of potentially injurious behavior under the auspices of an authority figure. Their emphasis is, of course, the uniqueness of the victim—the subject himself:

> On this point the conditions of the experiment contrast with those in
> Milgram's studies of obedience, where immunity from immediate dam-
> age to the self was explicit. Yet, despite this important difference in
> the expected locus of suffering, the results are closely comparable with
> Milgram's. (P. 352)

Martin et al. also suggest that their results support Milgram's contention that "aggression toward the helpless victim" is *not* a central dynamic in the obedience paradigm. Their reasoning is that their own
subjects' behavior could hardly be explained in terms of a disposition
to harm themselves. Common to both the Milgram paradigm and their
own methodology, however, is the issue of legitimate authority.

Martin et al. claim that obedience to authority, almost by definition, involves behaving in a manner that goes against one's natural
preference, that involves some "cost, deprivation, or pain" (p. 355).
They suggest that the experimenter in both the Milgram paradigm and
their own study is a *non-malevolent* authority—witness, for example,
Milgram's assurances regarding "no permanent tissue damage" and the
obvious merits of the scientific study of learning. Thus, the authors
are, implicitly at least, challenging Milgram's assertion that his experiment exposed subjects to "malevolent authority:"

> It is still to be shown that authority would be conceded if either (a) the
> E's declared goal were judged to be illegitimate or malevolent, or (b) the
> claim that the specified steps are necessary for its achievement were
> shown to be false. (P. 355)

The study by Martin et al. is instructive. By obtaining high levels
of "self-immolation," they force us to think about the laboratory and
what can occur there. While this matter will be given more thorough
discussion in Chapter Six, a brief reaction is appropriate at this point.
There is no doubt that the "legitimacy" factor is important. Considerable legitimacy pervades the context of a research laboratory, and we
should no longer be surprised at this fact. However, the Milgram paradigm, in my view, is so radically different from the procedures used
by Martin et al., that it is difficult to be persuaded by their arguments
regarding the non-malevolence of the authority.

As noted in Chapter One, the prods used by the experimenter were
vital in terms of operationalizing the authority concept. I think that
there is a reasonable doubt whether an experimenter can *legitimately*
say to a subject, "You have no other choice—you must go on." Martin et al. did not acknowledge this issue, nor did they refer to Milgram's Experiment 9, which featured the experimenter overruling an

explicit prior agreement made with the learner. These examples may not illustrate exactly what Martin et al. claim to be crucial, in that the basic purpose of Milgram's study (the experimenter's goal) was not shown to be illegitimate or immoral—but they do seem to approach such a conclusion.

Finally, there could be a serious question whether this experiment should in fact be termed an "obedience" study. The pressure—the agonizing conflict between an authority's commands and the subject's personal desires—seems missing, to a large degree. There really are no "orders" in this study, and the voluntary element of the subject's participation is continually emphasized. Although using the term "obedience" in their title, and elsewhere in the article, Martin et al. also use, seemingly interchangeably, the term "compliance." Compliance, I think, is different from obedience, and is a more accurate designation for what occurred in this research.

In conclusion, the study by Martin et al. displays, in a quite novel way, the power of an authority to influence people to perform acts of the most unusual kind. I think the point raised by Martin et al. that authority generally subsumes a set of behaviors which are not naturally preferred or gratifying, is also a relevant observation. Whether their behavior should be called obedience or compliance may be less significant than the fact that many of the subjects did not like what they found themselves doing—but they did it regardless.

DOCTORS' ORDERS: OBEDIENCE IN THE HOSPITAL

What will nurses do when receiving illegal instructions from a physician? This question received a provocative analysis by a group of psychiatrists and nurses (Hofling et al., 1966). In many respects this investigation was a remarkable parallel to Milgram's initial publication, although there is no mention of the Milgram study in this article, and it is likely that Hofling et al. were not aware of Milgram's research. What is special about this investigation is that it subjected a naturally occurring social hierarchy, namely the physician-nurse relationship, to an analysis in its natural context, the hospital.

Hofling et al. created the following scenario. A physician called a nurse at either a private or a general hospital and told her to administer 20 milligrams of a drug, "Astroten," in four capsules to one of the patients on her ward. This "event" violated several hospital regulations: the medication order was given by phone, the dosage limit specified 10 milligrams, the medication itself was not cleared for use, and the physician's name was fictitious and thus not familiar to any nurse.

An observer—a staff psychiatrist—was placed on each ward unit at the time of the phone call. His primary duty was to terminate the experiment prior to the nurse's entry into the patient's room, but he was also to reveal the experiment's actual purpose to all nurses who participated unwittingly in this study. This procedure was also designed to inquire about the nurse's reaction to the study, as well as to provide support for any negative emotional responses. It is important to note that the nurse was alone at the time of the phone call. A total of 22 nurses were subjects for this research.

Control Condition

Twelve graduate nurses, from another general hospital, constituted one of two control groups; the other was a group of 21 student nurses. The principal investigator provided a detailed verbal as well as written description of the experimental procedure, and asked the nurses to write down "exactly what you would say and do."

Results

The results with the nurses in the ward incident were striking. Of the 22 nurses, 21 would have given the medication as ordered. The phone calls were brief, and the investigators report that "essentially no resistance to the order was expressed to the caller" (p. 174). Thus, 95 percent of the subjects obeyed the physician under circumstances that were explicitly in violation of hospital regulations.

Based on subsequent interviews, the investigators report some additional findings of interest. Eleven nurses indicated an awareness of the discrepancy between the maximum dosage and the physician's orders, and 18 were aware of the impropriety of non-emergency telephone orders. Many agreed that it was not an uncommon violation. The authors report that in 17 cases, the nurses manifested signs of anxiety or "psychopathology of everyday life," ranging from erroneous recollections of the phone call itself to being unable to find the Astroten box when it was placed in a very prominent location in the medicine supply cabinet. None of the nurses became overtly angry or hostile, either during the phone conversation or during the interview. Reactions upon being told of the deception were variable, including scientific interest, mild anxiety, guilt or irritation, and "veiled anger."

Of the 12 graduate nurses in the control conditions, 10 reported that they would not have given the medication; each of the 21 student nurses indicated similarly that she would not have followed the physician's instructions. The investigators' conclusions are sobering:

> In a real-life situation corresponding to the experimental one, there would, in theory, be two professional intelligences, the doctor's and the nurse's, working to ensure that a given procedure be undertaken in a manner beneficial to the patient. . . . The experiment strongly suggests, however, that in the real-life situation, one of these intelligences is, for all practical purposes, nonfunctioning. (P. 176)

The implications of the control data are clear: Nurses have, in the abstract, an idealized and very correct view of what their behavior should have been under the circumstances of this experiment. Yet, in their behavior, they failed to act on the basis of such ideals.

The investigators also present an informative discussion of why nurses might typically trust physicians, and of the functional value of nurses being fundamentally oriented toward agreeing with doctors' instructions. Indeed the prospect of a nurse being *continuously attentive* to the prospects of illegal or inappropriate orders would seem bizarre and counterproductive of any reasonable degree of efficiency, particularly in any sort of emergency context. What seems to trouble the researchers here, however, is the "automatic" aspect of the nurses' behavior, that is, the fact that they were so quick to agree. Acknowledging that nurses have an understandable motive to be liked or approved of by physicians, Hofling et al. nevertheless argue that:

> The observance of professional courtesy and loyalty need not have precluded the making of relevant inquiries. It need not have precluded the nurses' making some sort of *appraisal* of the situation and then arriving at a *conscious decision* instead of an automatic response. . . . there appears to be room for greater intellectual activity—the pursuit of which need not be aggressive, destructive, or (to speak of the majority of nurses) unfeminine. (P. 179)

This study provides a highly instructive verification of one of Milgram's central arguments. Once again, we observe a sharp contrast between what people *think* they will do in a situation involving a conflict of conscience and what people *actually* do in such a circumstance. The care and precision with which Hofling et al. appear to have conducted their research are impressive, given the inherently difficult methodological hurdles associated with investigating this problem in a natural setting. Although this investigation bears only a faint resemblance to the Milgram paradigm in actual details—no prods, no unwilling victim, an authority figure not physically present—it seems to capture the essence of Milgram's concern: the realization of a hierarchical social structure, namely the physician-nurse-patient, in which the nurse's role is invested with a conflict deriving from (a) a proper course of action with respect to the patient, and (b) incompatible demands from a powerful authority figure. Unlike Milgram's subjects, the nurses in this study were not aware that their performance was being monitored. It becomes difficult, therefore, to attribute their behavior to influences which might be associated with the role or status of "experimental subject,"—an important methodological issue which will be examined in Chapter Six.

Another Look at Obedience in the Hospital

Rank and Jacobson (1977) were concerned with two features of the Hofling et al. study that seemed unrepresentative of hospital routine: first, that the nurses had no medical knowledge of the drug (the fictitious Astroten) and thus were completely dependent upon the physician, and second, that the nurses were not allowed to interact with anyone of equal or higher rank in the hospital concerning the order to administer the Astroten.

Rank and Jacobson replicated the essential procedure used by Hofling et al., but with the following changes: (1) The drug was a highly familiar one to all nurses (Valium), with the prescribed dosage (30 milligrams) being far above the recommended level (2-10 milligrams) in the *Physician's Desk Reference*. (2) The nurse was allowed to contact her supervisor or the pharmacy and to talk with other nurses—this "contact" had actually been a condition for terminating a nurse's participation in the Hofling et al. study. (3) The nurses were, technically, volunteers. For ethical reasons, all nurses were contacted several days prior to this experiment and were asked to volunteer for an experiment that would be conducted at a later date. The subjects in this study were obtained from those who had indicated a willingness to participate. (4) The physician phoning in the order gave the name of an actual staff doctor.

The major finding is that only 2 of 18 subjects actually proceeded as far as preparing the medication for delivery. The remaining nurses, 10 of whom in fact obtained the prescribed amount of Valium, attempted to check the physician's order in some manner, usually trying to contact the doctor for verification. Rank and Jacobson summarize their findings:

> Nurses aware of the toxic effects of a drug and allowed to interact naturally with each other will *not* administer a medication overdose merely because a physician orders it. In the absence of strong physician prodding, they will question the order in a variety of ways and will refuse to give the medication until they are given a reasonable assurance of its safety. (1977, p. 191)

Rank and Jacobson also obtained questionnaire responses from a group of 34 nurses who were given a description of the procedure, and asked for their likely course of action. *None* of these individuals predicted that they would have followed the physician's orders.

Why did Rank and Jacobson's nurses refuse to obey the physician's phone order immediately? The investigators' explanation is one of social support. The fact that these nurses were allowed—and took explicit advantage of—the opportunity to "check things out" with other hospital personnel appears to have reduced the authority of the physician. The investigators relate these findings to research which testifies to the effects of peer support when an individual is under strong social pressure (for example, Asch, 1955). Milgram's Experiment 17—two peers rebel—is cited in this context. The authors believe that their procedure was a fairer test of obedience than that used by Hofling et al. in that "most nurses . . . would find the inability to interact quite unusual and suspicious" (p. 192). They list other factors which could have facilitated the nurses' resistance to orders, for example, their volunteer status, the fact that since the time of the Hofling et al. study, physicians have become more open to criticism, that nurses perceive themselves to be more of an integral part of the health team, and that they are themselves open to malpractice suits.

Interpretation

It is difficult to reconcile the discrepant findings in the Hofling et al., and Rank and Jacobson investigations. Hofling et al. emphasize not only the virtually unanimous obedience but also the lack of delay or resistance once their nurses had received the call. In contrast, Rank and Jacobson note the considerable interaction and questioning of the order by their nurses. In fact, as noted earlier, Hofling et al. were explicitly concerned about their subjects' lack of appraisal, that is, their failure to engage in precisely the kind of search for a proper resolution that was in fact demonstrated by a majority of Rank and Jacobson's subjects.

If one considers these experiments as a conceptually linked pair of investigations, they provide a powerful field demonstration of Milgram's situational view of obedience. The Hofling et al. study tested obedience under conditions of virtual solitude for the nurse, and the obedience rate was very high. Rank and Jacobson tested obedience under conditions of peer support, and obedience dropped sharply. Rank and Jacobson are persuasive in asserting that their procedure more closely resembles the everyday social context of nurses. Yet, there clearly are times when nurses are alone, and, of course, it would require only one episode of the kind of obedience shown by Hofling et al. for a potentially fatal outcome to occur.

It should also be noted, in conclusion, that although Rank and Jacobson quite justifiably emphasize their subjects' independent reactions, it is nevertheless true that 67 percent of their subjects "got the prescribed amount of the drug and held it in their hands" (p. 191). Thus, there was considerable obedience at the most initial stage of their interaction with the physician. Their "achievement" was to engage in verbal dialogue with their peers—"In only one case did the nurse fail to make any comment to her co-workers concerning the order" (p. 191). It is difficult to say whether or not the nurses in Hofling et al.'s study would have performed similarly. My best guess is that they would have done so, were peers readily accessible as in Rank and Jacobson's procedure. What remains perplexing, however, is why the (isolated) nurses in Hofling et al.'s study did not make at least one phone call to recheck the order. It should be recognized that Rank and Jacobson acknowledged that it would have been methodologically advantageous had they included a *precise replication* of the Hofling et al. study as well as their own modification. However, this was prevented because the current hospital drug policy prevented access to undesignated medications (such as "Astroten" in the Hofling et al. research). Although the differences in the design of the two studies are sufficiently extensive to prevent a precise accounting of their radically different findings, it is very likely that the effect of peer interaction, as well as knowledge of the drug itself, were factors which "released" the nurses in this study from the kind of blind obedience shown by Hofling et al.

CONCLUSIONS

The major purpose of this chapter has been to establish the reliability of the obedience phenomenon, specifically to assess the replicability of Milgram's central findings in other laboratories.[5] Four of the investigations reviewed here—those by Mantell, by Kilham and Mann and the two experiments by Shanab and Yahya—were direct extensions of Milgram's paradigm. Each of these investigations was conducted in a country other than the United States, and involved different subject populations in terms of background or age. Considerable levels of obedience were observed in each case.

The study by Martin et al., although not designed primarily as a pure extension of the Milgram paradigm, addresses the issue of the subject's trust in the authority of the experimenter. Their focus upon the subjects' willingness to risk damage *to themselves* provides a unique kind of extension to the response measure—harm doing—which is of central importance in Milgram's research. The Hofling et al. study provides convincing evidence of obedience under *non-laboratory* conditions, and the Rank and Jacobson experiment, while clearly different in outcome, also speaks to precisely the kind of situational basis of obedience—or defiance—which is emphasized by Milgram.

Clearly, the phenomenon of obedience to harmful orders is generalizable beyond the confines of Milgram's laboratory. Despite the considerable ingenuity and sheer energy involved in performing research of this kind, a number of investigators have been able to gain impressive experimental control over the obedience problem. We turn now to a consideration of reactions to Milgram's work which have focused particularly upon its ethical (Chapter Five) and methodological (Chapter Six) dimensions. Although commentary on these matters often takes the form of critical essays and subjective appraisal, we will also encounter *empirical research*, that is, experiments that were themselves designed to answer ethical and methodological questions raised by Milgram's findings.

5

WHAT PRICE KNOWLEDGE? THE ETHICS OF THE OBEDIENCE EXPERIMENTS

It is potentially harmful to a subject to commit, in the course of an experiment, acts which he himself considers unworthy, particularly when he has been entrapped into committing such acts by an individual he has reason to trust.

—Diana Baumrind (1964)

The laboratory psychologist senses his work will lead to human betterment, not only because enlightenment is more dignified than ignorance, but because new knowledge is pregnant with humane consequences.

—Stanley Milgram (1964b)

The controversial status of the obedience experiments derives from two basic considerations. One concerns the *meaning* or *significance* of the research—the generalizations that one may draw from its findings. We review these issues in Chapter Six, where we discuss criticisms of the manner in which the research was conducted, and in Chapter Seven, where we focus directly on the inferences drawn from Milgram's research. The second consideration involves the *ethics* of the obedience experiments. It is curious that the obedience experiments, which in many respects are unique and unlike any other variety of behavioral research, have come to be the focal point for analyses and debates about research ethics. This has been true for almost 20 years. From their inception, the obedience experiments unleashed a storm of ethical controversy.

A strong case could be made to the effect that the debate between Diana Baumrind and Stanley Milgram in the *American Psychologist*

(1964) was the impetus for a renaissance of sensitivity to ethical issues in human experimentation. Their exchange is invariably cited in any serious review of research ethics. It was not simply that Milgram had used deception, for countless studies prior to his own had used this procedure, often to an extreme degree—the cognitive dissonance research being a case in point. Nor was the use of electric shock, or at least the prospect of delivering it, a key factor. Schachter's classic affiliation studies (1959) had explicitly threatened subjects with the severe pain of imminent shocks, yet this research is rarely, if ever, cited in terms of its ethical properties. There was, it seems, something about the obedience experiments which aroused a particularly hostile reaction in many readers, a reaction which often involved a general rejection of the experiments and, at least by implication, a personal attack on Milgram himself. It is also true, however, that the obedience research, because of its novelty and vivid impact, sensitized social scientists to a broad array of ethical issues which were, in principle, applicable to research in general, research of a more benign surface quality.

It could be reasoned, of course, that any research investigation that achieves the kind of celebrity status accorded to Milgram's work is likely to elicit criticism simply because of its visibility. However, this is not applicable to the obedience experiments, for they were the subject of an impassioned, and what turned out to be an extraordinarily influential, ethical criticism *less than one year* after Milgram's initial (1963) publication. It is important to note at this point that it was Milgram's response to Baumrind—and his published reactions to a number of other critics as well—that helped to construct an instructive and enriched scholarly foundation for the controversies which emanated from the obedience experiments. The student of the obedience research thus stands to profit, not simply in being able to arrive at a verdict in terms of whether Milgram "wins or loses" the debate, but rather in learning about the values and premises that generate questions about these experiments, and the strategies and resourcefulness of Milgram, and others, in answering them.

Because all of the developments regarding the ethics of the obedience experiments stem from Baumrind's initial critique (1964), it is appropriate to turn now to a detailed consideration of her analysis.[1] We will then attempt to chart, in essentially chronological order, subsequent lines of thought regarding the ethical ramifications of Milgram's experiments.

BAUMRIND'S CRITICISMS

The Experimenter's Responsibilities

Baumrind opens her article with a recognition that certain types of psychological research may prove unsettling to subjects. Noting that the experimenter is obliged to be attentive to the subjects' sense of well-being, particularly if the treatment has induced feelings of insecurity, anxiety, or hostility, Baumrind emphasizes the dependent posture of subjects in experimental settings. She concludes that this role or "mind-set" has important consequences in terms of what may be investigated:

> Because of the anxiety and passivity generated by the setting, the subject is more prone to behave in an obedient, suggestible manner in the laboratory than elsewhere. Therefore, the laboratory is not the place to study degree of obedience or suggestibility, as a function of a particular experimental condition, since the base line for these phenomena as found in the laboratory is probably much higher than in most other settings. Thus experiments in which the relationship to the experimenter as an authority is used as an independent condition are imperfectly designed for the same reason that they are prone to injure the subjects involved. They disregard the special quality of trust and obedience with which the subject appropriately regards the experimenter. (P. 421)

She thus opens her argument by emphasizing the vulnerability of the subject in the experimental setting, a factor which she views as having both ethical and methodological implications. Experimenters should assume a protective role in view of the emotional distress which could occur, and should recognize the implausibility of investigating phenomena which, as in obedience, are built into the subject's role. She does not rule out, in this paper, the use of deception or anxiety-evoking procedures, but stresses the need for sensitive, thorough post-experimental interactions between investigators and their subjects.

The Cost/Benefit Argument

What specifically are her objections to the obedience experiments? She begins by quoting, at some length, from Milgram's 1963 article. Her focus is on the tension experienced by Milgram's subjects, as in this passage: "I observed a mature and initially poised businessman enter the laboratory smiling and confident. Within 20 minutes he was reduced to a twitching, stuttering wreck, who was rapidly approaching a point of nervous collapse" (p. 422).

Citing Milgram's statement that "a friendly reconciliation was arranged between the subject and the victim, and an effort was made to reduce any tensions that arose as a result of the experiment" (p. 422), Baumrind expresses grave doubts: "His casual assurance that these tensions were dissipated before the subject left the laboratory is unconvincing" (p. 422). Thus, Baumrind appears to dismiss the validity of Milgram's assurance. Her use of the term "casual" could be taken as an implication of irresponsibility in Milgram's professional conduct, an implication also made when she then asks: "What could be the rational basis for such a posture of indifference?" (p. 422).

She asserts that in terms of research ethics, Milgram has taken a position that the "ends are worth the means." Because of the scientific value of his research, the costs, in terms of the distress experienced by his subjects, are viewed as acceptable. Baumrind does not agree. She selects a famous success in medical science to illustrate her position: "Unlike the Sabin vaccine, for example, the concrete benefit to humanity of his [Milgram's] particular piece of work, no matter how competently handled, cannot justify the risk that real harm will be done to the subject" (p. 422).

Her position here is that behavioral scientists cannot, in principle, have the kind of confidence that medical researchers would have regarding society's evaluation of their work: "The behavioral psychologist is not in as good a position to objectify his faith in the significance of his work as medical colleagues at points of breakthrough" (p. 422).

One is tempted to say, at this point, that Baumrind's conception of a "breakthrough" is naive, for rarely do we know when a breakthrough is before us—it is only *after the fact* that we recognize such a phenomenon in science, and invariably the "breakthrough" reflects decades of related research efforts, many of which were destined to "blind alleys" instead of public acclaim. She may also be suggesting that psychological research is, categorically, not as important as medical research, hence procedures which threaten research subjects with emotional stress are simply unwarranted. This, too, would be an "ends are worth the means" logic in that such stress would apparently be acceptable in medical research because of the long-term gains from its discoveries. Yet, the question of the value or "benefit to humanity" of Milgram's research is certainly reasonable to ask—this book is intended to provide some answers to it. Also, the cost/benefit framework raised, though hardly endorsed, by Baumrind, has been a very influential argument in subsequent analyses of ethical issues in research.

Consequences to Subjects

Baumrind outlines two unacceptable outcomes of the subject's participation in the Milgram paradigm. One is a shaken faith in authority: subjects may generalize their encounter with the deceitful experimenter and experience difficulty in their future relationships with authority figures. Second, the subject's self-image is threatened, in a manner which may be resistant to effective debriefing:

> The subject's personal responsibility for his actions is not erased because the experimenter reveals to him the means which he used to stimulate these actions. The subject realizes that he would have hurt the victim if the current were on. The realization that he also made a fool of himself by accepting the experimental set results in additional loss of self-esteem. (P. 423)

Baumrind's reference to the subject's "making a fool of himself" is based on her skepticism of the adequacy of Milgram's debriefing procedure—at least as presented in his 1963 article. Regarding her point on "personal responsibility," it is true that the obedient subject has performed certain actions which, logically, cannot be undone. The meaning of these actions is defined by the subject and, significantly, by the experimenter during post-experimental sessions, but in principle it can always remain problematic as to the precise interpretation carried by the subject. As Baumrind implies, it is largely irrelevant to tell the subject that no shocks were actually delivered, because the issue centers on the implications of the subject's behavior when he or she in fact believed that the shocks were being delivered to the learner.

The Implications of Milgram's Findings

Baumrind's critique then changes focus. Emphasizing her earlier argument regarding the high base line of dependency inherent in the role of laboratory subject, Baumrind takes exception to linking the obedience research to the genocide perpetrated by the Nazis. She notes that the SS officers (analogous to the teacher) were not under the impression that the ultimate authority, Hitler, was kindly disposed toward the victims. The victims were not (as in the obedience paradigm) social peers of the SS, but rather were dehumanized to an extreme degree. Baumrind contends that the conflict expressed by many subjects is evidence of their concern for the learner—again unlike the Nazi analogy—and that the subjects' tensions may have reflected their inability to comprehend the behavior of the experimenter as much as, or even more than, their misgivings about how they were treating the learner.

These are interesting issues which question the generalizability of Milgram's paradigm. We shall defer commenting on them until after considering Milgram's rebuttal to Baumrind. While the generalizability of a paradigm is, strictly speaking, a methodological rather than ethical problem, these two perspectives are often closely related. Thus, because one of Baumrind's central arguments rests on the trust and dependence of the subject with respect to the experimenter—that the experimenter is a "good" person who is kindly disposed toward human beings—it is precisely this perspective which, in turn, leads her to see the entire paradigm as unconvincing in its relevance to the Nazi death camps. Thus, the laboratory, to subjects, is a trustworthy and "safe" place. Milgram violated this presumption, and that was his ethical error. Yet, because the laboratory is still presumably invested with these qualities, one cannot interpret the subjects' behavior as reflecting destructive obedience with parallels to the Holocaust.

Baumrind concludes with a strong though not absolutist recommendation: "I would not like to see experiments such as Milgram's proceed unless the subjects were fully informed of the dangers of serious aftereffects and his correctives were clearly shown to be effective in restoring their state of well-being" (p. 423). As will become apparent, both of these issues raised by Baumrind—"informed consent" and harmful aftereffects—were to receive considerable attention by subsequent investigators.

MILGRAM'S REPLY TO BAUMRIND

Milgram's published response (1964b) to Baumrind's criticism appeared several months later in the *American Psychologist* (1964b). It should be remembered that Milgram had collected the *entire* set of data prior to the 1963 publication. As noted in Chapter One, Milgram makes reference in his 1963 publication to the fact that a larger data set had been collected. Footnote 5 reads as follows: "A series of recently completed experiments employing the obedience paradigm is reported in Milgram (1964)" (1963, p. 378). This refers to an article that appeared in 1965 in *Human Relations*. Another footnote (Note 3, p. 373) refers to a research proposal sent to the National Science Foundation in 1961 which contained relevant information concerning the apparatus and the initial reaction of subjects. Baumrind thus had made a decision to publish her ethical criticism *without first contact-*

ing Milgram and making inquiries pertinent to her objections. Whether or not she should have made this kind of inquiry is, of course, debatable. The point to emphasize, however, is that more information was available and was explicitly noted in Milgram's 1963 article.

Adequacy of Debriefing

Milgram (1964b) goes into considerable detail concerning the debriefing phase of his research. Subjects, regardless of their obedience or defiance, were each given an explanation that bolstered their sense of self-esteem and that supported their course of action. Subjects were also sent a report which presented various procedural details as well as findings. He emphasizes that "their own part in the experiments was treated in a dignified way and their behavior in the experiment respected" (p. 849).

The results of a questionnaire sent to subjects following their participation also support Milgram's view of the ethics of his paradigm. Eighty-four percent reported being glad or very glad to have been in the experiment; 15 percent reported neutral feelings, and less than 2 percent reported being sorry or very sorry to have participated. Over 75 percent indicated that experiments of this type are important and should be performed. Milgram states that his follow-up procedures were carried out "as a matter of course and were not stimulated by any observation of special risk in the experimental procedure" (p. 849). Thus, Milgram vehemently denies Baumrind's allegations that harm was inflicted upon his subjects and that he was indifferent to their welfare.

Psychiatric interviews were held with 40 subjects approximately one year after their participation. The conclusion reached by the psychiatrist, Paul Errera, was that "none were found by this interviewer to show signs of having been harmed by their experience" (Errera, in J. Katz, 1972, p. 400). Several subjects did display various recollections of having been angered or irritated in some manner, but no evidence of lasting trauma was apparent.

The report[2] sent to all subjects was a thorough description of the paradigm, the various deceptions employed, and the findings from several of the experimental variations. The situational or contextual nature of obedience was emphasized. Thus, the influence of group pressure was noted, in addition to the effects of the proximity of the learner or experimenter. Because *all* subjects received the identical report, it was important to present the information in a manner that would be minimally provocative or threatening to subjects, particularly those who had been maximally obedient or who had expressed severe indications of tension.

In my opinion, Milgram succeeded in presenting a sophisticated, informative, scientifically authentic analysis. It should be noted, however, that he did not attempt to conceal his concern about the destructive consequences of obedience. In order to indicate the relevance of the experimental analysis of obedience, at the close of his report he posed the question of whether a person (in another country) would obey orders to drop a hydrogen bomb on the United States. He also referred to the shock experienced when the consequences of obedience to authority in World War II were revealed. Thus, while it certainly would have been possible for a subject to conjure up distressing images after reading Milgram's summary, Milgram succeeded in his primary goals of (a) justifying the importance of a *scientific* analysis of obedience and (b) providing clarification and an accurate debriefing to the participants in his research. In addition, the report established a meaningful interpersonal contact with each of the subjects, so that it was possible for any of them to contact Milgram subsequent to their participation.

I find Milgram's rebuttal to Baumrind on the issue of "the adequacy of debriefing" to be convincing for several reasons. First, he presents empirical data concerning reactions of his subjects to their participation. This kind of postexperimental assessment is extremely rare in behavioral research. (He reported a 92 percent return rate for the questionnaires, an unusually high percentage.) Because the questionnaires were completed by the participants immediately after reading Milgram's written summary of the obedience research, it is possible that some of the participants were influenced by Milgram's communication and expressed more positive reactions to the research than they would have had they not seen the report. Nevertheless, the subjects were given an opportunity to express negative points of view and, as indicated, these were virtually nonexistent.

What is particularly impressive, in my view, is that subjects received *two* debriefings, one immediately after their participation in the laboratory, the other contained in the written summary subsequently mailed to them. The first debriefing, supportive regardless of the subject's behavior in the experiment, was designed to provide reassurance and to calm subjects, particularly in view of the high frequency of symptoms of conflict observed. In this phase of the research, subjects were given different information, depending, for example, upon whether they had been obedient or defiant, or whether they had maintained their composure or had manifested extreme agitation. In the second debriefing, which occurred considerably later, all subjects received an identical summarization of the research. Here Milgram's primary goal was informational, but the report was composed to be as nonthreatening as possible.

Thus, in terms of the thoroughness of the debriefing, as well as the empirical assessment of subjects' postexperimental attitudes, the procedures used by Milgram would seem to qualify as a model for laboratory research with human subjects.

Can Obedience by Studied in a Laboratory?

Recall that Baumrind criticized the choice of the experimental laboratory as a suitable context for the study of obedience because of the naturally occurring trust and dependency—hence the inevitably high base line of obedience—in that setting. Others have drawn the same conclusion (Chapter Six). Milgram, not surprisingly, takes a fundamentally opposing position on this matter:

> Here is one social context in which compliance occurs regularly. Military and job situations are also particularly meaningful settings for the study of obedience precisely because obedience is natural and appropriate to these contexts. I reject Baumrind's argument that the observed obedience does not count because it occurred where it is appropriate. That is precisely why it *does* count. A soldier's obedience is no less meaningful because it occurs in a pertinent military context. A subject's obedience is no less problematic because it occurs within a social institution called the psychological experiment. (P. 850)

Although, as mentioned earlier, this debate has strong methodological overtones, the ethical issue is clearly present as well. Baumrind's thesis is that the experimenter exploited the subjects. These were individuals who, in her view, were primed to do whatever the experimenter told them to do, simply by virtue of their role. Thus, they trusted the experimenter and depended upon him for guidance and direction. He then "took advantage" of their vulnerability and evoked destructive obedience.

Milgram denies this perspective of what transpired. He observes that a substantial number of subjects did in fact *disobey* the experimenter at some point, that in some of the variations—not accessible to Baumrind in reading the 1963 article—a majority of subjects defied the experimenter's orders. Speaking more directly to the ethical and moral dimensions of this problem, Milgram makes this crucial distinction between Baumrind's construction of events and his own:

> Baumrind feels that the experimenter *made* the subject shock the victim. This conception is alien to my view. The experimenter tells the subject to do something. But between the command and the outcome there is a paramount force, the acting person who may obey or disobey. I started with the belief that every person who came to the laboratory was free to accept or to reject the dictates of authority. This view sustains a conception of human dignity insofar as it sees in each man a capacity for *choosing* his own behavior. (P. 851)

One cannot simply assert that Milgram is correct or incorrect here. Before drawing conclusions, however, the reader may wish to reserve judgment until a number of other points of view on this matter have been considered. It would seem, at this point, that Milgram's most convincing argument rests with the data themselves—the variability of his subjects' behavior both within various experimental situations and, of course, across them. This variability does not support Baumrind's thesis that there is a kind of built-in obedience factor in the laboratory to which subjects must succumb.

The Analogy to Nazi Germany

Milgram agrees with Baumrind on the obvious differences between the historical events of the Holocaust and the laboratory paradigm. Although not "backing off" from the analogy, Milgram asserts, simply, that it was an analogy, that his intent was not to create a microcosm of the Holocaust in his laboratory, but rather to capture a social process that may have had vital significance in the Holocaust:

> How does a man behave when he is told by a legitimate authority to act against a third individual? In trying to find an answer to this question, the laboratory situation is one useful starting point—and for the very reason stated by Baumrind—namely, the experimenter does constitute a genuine authority for the subject. (P. 851)

As Douglas Mook (1983) has observed, it is a very simple matter to criticize psychological experiments on the grounds that they lack ecological validity or generalizability to non-laboratory events, but it is crucial to recognize that the goal of a direct application or extrapolation of experimental findings is not always intended by the investigator. (At times, it *is* intended—as in trying to forecast a political election by means of sampling polls).

Milgram's primary intent, therefore, was not to explain the Holocaust:

> Baumrind mistakes the background metaphor for the precise subject matter of investigation. The German event was cited to point up a serious problem in the human situation: the potentially destructive effect of obedience. But the best way to tackle the problem of obedience, from a scientific standpoint, is in no way restricted by "what happened exactly" in Germany. What happened exactly can *never* be duplicated in the laboratory or anywhere else. The real task is to learn more about the general problem of destructive obedience using a workable approach (P. 851)

We will consider the manner in which the obedience experiments have been interpreted with respect to the Holocaust and genocide in general more extensively in Chapter Seven. However, a brief comment is appropriate at this point. As mentioned in Chapter One, Milgram began his 1963 article with a reference to the Nazi death camps, and his work has continuously been linked to the Holocaust. It is common, for example, for textbooks to include a photograph of concentration camp victims at the point in the text in which Milgram's experiments are being described (see Worchel and Cooper, 1983, p. 446; Penrod, 1983, p. 386; Penner, 1978, p. 249). Pictures of the victims of the My Lai massacre of civilians during the Vietnamese War may also be linked to discussions of the obedience research (see Feldman, 1985, p. 351). The emotional imagery of the Holocaust *in combination* with the vivid, unexpected behaviors observed in the obedience paradigm create a compelling association in many readers. It then becomes virtually impossible not to make a kind of causal connection—namely, that what Milgram has shown did indeed play a crucial role in the Holocaust.

"How could it have happened?" This is the ultimate puzzle of the Holocaust. It becomes difficult—in part because of the manner in which Milgram's research is taught—to disengage the obedience experiments from assuming the status of an answer to that puzzle. It also needs to be recognized that although Milgram was disposed, in 1964, to make a sharp distinction between his *primary* research interests and the events of the Holocaust, there were enormous pressures placed upon him to make extensions from his laboratory findings to a variety of "real world" examples of destructive obedience to authority as these have periodically occurred in the course of history. Thus, the effective meaning of his experiments has been strongly determined by the manner in which *others* have interpreted his research—notwithstanding his own more conservative, scientifically oriented position. In practical terms, therefore, it would have been unrealistic to expect Milgram to continuously deny the social and historical implications of his findings even if he were personally more dubious about the certainty of the causal inferences than are others who have been so intrigued with his findings.

Subjects' Insights from their Participation

As stated earlier, Milgram denies the accusation that his subjects experienced psychological trauma of any significant duration. His post-experimental reports from subjects supported this view (although it would seem quite plausible for some subjects to conjecture that their behavior had put them in a class of rather unsavory people). Milgram then goes further, suggesting that many subjects had gained important insights regarding human nature, that they viewed the obedience paradigm as far more interesting than "the empty laboratory hour, in which cardboard procedures are employed, and the only possible feeling upon emerging from the laboratory is that one has wasted time in a patently trivial and useless exercise" (p. 850). Regarding Baumrind's concern that subjects would, as a result of their participation, have problems in relating to authority, Milgram makes two points. Given that she views the laboratory as an inappropriate—that is, non-generalizable—context for the study of obedience, Milgram is puzzled that Baumrind then worries about lasting (that is, generalizable) negative influences. But, more significantly, Milgram appears gratified by the potential insight gained on this score:

> I would consider it of the highest value if participation in the experiment could, indeed, inculcate a skepticism of this kind of authority. . . . Baumrind sees the effect of the experiment as undermining the subject's trust of authority. I see it as a potentially valuable experience insofar as it makes people aware of the problem of indiscriminate submission to authority. . . . If there is a moral to be learned from the obedience study, it is that every man must be responsible for his own actions. (P. 852)

Milgram could be accused of departing from his previously stated, more modest intentions, that is, of studying obedience in the interests of science. In this passage, he seemed to accept without reservation the moral significance of his findings, and to presume that the lessons inherent in his research would be worthwhile for the subjects who yielded its data. As we shall note, Milgram's presumption on this matter has not gone unchallenged.[3]

BAUMRIND'S RESPONSE TO MILGRAM

Baumrind refers to Milgram's research in a number of subsequent publications (1975, 1979, 1985). She extends her analyses beyond the obedience research per se, dealing with a variety of ethical issues in research. Her most venomous arguments center on the use of deception. We shall refer to some of these issues shortly, but it is appropriate to consider first an unpublished paper by Baumrind (1970) in which she responds directly to Milgram's rebuttal to her initial (1964) commentary.

Regardless of the motivation of the experimenter—his good intentions, his post-experimental caution—she regards "the use of the professional setting to inflict psychological pain . . . as an improper use of authority" (p. 2). A point not raised by Baumrind but relevant here is that although Milgram did not *anticipate* the prevalence nor the severity of the tensions experienced by his subjects, he nevertheless pursued this paradigm over a three-year period. Thus, he clearly made a decision to continue the research despite the extreme agitation demonstrated by subjects *at the outset of the program*.

Baumrind does not accept Milgram's assurance regarding harmful aftereffects. She does not view the psychiatric examination of 40 individuals as convincing, nor does she trust the positive self-reports in the questionnaires: "since one way to handle anger at being humiliated or hurt is to identify with the aggressor" (p. 4). Baumrind thus criticizes the validity of Milgram's ethical monitoring of his research. Short of an in-depth, repeated series of clinical interviews with every subject in his program, it does not seem that Baumrind would view any evidence as acceptable.

Obviously at this point the issue reaches an impasse. One is either inclined to accept Milgram's subjects' responses at face value—they did have the opportunity to express their opinions and feelings—or not. I am personally inclined to do so, however Baumrind's position on the unreliability of post-experimental verbal reports is not hers alone. There is evidence that people can, in retrospect, distort, in a positive direction, experiences which have been unduly stressful (Aronson and Mills, 1959). There is also evidence that people may persevere in holding impressions about others, or themselves, even when the initial evidence or basis for these impressions has been completely invalidated, as in an experimental debriefing (for example, Jelalian and Miller, 1984). Thus, for some subjects, at least, Baumrind's point is not implausible.

The issue of *responsibility* is of particular interest, not only because of its ethical ramifications, but because it is of substantive relevance to the problem of authority itself. Baumrind agrees with Milgram's argument that the experimenter does not determine the specific choice a subject makes in terms of obedience or defiance. However, she contends:

> He does use his professional status and setting as a lever to influence that choice, to put pressure on the subject to obey a bizarre and inhumane command. I object to the use of the psychologist's authority in that way. The psychologist cannot escape his responsibility to the subject by pointing to the responsibility of the subject for his own actions. (P. 5)

For Baumrind, subjects are endowed with certain rights—for example, to be treated with respect and consideration—because, among other things, they are in the presence of a *psychologist*, someone who, more than others perhaps, should be respectful and considerate.

Milgram (1964b), however, assumes the right to behave not only as a psychologist (as Baumrind construes this role) but as a *behavioral scientist* investigating a difficult but important social issue. Milgram indicates in several instances that the experimenter's behavior toward the subject was explicitly harsh, that it almost certainly violated the subject's expectations:

> The fact that trust and dependence on the experimenter are maintained, despite the extraordinary harshness he displays toward the victim, is itself a remarkable phenomenon. . . . He is an authority who tells the subject to act harshly and inhumanely against another man. (Pp. 851/852)

Milgram thus acknowledges, explicitly, that he has created a moral conflict for the subject. His purpose is to study how individuals resolve that conflict. Baumrind is arguing that Milgram does not have the right to pose that conflict in the first place.

Baumrind refutes the generalizability of Milgram's findings. Her position again rests upon what she views as the extraordinary *inappropriateness* of the experimenter's behavior, the incongruity between what subjects would ordinarily expect regarding the actions of a researcher and what they in fact observe in Milgram's paradigm. Thus, noting that it would be quite logical for an officer to command a soldier to fire upon an enemy, it simply is not logical for an experimenter to order a subject to shock another person, at least to severe levels of pain. She believes that subjects, also, perceive this incongruity and that regardless of their behavior, it is this "sense of the bizarre" which precludes the kinds of inferences made by Milgram and others. The issue of the incongruous or bizarre behavior of the experimenter has been given serious attention in methodological analyses of the Milgram paradigm, and will be discussed in the next chapter.

Baumrind has recently presented a more formal statement regarding her position on ethical issues in research (1985). Her major focus is the use of *deception* which, in her analysis, entails unacceptable costs in terms of its negative impact upon research subjects, the profession of psychology, and society itself. She again uses the obedience research as a vehicle with which to illustrate her position, repeating a number of misgivings which have been cited earlier.

Her position against the use of intentional deception in the context of a research setting is based on three values which are, in her view, compromised: the subject's right of *informed consent*, the implicit obligation of the researcher to be *trustworthy*, and the unacceptable *modeling influence* of a deceitful researcher, namely, that students would observe "lying" in the name of science and career (that is, the researcher's advancement).

Many of Baumrind's positions are eloquently stated, although most have been presented with even more impressive rationales in Kelman's seminal statements on the deception problem (1967). Her presentation of the "other side," that is, the benefits of deception, is far less well developed, a major theme being that laboratory experiments are generically suspect in so many ways that they do not justify the use of deception:

> Psychological processes do not occur in a psychosocial vacuum. When the task, variables, and setting can have no real-world counterparts, the processes dissected in the laboratory also cannot operate in the real world. In that case, deceptive research practices cannot be justified by their benefits to science and society. (1985, p. 171)

Of course, this perspective virtually ignores the point made earlier, expressed in a particularly compelling manner by Douglas Mook (1983), that the goals of research often are not primarily those of making immediate benefits to anyone, but endeavoring to conceptualize, to *understand*, from a theoretical perspective, a phenomenon. Thus, I would disagree with Baumrind's thesis that "if the phenomenon being studied is socially important it can be studied in natural or clinical contexts that do not require laboratory manipulation to produce (1985, p. 170).

Baumrind's ethical position—which she terms "rule utilitarianism" —holds that the locus of control should be within the research participant. The subject should have the right to decide whether the likely benefits to self or society outweigh the costs of being in a particular study. The principle of informed consent allows the subject to do this. In her view, "a subject whose consent has been obtained by deceitful and fraudulent means has become an object of the investigator to manipulate" (p. 169). The issue of informed consent is, without question, central. Milgram's paradigm is, of course, permeated by various deceptions. Thus it is crucial to examine his response to this critical ethical matter, which we will do momentarily.

In concluding a synopsis of Baumrind's (1985) recent position, I must confess to disagreeing with much of her reasoning. In effect, she dismisses the value of experimental research in social psychology: "The mechanistic model of development implied by experimental social psychological procedures is not really applicable to social psychological phenomena" (p. 172). I find her alternatives unconvincing: "Experimenters could act as subjects in their own experiments and employ introspection" (p. 172).

Her position on debriefing is somewhat unclear. In her most recent statement (1985), she takes a relatively nonabsolutist stance: "If an investigator does elect to use deception, he or she must include an effective debriefing procedure in order to reduce the long-range costs of deception and offer partial reparation to subjects" (p. 172). In another citation, however, Baumrind is far more restrictive, particularly in the case of Milgram's work:

> In the Milgram experiment, debriefing would not reinstitute the subject's self-image or ability to trust adult authorities in the future. The subjects did after all commit acts that they believed at the time were harmful to another, and they were in fact entrapped into committing those acts by an individual whom they had reason to trust. In my view the investigator must forego the opportunity to engage in research that permits only two possible alternatives: *deceptive debriefing* (in which the truth is withheld from the subject because full disclosure would lower the subject's self-esteem or affect the research adversely); or *inflicted insight* (in which the subject is given insight into his or her flaws, although such insight is painful and he or she has not invited such insights). (1979, pp. 3-4)

Baumrind (1985) does endorse Mills' (1976) treatment of the debriefing process, which is widely acknowledged as the most thorough and sensitive presentation of this issue.

MILGRAM'S POSITION ON RESEARCH ETHICS

Milgram's final pronouncements on the ethics of the obedience experiments are to be found in his 1974 book and in an article in the *Hastings Center Report* (1977b). His major argument is the following:

> *The central moral justification for allowing a procedure of the sort used in my experiment is that it is judged acceptable by those who have taken part in it. Moreover, it was the salience of this fact throughout that constituted the chief moral warrant for the continuation of the experiments.* This fact is crucial to any appraisal of the experiment from an ethical standpoint. (1974, p. 199)

Milgram thus reaffirms his belief in the significance of his subjects' post-experimental reports. Given his perspective, that of a practicing social scientist, empirical evidence pointing to a *lack of harmful effects* was crucial. He expresses surprise at how such evidence is often interpreted:

> These data have been ignored by critics, or even turned against the experimenter, as when critics claim that "this is simply cognitive dissonance. The more subjects hated the experiment, the more likely they are to say they enjoyed it." It becomes a "damned-if-they-like-it and damned-if-they-don't" situation. (1977, pp. 21-22)

He makes a strong distinction between biomedical and psychological research. In the former, he acknowledges that risk is involved, but he denies this in the case of psychological research: "In all of the social psychology experiments that have been carried out, there is no demonstrated case of resulting trauma" (1977b, p. 22). He recognizes that this would not rule out the possibility of negative outcomes, but claims that this potentiality cannot serve as *documentation* that harm inevitably results.

Milgram's position reflects a set of values that not all would endorse. It is important to recognize this fact because it bears on the nature of all debates concerning ethical issues. Some questions are resolvable in terms of observable events. Thus, if one asks this question: "Is participation in the Milgram paradigm psychologically damaging?," the best evidence is that the answer is "no." However, if one asks a slightly different question: "Does a research psychologist have the right to expose subjects to intense stress and conflict?," the answer is less clear. Is there *evidence* that would bear on such an answer? I think not. It becomes a question, then, of values, of priorities, of what one views as important knowledge, and whether the price of that knowledge is worth paying:

> If we assert categorically that negative emotions can never ethically be created in the laboratory, then it follows that highly significant domains of human experience are excluded from experimental study. For example, we would never be able to study stress by experimental means; nor could we implicate human subjects in experiments involving conflict . . . historically, among the most deeply informative experiments in social psychology are those that examine how subjects resolve conflicts, for example: Asch's study of group pressure studies the conflict between truth and conformity; Bibb Latané and John Darley's bystander studies create a conflict as to whether the subject should implicate himself in other peoples' troubles or not get involved; my studies of obedience create a conflict between conscience and authority. If the experience of conflict is categorically to be excluded from social psychology, then we are automatically denying the possibility of studying such core human issues by experimental means. I believe that this would be an irreparable loss to any science of human behavior. (1977b, p. 21)

DEVELOPMENTS REGARDING THE ETHICS OF THE OBEDIENCE EXPERIMENTS

After the 1964 exchange between Baumrind and Milgram, there were three general types of reaction or impact. First, numerous "position statements" were presented by a large number of social scientists. These were usually brief comments, in a variety of outlets—journals, books, edited anthologies, mass media—which took an essentially "pro" or "anti" position on the ethics of the obedience research. We will chart at least a representative number of these reactions, to see if there is a reasonable consensus of opinion, and to examine the rationales underlying specific positions.

A second, related intellectual development was a progressively intense interest in the general subject of ethical issues in behavioral research. Stemming from a variety of influences—the Baumrind-Milgram exchange being a crucial, but by no means the only, factor—a number of major publications appeared which dealt with such problems as the use of deception, the necessity of proper debriefing, the role of informed consent, alternative research methodologies, and ethical problems with special subject populations (for example, Beauchamp, Faden, Wallace, and Walters, 1982; Diener and Crandall, 1978; Kennedy, 1975; Miller, 1972a, 1972b; Schuler, 1982; Sieber, 1982a). It also became routine in the 1970s for textbooks in social psychology to give reasonably thorough treatment to ethical issues and dilemmas involved in social research.

A major theme in these presentations was that the prevailing research establishment was ethically negligent, that it fostered, perhaps unwittingly, a "dehumanization" of human beings in the name of "science."[4] Most of these reactions were not simply jaundiced views from the "outside," but reflected a growing crisis of confidence within social psychology. One concern, in this context, was the unfavorable image of the discipline which was being perpetrated by its characteristic research practices. Inevitably the obedience research became a focal point for all such ethical probing. This book clearly is an inappropriate place to review this vast literature, but we will, at least briefly, examine the views of Herbert Kelman, who has been the leading ethical scholar within the discipline of social psychology.

A third reaction was empirical. A number of investigations were conducted, directed at specific ethical problems or facets of the obedience paradigm. There is a kind of twofold advantage to this kind of endeavor—one learns not only about the ethical issue but also, more generally, about obedience to authority. The difficulty lies in drawing generalizable ethical conclusions on the basis of these empirical studies. It is, I think, a special virtue of social psychology that it has at least attempted to apply an empirical orientation to questions concerning its methods and ethics. We will first deal with this unique kind of research, and then examine the ethical commentaries of a more reflective or ideological nature.

Research on Harmful Aftereffects

Kenneth Ring and his colleagues performed what may have been the first replication of the obedience paradigm in order "to provide an independent assessment of the immediate and long-term consequences of participation in a Milgram-type experiment" (p. 69). Citing the ethical criticisms of Baumrind (1964) and Kelman (1967), Ring et al. noted that although Milgram's data—that is, his subjects' self-reports—were highly supportive, they would be viewed as self-serving and discounted by those who were skeptical of the paradigm's ethical status.

The procedure was similar to Milgram's paradigm, with the following exceptions: punishment involved the (apparent) use of increasingly noxious auditory stimuli delivered through earphones; Milgram's fourth prod—"you have no other choice"—was not used; the experimenter was not impassive but maintained a somewhat surprised expression at the protests of the learner. As in the obedience paradigm, protests from the learner were contingent upon the intensity of the punishment, the last protest taking the form of "(in anguish), Please, I really can't take it anymore. This (pause, as if gasping for breath) constant buzzing in my head now. (Begin sobbing and continue sobbing on and off for the duration of the trials.) This is inhuman" (p. 72). The subjects were female college students; the experimenter was male.

Upon completion of the punishment series or after refusing to continue, subjects were randomly assigned either to a control group or to one of two experimental conditions. For those in the experimental conditions, an initial debriefing was given in which all deceptions were explained and the experiment's purpose was described as dealing with factors affecting conformity to an authority. The experimenter then went into a fictitious elaboration in terms of his interest in detecting personality differences between those who did or did not continue punishing the learner. In the *obedience justification* (OJ) condition, subjects were told that those who persisted were psychologically better adjusted, more mature, etc; in the *defiance justification* (DJ) condition, subjects were told that those who refused to continue punishing the learner were psychologically superior, able to avoid submissiveness to authority, etc.

Subjects were thus given, after the fact, one of two "authentic" bases for evaluating their performance. The DJ condition was used to produce in obedient subjects the kind of anxiety which Baumrind (1964) and Kelman (1967) had indicated would be a probable occurrence. Subjects in the *control group* were given no information other than the original, factually accurate debriefing.

Subjects then filled out a five-page questionnaire concerning diverse reactions to the experiment. To increase candor, subjects were assured that the experimenter would not see their responses. They were enclosed in an envelope and handed to the department secretary. After turning in this questionnaire, subjects were given a debriefing that was complete and truthful, but designed to be emotionally supportive as well.

The results were as follows: Fifty-two of 57 subjects (91 percent) were completely obedient. The effects of the experimental conditions were analyzed only for these subjects. Emotional reactions during the punishment phase varied, ranging from no overt distress to extreme agitation (with three subjects in tears near the conclusion). Thus, in terms of obedience per se, this study constituted a powerful replication of Milgram's paradigm, demonstrating its generality in terms of a different gender combination (female-female) for the teacher and learner roles as well as an alternative procedure for administering punishment.

On a variety of self-ratings—degree of upset, anger at experimenter, depression, embarrassment—subjects in the OJ condition indicated less negativity than subjects in the DJ and control groups. Thus, the manner in which subjects were debriefed *did make a difference* in their emotional state immediately following the experiment. Subjects who were given a supportive debriefing were less distressed than those given no debriefing or one which, though more "truthful" (DJ), was not supportive of the subjects' behavior.

When asked "Was the experiment instructive about psychology?" or "Should the experiment be permitted to continue?" subjects, provided that they were informed of the deception, were clearly positive about the experiment. Ring et al. note, "In our judgment . . . virtually none of these subjects resented being deceived, regretted being in the experiment, or thought that it involved anything unethical or should be discontinued" (p. 80).

It was the no-debriefing control condition that produced relatively negative attitudes toward the experiment itself. Thus, the sheer enactment of a thorough debriefing (regardless of its specific reference to the desirability of the subject's behavior) is an important procedure in terms of enabling subjects to form positive impressions of the research enterprise. Ring et al. note that their findings "accord perfectly well with Milgram's accounts which make clear that while many subjects are upset by the experimental procedure itself, they value the experiment and their participation" (p. 80).

The results of follow-up interviews, obtained two to five weeks later from phone conversations with 20 subjects, were similarly supportive. Approximately 90 percent expressed overwhelmingly positive opinions regarding the experiment's purpose and their treatment in it. Approximately 50 percent of these subjects said, however, that "they would now be more suspicious of psychological experiments and more wary about being deceived" (p. 82). Other subjects expressed reservations about what they had done or about having been deceived, or indicated that they were having difficulties in trusting adult authority figures.

Ring et al. make no attempt to play down the significance of negative reactions or to deny that a critic of the obedience research could find one or more objectionable features in their data.[5] Their major conclusion, however, is clear, "the data from this study fail to substantiate the charge that there are likely to be widespread and persistent negative aftereffects from Milgram-type obedience experiments" (p. 83). This conclusion is particularly significant because Ring et al. do *not* share Milgram's confidence regarding the ethics of this paradigm:

> Despite our initial and persisting sympathy with Baumrind's position, it seems to us that effective arguments against the Milgram-type experiment cannot any longer be predicated on the assumption of its generally adverse effects on subjects. (P. 85)

Ring et al. suggest that a detailed, personally involving debriefing is clearly useful. More crucial, however, may be the nature of this debriefing:

> Deception experiments particularly require that in order to protect a subject's welfare the full truth about an experiment be withheld from him. Whenever such disclosure might lower a subject's self-esteem, it would seem advisable to sacrifice complete honesty with him. It may be that a subject would be better off knowing the truth, but as Kelman (1967) rightly points out, when he volunteers for an experiment, a subject doesn't bargain for such potentially upsetting insights. (P. 84)

The exasperating nature of the ethical dilemma is, however, well illustrated by Kelman's position on the content of post-experimental disclosure:

> If we hope to maintain any kind of trust in our relationship with potential subjects, there must be no ambiguity that the statement "The experiment is over and I shall explain to you what it was all about" means precisely that and nothing else. (1967, p. 9)

To the extent that one cannot provide two different "truths," that is, to obedient and defiant subjects, the Milgram paradigm lacks, in Kelman's view, the possibility of an ethical debriefing. However, one could raise the issue of whether *the truth* actually exists regarding this research (or, for that matter, most experiments). Would it not be possible to provide different emphases depending upon a subject's performance, without fabricating substantive realities? The viewpoint expressed by Ring et al. is, in my view, one of the most sophisticated discussions of the ethics of the obedience paradigm. The fact that their perspective is based upon direct experience with the paradigm strengthens considerably their line of reasoning.

Do the Findings of the Experiment Influence One's Ethical Reaction?

Among the complexities involved in a consideration of the ethics of the obedience research is the simple fact that we know what happened. One's ethical stance could be biased by one's evaluative reaction to the subjects' behavior. Put simply, if one doesn't like the message, one may not feel kindly toward the messenger. Milgram addresses this possibility in his first reply to Baumrind:

> Is not Baumrind's criticism based as much on the unanticipated findings as on the method? The findings were that some subjects performed in what appeared to be a shockingly immoral way. If, instead, every one of the subjects had broken off at "slight shock," or at the first sign of the learner's discomfort, the results would have been pleasant, and reassuring, and who would protest? (1964b, p. 849)

It would clearly be untenable to base one's ethical reaction strictly on the basis of the results of an investigation, because these cannot be known in advance of doing the experiment. Fortunately there is evidence on this difficult issue.

Bickman and Zarantonello (1978) asked a number of individuals to read one of four prepared versions of the Milgram obedience experiment. Two of these included reference to the deceptions involved, namely, that the learner was an accomplice and that shocks were not actually administered. The other versions described the experiment as if the subjects were told, initially, that the learner was the experimenter's assistant and that they were to pretend that the shocks were being given. The described outcome of the experiment was also varied. In two cases, the results were presented as indicating that almost all of the subjects obeyed instructions to deliver "very dangerous" shocks. In the other versions, the results indicated minimal degrees of obedience on the part of a majority of subjects.

Thus, subjects read one of four versions: deception plus high obedience; deception plus low obedience; no deception plus high obedience; no deception plus low obedience. Subjects were then asked to respond to a variety of items concerning their opinion of the study.

Whether or not deception was described in the account had no impact on subjects' evaluations of the experiment. The degree of observed obedience, however, was an important factor. Subjects in the *high-obedience* condition (relative to those in the low-obedience condition) indicated that the experiment would be more harmful to its participants, that it spoke more unfavorably about human nature, that the participants had a worse experience in it, and that the participants behaved more irresponsibly. Bickman and Zarantonello echo Milgram's own reaction:

> One may wonder if the Milgram study would have been the subject of public outrage if the results had turned out differently. These data suggest that if most of Milgram's subjects had disobeyed, his experiment would have not received as much condemnation. . . . Critics may be responding to the unflattering portrayal of human nature discovered using deceptive methodologies rather than the act of deception itself. (Pp. 84-85)

This study is small-scaled and should not be viewed as the definitive investigation of this issue. Yet, the conclusion is thoughtful. Remember that in a number of Milgram's experimental variations, obedience was in fact extremely low. Had *these* particular studies been the focus of attention, ethical misgivings would likely have been greatly reduced. But, of course, it was the 1963 publication, featuring the 65 percent obedience rate, which prompted the ethical controversies. As noted in Chapter One, it was not only the obedience per se but the emotionality of many of the subjects—framed in Milgram's arousing, picturesque account—which may have triggered the eventual critical reactions. It is difficult, therefore, to isolate one particular aspect of an investigation, such as the degree of obedience, and claim that it was *the* crucial factor. Yet Bickman and Zarantonello force us to consider it as a strong possibility in the case of Milgram's paradigm.

It should be noted that the use of deception, as a research strategy or methodological tool, appears to be generally acceptable to people. A number of investigations have probed for subjects' reaction to a variety of research practices (see, for example, Collins, Kuhn, and King, 1979; Epstein, Suedfeld, and Silverstein, 1973; Smith and Berard, 1982). Subjects are far more likely to express negative attitudes toward being mistreated or toward *not* being given a clear explanation about the experiment at its conclusion than to the use of deception per se. Perhaps the "Candid Camera" mind-set has infiltrated society to the degree that people recognize the utility of observing behavior under conditions which minimize the actors' ability to distort or bias their own actions. This by no means legitimizes the use of deception, but suggests that in the context of behavioral research, the usefulness of deception is at least recognized by many people. What appears to be a recurrent complaint is not that deception is, categorically, unethical, but that it too often is used *routinely*, without serious consideration to alternatives (see, for example, Rubin, 1983, 1985).

Schlenker and Forsyth (1977) have conducted one of the most elaborate investigations bearing on the ethics of psychological research. Using the Milgram obedience paradigm as an illustration, they were interested in two basic questions. The first was the degree to which individuals would be influenced in their appraisal of Milgram's research by the degree of obedience as well as the extent of psychological stress observed in this paradigm. The investigators presented various scenarios of the Milgram experiment,[6] in which subjects—naive to the actual research—were told that the obedience rate was either low or high and that either very few or a considerable number of individuals had experienced severe stress and anxiety. In this respect, the Schlenker and Forsyth experiment resembles that of Bickman and Zarantonello (who had varied obedience level and the use/non-use of deception).

The second question involves the matter of ethics per se. On the basis of an extensive questionnaire, containing items dealing with perceptions of research ethics—attitudes toward deception, harm to research participants, importance of science—subjects were categorized into one of three basic groups:

Idealists—Universal Rules—These individuals adhered to a position, associated with Kant, known as deontology. The central feature is an absolute ethical position prohibiting the use of deception and arguing against a cost/benefit approach to judging the ethical propriety of a research endeavor. Scientific ends, no matter how noble, would not justify means that would, under non-research conditions, be regarded as morally unacceptable. Schlenker and Forsyth quote Baumrind (1971) as an illustration of this ethical position:

> The risk/benefit ratio justifies the sacrifice of the welfare of the subjects in the name of science, thus creating moral dilemmas for the investigator, and, as such, is not moral. (P. 890)

Pragmatists—Universal Rules—These individuals subscribed to a position, associated with Socrates, Plato, and John Stuart Mill, known as teleology. The key principle is that the morality of an action is based upon its consequences. According to Schlenker and Forsyth:

> a teleological approach to research ethics advises that the potential benefits of the research (e.g., advancement of science) must be weighed against the potential costs (such as harm to subjects). (Pp. 370-71)

A proponent of this position is Zick Rubin who, in a 1970 article in *Psychology Today*, wrote a scathing criticism of the ethics of laboratory research. His specific target was the widespread use of deception, which he argued was dehumanizing to research subjects and embarrassing to the discipline of psychology.[7] Yet, his position on the obedience research was surprisingly positive:

> Milgram's work has a social importance that, in my view, vastly outweighs any psychological harm it may have inflicted, and which was probably minimal. He carefully screened his subjects before the experiment, painstakingly dehoaxed them afterward, and had a psychiatrist follow up on them. (Pp. 23-24)

This approach is also descriptive of the current (1981) "Ethical Principles" of the American Psychological Association, as in the following section:

> Methodological requirements of a study may make the use of concealment or deception necessary. Before conducting such a study, the investigator has a special responsibility to: (1) determine whether the use of such techniques is justified by the study's prospective scientific, educational, or applied value; (2) determine whether alternative procedures are available that do not utilize concealment or deception; and (3) ensure that the participants are provided with sufficient explanation as soon as possible. (Principle 9, Section [e])

Thus, restraints on certain procedures are clearly recognized, but exceptions to these restraints are, in principle, acceptable provided that the ultimate consequences are highly valued.

Skeptics—This category involved two varieties of an ethical position referred to as *Skepticism*. The key feature is an absence of a set of universal ethical principles. A proponent of Skepticism, according to the investigators, is Kenneth Gergen who argues against the idea of a fixed code of moral principles or rules, because these are likely to discourage research and impose restrictions based on hypothetical images of danger (1973).

Schlenker and Forsyth were successful in identifying among a college student population individuals who adhered to one of these major ethical orientations, positions which have been identified essentially in scholarly academic debates on the ethics of psychological research.

The findings of this complex investigation can be readily summarized. Regarding their initial question concerning the relative impact of the degree of obedience and the amount of stress on ethical evaluations of the research, the results clearly indicated that it was the *degree of obedience and not the amount of stress* that was crucial. For example, on the item, "How much do you feel the experiment threatened the dignity and welfare of the subjects?'' the perceived threat was significantly higher if the results had shown high, as opposed to low, rates of obedience. The factor of stress or psychological conflict was not a significant variable on this item (or related items). Subjects also indicated that the obedience research was less moral under the high-obedience condition. Like Bickman and Zarantonello, Schlenker and Forsyth conclude that:

> The results on the threat and morality items provide support for Milgram's contention that the behaviors of the participants in an experiment will affect the moral judgments made about it . . . as Milgram asserted, the social undesirability of the participants' behaviors may have reflected negatively upon the ethics of the study. (P. 387)

The findings also suggest that the specific ethical orientation held by the evaluator was a decisive influence on reactions to the obedience research. Subjects in the "pragmatic-universal rule" category manifested the teleological position. Their judgments of the experiment's moral and ethical qualities were positively associated with their impressions of its scientific value and contribution to knowledge, and not associated with estimates of the degree of harm likely to have occurred.

Subjects categorized as "idealists" displayed the deontological position quite strikingly. Their ratings of the moral and ethical features correlated *significantly* in the negative direction with the cost factors, such as the experiment's threatening quality, but did *not* correlate with the benefits of the research (such as scientific value). Schlenker and Forsyth relate these findings to the Baumrind-Milgram debate:

> This pattern strongly supports one of Milgram's charges against Baumrind. In replying to Baumrind, Milgram (1964, p. 852) noted the existence of a "cleavage in American psychology between those whose primary concern is with *helping* people and those who are interested in *learning* about people." Our results certainly indicate that some people (deontologists) are so concerned with helping or protecting that they neglect the informational benefits of research. (P. 391)

Subjects classified as "skeptics" tended to associate the ethics and morality of the research with *both* the positive benefits to be gained and the lack of costs incurred.

Schlenker and Forsyth offer an interesting rationale for their earlier finding concerning the impact of the obedience rate on ethical evaluations. In the high-obedience condition, subjects (that is, evaluators of the obedience study) were presented, in effect, with two pieces of information: (1) strong or severe behavior, and (2) socially undesirable behavior. Both of these factors—undesirability and severity—have been shown to influence attributions of responsibility. That is, more responsibility is attributed to a person who commits negative (as opposed to positive) actions and who commits strong, consequential acts as opposed to minor, less serious actions (Walster, 1966). These findings relate, of course, to a major argument advanced in Chapter Two regarding the inclination to see the actions of the obedient subject in *personal causal terms*. Thus, for quite "natural" reasons—attributional processing—individuals are likely to be influenced in their moral evaluation of an experiment by the behaviors revealed in that experiment. To the degree that the investigator is not, in principle, responsible for the behaviors observed in his or her research, the findings here suggest the operation of a bias that could work against the interests of the investigator.

Furthermore, the evidence here clearly suggests that the ethical status of a particular research project resides, to a significant extent, in the eye of the beholder. This helps to explain the impasse which characterizes debates on this difficult subject. Milgram, according to the analysis of Schlenker and Forsyth, would be termed a "teleologist," one who is focusing primarily upon the consequences of his research (although hardly to the exclusion of a concern with the welfare of his subjects). His position that the final arbiters of the ethics of his experiment should be the participants themselves is perhaps the epitome of the teleological perspective. Baumrind, on the other hand, is clearly in the general position of a deontologist. Schlenker and Forsyth conclude:

> Whenever a teleologist and a deontologist discuss morals, there will be an inevitable value conflict. The fundamental moral guide for the teleologist is the test of consequences, a consideration that the deontologist cannot abide. (P. 373)

The prospects for compromise or rapprochement would seem remote, given that the disagreement is based upon fundamental philosophical values or priorities. As a practical implication, Schlenker and Forsyth's research is of value in informing those who favor the operation of institutional review boards in deciding matters pertaining to the ethics of proposed research. The specific orientation of the members of these committees should be identified so that there can be a proper representation in terms of the biases likely to influence the evaluations of these individuals. (For an extension of this research perspective, see Forsyth and Pope, 1984.)

POSITIONS ON THE ETHICS OF THE OBEDIENCE EXPERIMENTS

Although it was hardly Milgram's intent, one of the most influential and lasting consequences of the obedience research has been a "consciousness raising" in terms of ethical issues in social research. It is perhaps less important to know whether Milgram's research *was* or *was not* ethical than it is to engage in serious reflection about this matter. The studies of Ring et al., Bickman and Zarantonello, and Schlenker and Forsyth, reviewed in the last section, are illustrations of how this sensitization to the ethical dimension has been translated into empirical research.

However, as noted in Schlenker and Forsyth, the ethical base of a research investigation is not solely an empirical matter, but depends considerably upon one's point of view on such issues as the cost/benefit model, the role of informed consent, and the use of deception. It was particularly this latter issue, that of deception in social research, which, historically, became the core problem for most of the published debates on research ethics. Because the obedience paradigm involved extensive use of a number of deceptions, Milgram's research became the most frequently cited target in the debates on the deception problem. We shall not review that literature, because most of it was not directed at the obedience experiments per se but at more general procedural and ethical issues. However, it will be instructive to survey a representative number of position statements on the ethics of Milgram's research. To begin, it is appropriate to cite the views of Herbert Kelman, for it was his 1967 article in the *Psychological Bulletin* that set into motion a subsequent wave of interest in the ethical problems of deception. Not surprisingly, he was critical of the obedience experiments.

Kelman's Position

Kelman is equivocal on the ethics of Milgram's research. Kelman's personal involvement with issues of genocide and the Holocaust gives him a substantive interest in the problem of obedience to authority. However, his views echo those of Baumrind on the threat to self-esteem in at least some of Milgram's subjects, and he is also unimpressed with Milgram's claim that there were valuable insights to be gained in his paradigm. Kelman's thesis is that because subjects were deceived from the outset, they had *no choice in terms of acquiring potentially disturbing knowledge about themselves*. He asks:

> If this were a lesson from life, it would indeed constitute an instructive confrontation and provide a valuable insight. But do we, for the purpose of experimentation, have the right to provide such potentially disturbing insights to subjects who do not know that this is what they are coming for? (P. 4)

Kelman does not answer this question with an unequivocal "no," however, as his essential purpose was to sensitize researchers to the ethical implications of the use of deception—he was not passing judgment on specific experiments.

One can appreciate the scope of the controversy by considering the use of the term "deception." Milgram, taking the view that deception is absolutely necessary in many social-psychological investigations, was critical of the term itself:

> The term "deception" . . . biases the issue. It is preferable to use morally neutral terms such as "masking," "staging," or "technical illusion" in describing such techniques, because it is not possible to make an objective ethical judgment on a practice unless it is described in terms that are not themselves condemnatory. (1977b, p. 19)

For Milgram, then, it is the *context* or purpose of deception that is critical. He points to numerous examples in everyday life where "deception" is tolerated, if not championed, such as the illusion of "Santa Claus," the deception involved in a surprise birthday party, the privileged communication given to a defense attorney, the illusions in theater, and so on. One could point to the "placebo" control in biomedical research as another legitimate use of a form of deception. Thus, for the purpose of scientific research, deception should be given its proper meaning. In effect, he was asserting that to equate the "research" application of deception with "cheating on one's spouse" is ethically naive.

Yet Kelman seems to take essentially the opposite point of view:

> I am reminded . . . of the intriguing phenomenon of the "holiness of sin," which characterizes certain messianic movements as well as other movements of the true-believer variety. Behavior that would normally be unacceptable actually takes on an aura of virtue in such movements through a redefinition of the situation in which the behavior takes place and thus of the context for evaluating it. A similar mechanism seems to be involved in our attitude toward the psychological experiment . . . de-

ception—which is normally unacceptable—can indeed be seen as a positive good. (P. 5)

It should be noted that Milgram (1977b) was explicit on the matter of priorities:

> One thing is clear: masking and technical illusions ought never to be used unless they are indispensable to the conduct of inquiry. Honesty and openness are the only desirable basis of transaction with people generally. This still leaves open the question of whether such devices are permissible when they cannot be avoided in a scientific inquiry. (P. 20)

Kelman, I suspect, was more in agreement with Milgram than might be apparent from the quotations above. Yet, his argument is essentially that "a lie is a lie is a lie." As with numerous critics of the research establishment (such as Ring, 1967; Geller, 1982), Kelman was particularly troubled by the widespread routine use of deception.

One of Kelman's recommendations is the exploration of research strategies that would not require deception. He focuses upon "role playing" as an alternative methodology, and it is this technique that is featured in a number of subsequent obedience experiments. We shall consider these developments in the next chapter.

Negative Commentary on the Ethics of the Obedience Experiments

Heinz Schuler (1982)

Schuler suggests that Milgram's subjects were mistreated in view of an implied contract existing between the subject and researcher:

> To be sure, you don't understand why I'm making you do this. You think it's foolish or dangerous, immoral or even completely insane. But my position proves that I can make the right decisions, that I am competent to judge the results of my actions. I'll be responsible, and you do what I say (P. 63)

Using this "contractual" perspective—one that emphasizes the power that one person has over another in a variety of contexts—Schuler notes that most people would follow the instructions of an auto mechanic to rev up an engine beyond the red line on the tachometer if he said that he would not fix the car unless this were done. A nurse would likely obey a physician to administer a dosage that seemed dangerous. Like Baumrind, Schuler feels that obedience is appropriate to the subject's *role*. The ethical problem arises because the experimenter transfers the responsibility to the subject who, presumably, has behaved largely out of a sense of "trust."

Schuler then extends his analysis to an inference regarding Milgram's motivations:

> This experimenter failed to keep his word. The terms of an implicit social contract were not observed, and the trust of the subjects was misused. Attention was distracted from this breach of contract by means of spectacular association of the subjects' behavior with crimes committed in concentration camps. Milgram's strategy aims at stirring up excitement among the readership. If the strategy succeeds, it is hard for readers to think about the experiment from another perspective. (Pp. 63-64)

Since most scientists probably wish to "stir up excitement" (in one form or another), Schuler is weak on this point. His observation that the association of Milgram's research with the Holocaust complicates a more detached appraisal of the experiments is, however, quite accurate.

Perhaps Schuler's strongest ethical case against the obedience research is his accusation that Milgram violated the subjects' right to terminate their participation:

> The principle that a subject can discontinue participation in an experiment at any time (blatantly disregarded in Milgram's studies of obedience) should be placed very high in the hierarchy, because not following this principle amounts to the experimenter's assuming responsibility for all consequences of the original decision to participate, including unforeseeable consequences. (P. 125)

What this leads to, of course, is Schuler's ultimate denial of the experiment's generality or significance—another illustration of the close interplay between the ethical and substantive (or, generalization) facets of research.

Principle 9, Section f of "Ethical Principles of Psychologists" (American Psychological Association, 1981) states:

> The investigator respects the individual's freedom to decline to participate in or to withdraw from the research at any time. The obligation to protect this freedom requires careful thought and consideration when the investigator is in a position of authority or influence over the participant. (Schuler, 1982, p. 215)

Milgram's paradigm may well have failed to respect the subject's "freedom to decline to participate." From Milgram's point of view, of course, the subjects in fact had every right to withdraw—they were not explicitly threatened with any consequences for refusing to continue—and, in fact, many subjects did withdraw. However, we are speaking here of "respect" for the subjects' rights. Milgram's fourth prod—"you have no other choice, you must go on"—is but one illustration of the fact that his primary interest was in challenging the subjects' right to withdraw and observing how such subjects responded to this challenge.

Schuler's discussion regarding the "right to withdraw" may be one of the most convincing ethical arguments against the obedience research. This issue pertains to the basic design or paradigm itself, as distinct from the emotional reactions in subjects, the perseverance of their negative self-image, etc.

Steven Marcus (1974)

Steven Marcus, in his review of Milgram's book *Obedience to Authority* in the *New York Times*, takes a negative view on the ethics of the research, although he stops short of dismissing the value of the work itself:

> The high levels of deceit, fraud, misrepresentation and chicanery necessary to perform such research were also attacked as being incompatible with the conduct of science. At times it became difficult in the furor to know which was to be more condemned—the results of the experiments or the experimental activity itself . . . it may be reasonable to propose that although it is a useful thing that we have the knowledge that came out of these experiments, it is at least as desirable that research conducted according to such methods be interdicted. (P. 2)

This kind of ambivalence is encountered quite frequently in commentaries on Milgram's experiments.

Marcus is decidedly unequivocal in criticizing what he feels to be Milgram's excessive moralizing—as shown in this account of one subject:

> When the learner first complains, Mr. Batta pays no attention to him. . . . All the while he maintains the same rigid mask. The learner, seated alongside him, begs him to stop, but with robotic impassivity, he continues the procedure. What is extraordinary is his apparent total indifference to the learner; he hardly takes cognizance of him as a human being. (P. 2)

Marcus indicates that this kind of description—and there are a number of similar narratives in Milgram's book—implied a low personal regard for his subjects and an insensitivity regarding how these accounts would influence his readers.

Two points can be raised here. First, in contrast to Milgram's interpretations of his subjects' behavior, one might note the extreme sensitivity with which he treated his subjects as evidenced by the highly individualized post-experimental debriefing period, the written summary sent to subjects, and his interest in their post-experimental attitudes and opinions. As noted earlier, this activity is, unfortunately, rare in social research. Milgram's procedures could reasonably be viewed as a model of how subjects should be treated.

As far as Milgram's personal opinion of his subjects' behavior is concerned, there is no question that he views obedience as a *moral failing*. His stated intention was to pose a moral conflict for his subjects. Those who obeyed the experimenter chose the wrong course of action. As I see it, Milgram is very clear on this.

Marcus quotes Milgram who, in his preface, states his goal as follows:

> The dilemma inherent in obedience to authority is ancient, as old as the story of Abraham. What the present study does is to give the dilemma contemporary form by treating it as subject matter for experimental inquiry, and with the aim of understanding rather than judging it from a moral standpoint. (1974, p. xi)

Contrasting this latter sentence with Milgram's account of Mr. Batta (above), Marcus notes that "I have rarely read a book that is so moralistic, so obtrusively preachy, as 'Obedience to authority'" (p. 2).

Marcus may, of course, be correct, in having detected a basic flaw or contradiction in Milgram's work. An alternative view is that Milgram's intent in his preface was to emphasize his basic *empirical* orientation to the analysis of obedience, as contrasted with purely *theological* or *philosophical* treatments of the issue. Thus, he may never have intended to be neutral on the meaning of destructive obedience in his laboratory or anywhere else. Regardless of these considerations, Marcus is correct in stating that the *style* of Milgram's portrayal of individual subjects is, on occasion, unsettling. In describing Fred Prozi, who obeyed to the maximum voltage level despite intense agitation, Milgram concludes, "The subject's objections strike us as inordinately weak and inappropriate in view of the events in which he is immersed. He thinks he is killing someone, yet he uses the language of the tea table" (1974, p. 77).

While I do not agree with the substance of Marcus' criticism, I do agree that for *some readers*, Marcus is correct in stating that "these characterizations are being written from a very high horse, and that they communicate to the reader a distinct impression that Milgram regards their objects with outright contempt" (p. 2).

Donald Warwick (1982)

Donald Warwick, in a sophisticated discussion of the harm that may be experienced by research subjects, is critical of Milgram's reliance upon post-experimental surveys:

> The use of self-report data is particularly ironic in studies using deception, since the usual justification for deception is that the reports of subjects are not to be trusted in sensitive areas of behavior. In his famous studies of obedience, Stanley Milgram surely would not have used an item such as the following as the basis for his conclusions: "If you were put in a situation where you were told by the experimenter to give electric shock to other people, how much shock would you be willing to give? . . . Yet in testing for subject reactions to his experiments—including areas of behavior notably susceptible of bias—Milgram used precisely that approach. (P. 102)

Warwick's point is that Milgram was inconsistent. Willing to invest his subjects' verbal reports with validity regarding their self-esteem and attitudes toward his experiment, Milgram was hardly as enthusiastic about the validity of the verbal estimates made by subjects who were asked how far they personally would have gone had they been in the experiment.

Warwick's point is not without merit. Milgram's subjects were, from all indications, treated in a very responsible and dignified manner during the post-experimental phases of his research. Paradoxically, this could have influenced them to refrain from being completely candid regarding negative aftereffects. Warwick suggests that deception might be required to check on post-experimental harm—simply asking subjects is insufficient because, among other things, many subjects do not wish to "spoil things" for the experimenter.

The resolution of Warwick's point seems to rest upon what constitutes a *reasonable* course. Milgram presented a variety of response alternatives regarding subjects' opinions of his research. A majority checked "positive." Were there lingering doubts, more subjects would likely have checked a more neutral response option. During the experiment, many subjects, regardless of the number of shock levers pressed, were extremely vocal in protesting the experimenter's insistence that they continue. Why should they then become totally silent regarding negative emotional thoughts in the security of their homes as they reflected on their participation?

Warwick is correct in asserting that it is difficult to be *sure* that no harm occurred, and that verbal assurances may be treated too uncritically by researchers. From another perspective, however, Milgram's procedure seems reasonable. He invited reactions from his subjects and proceeded in a very *public* manner. His address was known to all who participated.

Rom Harré (1979)

Rom Harré, a prominent critic of traditional experimentation in social psychology, has objected to the obedience experiments on a number of grounds. Similar to Baumrind, he emphasizes the "trust" factor. Once subjects have been assured that the learner will not suffer permanent damage—an assurance that occurred very early in the shock series for most subjects—their subsequent responses are acts of faith or trust in the experimenter, not destructive obedience.

After dismissing the significance of the research on this methodological point, Harré presents the following ethical criticism:

> Milgram's assistants were quite prepared to subject the participants in the experiment to mental anguish, and in some cases considerable suffering, in obedience to Milgram. The most morally obnoxious feature of this outrageous experiment was, I believe, the failure of any of Milgram's assistants to protest against the treatment that they were meting out to the subjects. At least the citizens of New Haven in the measure of one in three had a finer moral sensibility than any of those who assisted Milgram in this unpleasant affair. (P. 106)

The accusation that Milgram's personnel were, themselves, obedient is, to say the least, novel. Where are the orders, the conflict, the tension, etc.? Were not these individuals *investigating* obedience rather than displaying it? Harré's argument is that Milgram was the "authority" figure in a hierarchy—the research team—which brutalized subjects.[8] Lewis Brandt, a psychoanalytically oriented critic of methodology in social psychology, has expressed a similar point of view:

> A . . . deceit of the profession was perpetrated as a result of lack of self-reflection by Milgram (1963) who had no logical or psychological basis for claiming that he investigated "obedience" as demonstrated by Orne and Holland (1968) and myself (Brandt, 1971). Had Milgram critically analyzed his experimental procedure before carrying out his experiments, he would have . . . known the results beforehand (since he was willing to make his participants suffer in the name of science, his participants would do the same) (1978, p. 65).

Bruno Bettelheim (1978)

Hans Askenasy, a clinical psychologist who spent his adolescence under Nazi control in Frankfurt, has written an analysis of genocide (1978). The obedience experiments are featured in Askenasy's account, which will be described briefly in Chapter Seven. It is appropriate here, however, to note a reference by Askenasy to the views of the prominent psychiatrist, Bruno Bettelheim. In a correspondence with Askenasy, Bettelheim took the following position on the obedience research:

> You by implication quote Milgram favorably, as one of the great experiments of our time. I detest it, as I detest Zimbardo's experiments. These experiments are so vile, the intention with which they were engaged in is so vile, that nothing these experiments show has any value. To me they are exactly in line with the inhumanity of a Skinner who first starves pigeons nearly to death and then says he uses only positive reinforcers. They are in line with the human experiments of the Nazis. They, too, considered them most valuable experiments. Never mind what it did to the subjects so experimented on. Having been one of those experimented with, I can see no redeeming merit in these experiments. Milgram, Zimbardo did them to promote their own professional advancement. (Askenasy, 1978, p. 131).

The reader will, of course, have his or her own reactions to these arguments. For myself, the position taken by Bettelheim, as well as the closely related ideas of Schuler, Harré, and Brandt, illustrate the manner in which ethical criticisms of the obedience research have extended to personal attacks on Milgram. Thus, it is claimed that Milgram forced his assistants to do the dirty work of the experiment, that he engaged in needless research when he should have been able to foresee what people would do in the name of science, and that the experiments were a product of Milgram's personal motive of career advancement. Askenasy suggests that Bettelheim failed to distinguish between the ethical considerations involved in conducting the obedience experiments and the results of the obedience research. Askenasy expresses "deep emotional sympathy" with Bettelheim's views but argues that his conclusions were patently false. Askenasy's position is that the obedience research is of the most profound importance.

Steven Patten (1977a)

Steven Patten, an English philosopher, has found what he views as a basic inconsistency or contradiction in Milgram's experiments. In

Patten's analysis, Milgram is portrayed as making two central arguments: first, that his obedient subjects behaved in an immoral fashion; and second, that the experiment, itself, was ethical. Patten disagrees. He argues that if Milgram is correct in arguing that the experiments were ethical, then the behavior of his subjects must also be vindicated and *not* be viewed as unethical obedience. He notes that Milgram claimed that his research was ethical because it involved only momentary stress or excitement rather than permanent harm. Patten then asks why Milgram's *subjects* cannot make the same claim, namely, that they were only causing the learner momentary pain (the experimenter even assured subjects on this point).

Milgram also indicates that his research was ethical because the subjects themselves endorsed it in their post-experimental survey responses. Patten has considerable difficulty accepting such reports (they come from morally flawed individuals, or individuals who are just as likely to be submissively approving after the experiment as they were during it). Just as Milgram was able to elicit praise from his subjects, Patten suggests that his subjects would conceivably have been able to elicit similar endorsements from the *learners* if they really existed. From this perspective (and perhaps with some intended facetiousness), Patten argues that Milgram would have no justification in accusing his subjects of having failed the moral conflict posed to them in his experiment. That is, they would have been as justified in harming the learner as Milgram was in exposing them to the agonizing conflict in their role as teacher.

Patten also argues that Milgram clearly intended to create severe stress and conflict in his subjects—if not, he would have terminated the experiment early in the program when it had become obvious that this was a highly frequent response. Milgram also used this kind of emotional reactivity to buttress his argument regarding the realism of the conflict experienced by the subjects. Patten thus dismisses Milgram's claim, made originally to Baumrind, that the emotional stress was *unexpected*. If Milgram was ethical in creating conditions which would produce uncontrollable seizures and convulsions, then Patten argues that perhaps Milgram's subjects were also ethical in terms of what they were doing to the learner.

Patten does not view Milgram's arguments on behalf of his own ethics to be persuasive, but his major thesis is not to prove that Milgram himself was unethical. Rather:

> I have been concerned to maintain primarily that the only vindications
> Milgram offers for himself which are at all plausible would, if adequate,

also serve to rescue his supposedly obedient subjects from the charge of immoral behavior. . . . Thus, on pain of inconsistency, he will have to accept that there is nothing immoral in the actions of his subjects. This in turn will mean that his experiments cannot have their announced import simply because it will no longer be possible to classify the behavior of his subjects as *unethical* obedience. (P. 361)

Patten then notes that regardless of the issues raised above, one might simply argue that Milgram's subjects should have realized that it was unreasonable for the experimenter to insist that the protesting learner be subjected to more shocks—that notwithstanding the expertise and legitimacy of the research setting, *in this paradigm, things were out of control and subjects had the moral obligation to act on such a state of affairs*. If this is accepted, then Patten asks:

What is to prevent the subject of the experiment from arguing in an exactly analogous fashion? "What of *my* pain?" he will ask. "What is one to say of my sweating, my nervous laughter, my fits, and my seizures?" Should not one be able to *just see* in this case as well that the rationale of the Milgram experiments could never vindicate the suffering of the subjects? . . . And do not say that the significant difference is that the subjects of the Milgram experiments had a choice as to whether to continue with the experiments. For Milgram and his helpers had precisely the same choice. (P. 363)

So, if Milgram's subjects were unethical—and this is his major claim—then, Patten indicates, Milgram also was unethical. Patten concludes with a simple statement of his complex analysis—"Milgram-type experiments are themselves unethical or . . . they tell us little about unethical obedience" (p. 364).

Patten's analysis is impressive. He demonstrates a thorough familiarity with the obedience experiments and the literature relevant to a critical understanding of Milgram's work. He is concerned about *unethical obedience*, a very precise issue of central significance to an understanding of Milgram's work. At several places, he makes useful distinctions in terms of conceptualizing authority as well as harmful obedience. He notes, for example, that even if Milgram's subjects did endorse their participation, that, in itself, does not automatically justify the research from an ethical standpoint. His paper will be difficult for some—it took several readings on my part—but is extremely valuable in forcing one to think about the obedience research in a unique and quite provocative way.

This having been said, I must disagree with Patten on several counts. Some of his ideas simply seem intellectually "thin." Thus, when Patten suggests that the subjects' post-experimental reports should not be taken seriously because these individuals, having been obedient, are "morally flawed," he is introducing a kind of permanent condemnation of these individuals that is certainly not in keeping with Milgram's analysis. When he suggests that the subjects would have been able to obtain endorsements from the *learners* (had there been genuine learners) just as Milgram obtained endorsements from his subjects, I totally disagree. The learner was portrayed as initially agreeable, but increasingly resistant and ultimately in agony.

Patten's strategy of equating the behavior of Milgram (or his confederate) and that of his subjects *may*—and I stress that I am not certain on this point—be another manifestation of using the results of the experiment to personally attack Milgram's own ethics. Some of Milgram's subjects obeyed to a point at which it appeared that extreme pain was being inflicted on the learner. Milgram, of course, wants this phenomenon to be taken seriously. Patten implies that the pain of Milgram's *subjects* (uncontrollable laughter, sweating, etc.) is not taken with equal seriousness in order to justify the ethics of the obedience experiments. I think he is wrong here. I feel that Milgram addressed the emotional reactions of his subjects with perhaps unprecedented care and made a decision to pursue the research with this information available to him.

In my view, Patten fails to deal with the role of the behavioral scientist in studying a phenomenon such as harmful obedience. His approach of drawing continuous analogies between what Milgram is doing to his subjects and what they are doing to the learner is provocative and will strike some readers as convincing. Another view is that it is confusing and misleading, that it presumes that one must evaluate the researcher's behavior and that of research subjects on the same ethical basis.

Patten claims that he is open regarding the "final truth," that it is still possible that someone could present an argument that "would serve to justify the experimenter and not the subject" (p. 364). But he thinks such a defense will be difficult to construct, that we are likely to be left with two options—either the research was unethical or they tell us little about destructive (that is, unethical) obedience. In my own view, the thrust of Patten's argument is that he views the experiments and Milgram as unethical. However, Patten has also analyzed the obedience paradigm from a methodological perspective. We will consider this analysis in Chapter Seven, and will reconsider what appears to be his fundamental position at that time.[9]

Positive Commentary on the Ethics of the Obedience Experiments

Notwithstanding the intensely critical position of various commentators, there have been numerous, enthusiastic endorsements regarding the ethics of Milgram's obedience experiments. Similar to those critics who extended their arguments to a personal attack on Milgram himself, those with positive regard for the research have often praised Milgram for his ingenuity and pioneering efforts on the problem of harmful obedience. We have noted that a basic ethical criticism of research *in general* has been directed at the use of deception. Those who have taken a strong stand against it—Baumrind (1985) is a case in point—are inclined to disapprove of the obedience research. Similarly, those who explicitly deny a cost/benefit, "means are worth the end" approach to research ethics will be critical of the obedience experiments. Yet, many do not object, categorically, to the use of deception in social research and readily endorse the cost/benefit rationale. The vast majority of textbook writers in social psychology—and related disciplines in psychology, sociology, and other social sciences—fall into this latter grouping. These individuals are extremely positive in their characterization of the obedience research. For many, this research is the "very stuff out of which social psychology is made." We will not review the positions of textbook writers, however, but reserve discussion for a number of analyses which have been specifically directed at the obedience research.

Harry Kaufmann (1967)

In a short but incisive essay, Harry Kaufmann was one of the first to publish a defense of the obedience research on ethical grounds. His position is a classic illustration of the teleological orientation:

> Milgram's experiments can be argued to have provided us with insights about social behavior comparable to few other experimental studies. Whether the anxieties aroused in the subjects realizing their moral flaws are really intense and durable enough to warrant the cry that the price paid is too high, is a suitable topic not so much for debate, as for empirical inquiry. Milgram's own . . . follow-up work seems to show very little lingering discomfort, amply counterbalanced by the subject's gratification for having participated in a really meaningful experimental situation, a rare enough event. (P. 322)

Kaufmann makes explicit reference to the Holocaust, noting that Milgram's subjects—and by extension, those studying them—were given an opportunity to learn "that it can happen here, with me as an instrument of murder" (p. 322).

The title of Kaufmann's essay—"The price of obedience and the price of knowledge?"—is, in itself, telling, eloquently capturing the researcher's dilemma. Unlike Kelman or Baumrind, Kaufmann was prepared to inform subjects about things they may not have wished to learn, "The social theory of evil may be distressing and humiliating to the stature of man, but then, learning to know oneself is seldom a gratifying experience, yet one which few of us would forego" (p. 322).

Milton Erickson (1968)

Citing numerous instances of genocide, the Holocaust being but one glaring example, Erickson presents a glowing endorsement of the obedience research. He suggests that people—social scientists among them—have a tendency to emphasize the positive aspects of human behavior. If evil is considered at all, it is invariably explained by reference to the pathology or evil nature of "those" people. Erickson, a psychiatrist, offered an account of his own regarding negative reactions to Milgram's work:

> That his pioneer work in this field is attacked as being unethical, unjustifiable, uninformative, or any other derogative dismissal, is to be expected, simply because people like to shut their eyes to undesirable behavior, preferring to investigate memory, forgetting of nonsense syllables, conditioned reflexes, span of attention and similar kinds of behavior that do not arouse inner distress and anxiety. (P. 278)

This is hyperbole, as there is obviously no necessary relationship between an interest in the more benign issues of behavior and "shutting one's eyes to evil." Erickson's major point, however, is attributional (Chapter Two), namely, that it is wrong to perceive evil as solely dispositional in its causation. His positive view of the ethics of the obedience research is linked to his belief in the "inhumanity of ordinary people:"

> Here is a pioneer willing to say simply and emphatically . . . that normal and average human beings can be manipulated into inhumane behavior, and that the need is great to study the normal man from this aspect rather than to continue to regard such behavior either as incomprehensible or as evidence that the person involved is somehow aberrant, abnormal, and atypical. . . . To engage in such studies as Milgram has requires strong men with strong scientific faith and a willingness to discover

that to man himself, not to "the devil," belongs the responsibility for and the control of his inhumane actions. (P. 279)

Gary Stollak (1967)

Gary Stollak raises an interesting question pertaining to *debriefing* in the obedience paradigm. He first cites Kelman (1967), who had stated that debriefing, because it must be completely truthful, could be harmful to (at least some) subjects who would learn about their potentiality for destructive obedience. Stollak then asks whether all subjects should in fact be debriefed by telling them the (same) truth. Could it not be particularly stressful for subjects to leave the experiment knowing what they did and what it means—and knowing that the experimenter knows it as well?

> Is it possible that we could produce less side-effects, and is it perhaps more kind and ethical to either have no debriefing, or a specific kind of debriefing which does not inform subjects of the true nature of the experiment? . . . Does the truth always set our subjects free? Is truth always more important than compassion? (P. 678)

Of course, people differ in their answer to Stollak's thoughtful questions. Baumrind (1985) has stated that if a researcher cannot give a truthful as well as emotionally supportive debriefing, then the research should not be conducted. My impression, however, is that Stollak's question has been answered by the prevailing research establishment on the side of compassion, with an emphasis upon providing a meaningful, accurate account without necessarily giving every subject the same, most negativistic or morally unsettling sort of information.

Stollak thus raises an issue which would itself prove to be troublesome and controversial: What should one tell subjects in the obedience paradigm—and should their behavior determine what is said to them afterward? He does not directly endorse Milgram's research, but the very raising of the issue suggests that he holds a teleological position, that is, that the research could be of sufficient importance to consider not debriefing subjects at all (a view never to receive any sort of popularity) or to construct a debriefing to meet the emotional needs of the subject.

Thomas Crawford (1972)

Thomas Crawford has defended the obedience experiments in terms of their substantive contribution. He sees a paradox in Kelman's criticism, namely that the obedience problem relates precisely to issues—of control, manipulation, freedom—which are of central concern to Kelman's fundamentally humanistic perspective:

> Kelman (1965) tells us that "In order to build some protection against manipulation into the social structure, we will have to extend our research on processes of resistance to control" . . . I submit that Milgram's research, along with the studies of Asch and Sherif on conformity and McGuire's work on inoculation and resistance to persuasion, is precisely aimed at achieving the admirable goal which Kelman sets before us. We can hardly read the study without becoming more sensitized to analogous conflicts in our own lives. (P. 183)

Crawford suggests, then, that we cannot have it both ways—we cannot be seriously concerned about problems of destructive social influence and at the same time hold to an ethical position that prevents the conduct of research aimed at understanding these phenomena.

Citing the testimony of Milgram (1964) as well as of Ring et al. (1970) on the lack of demonstrated harm to subjects, Crawford agrees with Kelman's thesis, that the purpose of research is not to provide self-knowledge to subjects. However, he maintains that, "the postexperimental debriefing served to *heighten their awareness that choice was possible* in a situation in which they had been willing to relinquish autonomy. Therefore, the study performs the very service which Kelman says justifies manipulations of human behavior—it enhances awareness of freedom of choice and thereby maximizes the attainment of individual values" (p. 183). Thus, one of Crawford's central arguments is that the obedience experiments inform us about *disobedience*. This, for Crawford, makes the obedience research not only ethical but "one of the most important studies ever done in social psychology. . . . It is an allegory for our times" (p. 181).

Alan Elms (1972, 1982)

Alan Elms was a graduate assistant to Milgram during the actual conduct of the obedience research. He went on to become a social psychologist, specializing in the application of social psychology to political issues. His involvement with the research was thus very intimate, and his perspective, though understandably biased, is unique in terms of his background. He has discussed the obedience experiments in his text *Social Psychology and Social Relevance* (1972) and in a recent chapter devoted to the ethics of deception (1982). His basic position is readily seen in the following:

Milgram, in exploring the external conditions that produce such destructive obedience, the psychological processes that lead to such attempted abdications of responsibility, and the means by which defiance of illegitimate authority can be promoted, seems to me to have done some of the most morally significant research in modern psychology. A number of ministers who have based sermons on this research, and the Germans and Israelis who were the first to publish translations of Milgram's papers, apparently agree. (1972, p. 146-47).

Elms, like Crawford and Erickson, invests the obedience research with profound moral significance, based on the association of obedience to authority with political and historical events.

One of the most striking features in Elms's 1972 analysis is his venomous criticism of Diana Baumrind, who had been, of course, Milgram's first and most influential critic. Sarcastically, Elms notes that because Baumrind herself is a developmental psychologist, she views Milgram's subjects as if they were children: "The volunteers are all children at heart, unable to resist the experimenter's wiles and therefore needing protection by someone who knows better, namely Dr. Baumrind" (p. 151).

Elms adopts Milgram's view, that the subjects were given a *choice* in the obedience paradigm—that their behavior was neither inevitable nor controlled by Milgram. Elms cites research in which Baumrind intentionally made children fail at a task in order to observe their responses to failure. Elms views her subjects' lack of choice in such a setting to be unethical.

As in previous commentaries, Elms's position is clearly teleological. Recognizing that reasonable caution must be exercised on matters pertaining to the welfare of subjects, Elms views the importance of the research as paramount. He introduces a novel role for the reader, a kind of pre-Holocaust perspective:

> It happens to be quite true that the obedient volunteers were willing to shock innocent human beings upon command, and each volunteer proved this to himself. Should we instead leave people to their moral inertia, or their grave moral laxity, so as not to disturb their privacy? Who is willing to justify privacy on this basis? Who would have done so, with foreknowledge of the results, in pre-Nazi Germany? (P. 156)

Elms is again unreserved in his criticism of Baumrind, as when he asks: "But what of the broader position advanced by Baumrind (who is mainly a clinician rather than an experimentalist), the idea that psychological experimentation as a whole is so worthless that its value can be counted as zero in any moral equation?" (p. 159). He well may be venting here, at least in part, the personal insult he feels Baumrind unjustifiably directed at Milgram. Elms is far more impressive, I think, when arguing for the social relevance of research:

> Some social scientists and ethicists find it implausible that laboratory studies of individual psychological phenomena could yield any useful understanding of the dynamics of a Holocaust. I find it even more implausible to assume that research with the broad dissemination and emotional impact of Milgram's studies has not already generated enough introspection and discussion to diminish significantly the likelihood of another Holocaust-like phenomenon, at least in this country. (1982, p. 240)

One could, of course, endorse the value of the obedience research without this kind of unbounded praise. Yet, I find a sober conviction in Elms's discussion that is very moving. Here, one can sense the value of all of the criticisms and rebuttals, the point-counterpoint nature of what we have been considering in this chapter. For it is unlikely that Elms or anyone else would have been prompted to engage in this kind of informative—at times truly passionate—analysis, were it not for the spirit of intellectual combat generated by the stimulating ideas of people such as Diana Baumrind. The reader may take sides or attempt to integrate the views expressed in these pages, but the result, whatever its resolution, is a clear "plus" in terms of having produced a highly sensitized, aware community of scholars and students.

M. Brewster Smith (1976)

M. Brewster Smith, like Herbert Kelman, stands as one of the premier humanists in social psychology, an individual with a prestigious research career who has consistently argued for a compassionate, humane perspective on research methodology. He is very cautious on the use of deception, for example, and unimpressed by Milgram's answer to Baumrind, namely that his use of deception was inappropriately singled out, given its ubiquitous use by other researchers. Smith is skeptical regarding insights gained in participating in the obedience experiments: "Maybe so—but it does take considerable *chutzpah* to regard the bestowal of unwelcome truths about others as a benefit to them—even if, after the fact, people say they like it" (p. 449).

Smith recognizes the logic and apparent usefulness of the cost/benefit approach to ethical decision making, but concludes that the actual calculation of such a ratio is impossible. It is nebulous, confronting on the one hand values to science and society, but on the other, risks to *individuals*. The question of "who is to decide the issue" is also of obvious complexity. Smith feels that ethical judgments do not lend themselves readily to pat formulas or abstract analysis: "Complex human judgments are involved, ad hoc judgments guided by precedent and debate, in which movement toward consensus can be stimulated but hardly dictated by ethical analysis" (p. 450).

However, Smith's overall assessment of the obedience research is quite unique. He sees it as an *exception*, one that should be tolerated, if not admired: "For myself, I find it quite possible to justify a Milgram study, as a carefully weighed exception, an important study that raises serious ethical questions but can be undertaken with heavy ethical responsibility falling on the investigator's shoulders. I wouldn't do such a study, but I really respect Milgram's right to have done it" (p. 452).

One senses a similar attitude on the part of Herbert Kelman. Almost everything about the obedience paradigm is offensive to Brewster Smith, with the exception of the subject matter, destructive obedience. That is a problem that in his view simply must be addressed, thus his begrudging endorsement of Milgram's research.[10]

ETHICAL CONTROVERSY IN SOCIAL SCIENCE: A HISTORICAL NOTE

A convincing argument can certainly be made for the landmark position of the obedience research in sensitizing social scientists to ethical issues. However, it should be recognized that there have been a number of research projects, in disciplines other than social psychology, that have also achieved a highly controversial ethical status. This reflects, at least in part, the diversity of methodologies in the social sciences. Often there are unique ethical ramifications associated with specific research procedures. Within the social sciences, for example, anthropology, sociology, psychology, the process of codifying ethical principles has been a painstaking enterprise, characterized by heated debates and numerous revisions. These discussions have not taken place in a vacuum, however. Invariably, it has been specific research projects that have served as catalysts for ethical decision making and legislation (for example, Barnes. 1979, Chapter Eight).

An illustrative case, in sociology, was Laud Humphreys' doctoral dissertation. Conducted in the mid-1960s, this research was concerned with the determinants of impersonal sexual gratification in public restrooms. Humphreys collected part of his data by positioning himself as a "watchqueen," serving as a lookout for interruption by the police or by strangers of ongoing homosexual acts. He thus disguised himself as a homosexual, obtaining the trust of the men he observed. He secretly followed some of these men, and by obtaining their automobile license numbers he was eventually able to identify their names. Months later, disguised as a health survey interviewer, Humphreys visited these men and obtained considerable personal information regarding their lifestyles, attitudes, etc.

The controversial nature of this research should be evident (Humphreys, 1978). Humphreys was resoundingly accused of spying on his subjects, of invading their privacy, of endangering their social standing, of using false pretenses to gain access to homes for his interviews. Were his data subpoenaed, it is conceivable that some of his subjects might have been arrested, for it was this form and location of homosexual activity that accounted for a majority of arrests in this country. Sieber (1982b) notes that some faculty members of the sociology department at Washington University who were not on his doctoral research committee upon learning of Humphreys' methodology were provoked to the point of urging that his degree be withheld. Invasion of privacy was perhaps the most fundamental criticism (for example, von Hoffman, 1970). One could hardly imagine a more blatant violation of the principle of informed consent—or a more necessary one, given the need to obtain valid behavioral information. The subjects in Humphreys' study, unlike those in the obedience experiments, were never aware that a study was even being conducted.

Sieber (1982b) also reports, however, that Humphreys' research was praised by various gay communities and was instrumental in changing the arrest policy of police departments in several cities. His research received a prestigious award from the Society for the Study of Social Problems. Humphreys viewed his research as a significant scientific contribution to an area beseiged by ignorance and destructive stereotypes. He also received support from the academic community as well. Irving Louis Horowitz and Lee Rainwater expressed the view that without the right to pursue this type of research, the social scientist's ability to illuminate a variety of serious problem areas would be in severe jeopardy.

As in the Milgram-Baumrind exchange, the controversy regarding Humphreys' research could be viewed as a truly vexing dilemma. On the one hand, there were those who criticized Humphreys for violat-

ing the rights of his subjects. On the other, there were those who supported Humphreys' right to engage in meaningful scientific inquiry.
Like Milgram, Humphreys defended his research in terms of the value
of his findings. This approach, however, was ineffective in silencing
his critics because it was his *methodology* rather than his findings that
was the object of ethical debate.

We can see in this example, then, another expression of a familiar
refrain—are the ends worth the means? Put succinctly if not delicately,
the issue often seems to come to this: Either one is going to do the
research and pay the ethical costs, or one will remain ignorant about
this particular arena of social life. The assumption can usually be
made, in this context, that if there was an alternative methodology
that would (a) involve fewer potential ethical pitfalls and (b) would
yield data with equivalent informational value, this methodology
would have been used.

An interesting commonality to the diverse research controversies
noted in this discussion[11] is that in each case, the *timing* of the initial critical reaction occurred at approximately the same period, that
is, mid to late 1960s. In psychology, of course, this period was the
occasion of the Baumrind-Milgram exchange as well as Herbert Kelman's profoundly influential essays on the use of deception. The fact
that such an abundance of ethical debate and controversy in the
various social sciences occurred at approximately the same time may,
of course, be a coincidence. However, Aronson, Brewer, and Carlsmith, in the third edition of the *Handbook of Social Psychology*, have
recently suggested a more rational basis for the zeitgeist of ethical
scrutiny. They speak primarily in reference to experimental social
psychology, but clearly their perspective could be generalized to the
other social sciences as well:

> Critics both inside and outside the field began to question using decep-
> tion . . . and those generating extreme anxiety as in the well-known re-
> search of Milgram . . . and Zimbardo and his students. . . . The strength
> of this reaction was perhaps more influenced by societal events than by
> any clear evidence of gross insensitivity to the rights of experimental
> subjects or of harm having been done by experimenters. . . . For exam-
> ple, in the late 1960s and early 1970s, most of us were strongly affected
> by the cynical, self-serving duplicity employed by our national leaders
> during the Vietnam War and during the Watergate investigation. In this
> atmosphere, many social psychologists grew alarmed lest we as a pro-
> fession might lose the confidence of the public by behaving in a way
> that bore any resemblance to that exposed in Watergate investigations—

no matter how superficial that resemblance might be. The rapid growth in government regulations on the protection of human subjects also reflected the same concerns. (1985, p. 442)

Aronson, Brewer, and Carlsmith point out that in social psychology there have been important consequences to the ethical sensitization noted above. Far less dramatic experimental treatments or manipulations are used. Deception, while still prevalent, is generally of a more benign quality, and stressful laboratory experiences are relatively infrequent. The marked increase in research on social cognition and human judgment is, in their view, a reflection of a methodological reorientation in which research operations have relatively little direct impact on subjects. Finally, there is more field research. Ethical issues can, of course, be as critical here as in the laboratory, but in practice, the controversies have been minimal, a reflection of the generally nonintrusive manipulations characterizing field experimentation. These writers suggest that to the degree that the sociopolitical climate of the culture influences ethical decision making, it is not inconceivable that a more permissive consensus regarding the use of high-impact research methods could ultimately regain currency. Their position is cogently summarized in this restatement of the ubiquitous ethical dilemma:

> The major thrust of our argument here is that we are opposed to defining for the experimenter what *is* and *is not* a justifiable decision. Rather, it is to plead for care and concern for the welfare of subjects and at the same time to suggest that we do not abandon totally the hope of testing interesting hypotheses in powerful ways simply because such tests do not come in packages that are ethically impeccable. . . . There are no pat solutions in any era, much less for all time. (P. 469)

CONCLUSIONS

It is almost irresistable, after reviewing the ethical commentary on the obedience research, to avoid an integrative point of view. How simple it would be to say, with conviction, that "there are good points on both sides!" I will resist this temptation, however, and take a strongly affirmative position on the ethics of the obedience experiments.

Baumrind contrasts the obedience experiments with medical research, such as that related to the Sabin polio vaccine, and argues that Milgram could not be in a comparable position, before engaging in his research, to justify the risk that might be incurred by his subjects.

I appreciate Baumrind's line of reasoning. Certainly there is a vividness, a sense of urgency or immediacy regarding the devastation of physical illness that seems to justify almost anything done in the name of trying to find a cure. In fact, "anything goes" is hardly the case in biomedical research, where ethical guidelines are often extremely restrictive. I would argue, however, that the phenomenon of destructive obedience, which was one of the major facilitators to the success of the genocidal social policy in Nazi Germany, is as worthy of serious research as is cancer, heart disease, or poliomyelitis. "Real harm" (Baumrind's phrase) could result from *not doing* research on destructive obedience. Thus, I agree with Alan Elms when he states that "better and wider public understanding of the conditions most likely to promote destructive obedience on a small scale could have a prophylactic effect with regard to destructive obedience on a large scale" (1982, pp. 239-40). If one reads Milgram's (1961) research proposal (which was funded by the National Science Foundation) it is hard to imagine a more convincing presentation in terms of the usefulness of a basic research project.

We are fortunate that the ethical controversy reviewed in this chapter has been aired in accessible sources—in journals and, with increasing frequency, books devoted to the vexing ethical problems involved in social research—and that the discussants have been generally so articulate and thoughtful. To say that we are better off for having considered the ethical dimension of the obedience paradigm may sound trite, but it must certainly be the case. Among the beneficiaries, doubtless, are legions of research subjects who have been treated in a more humane and informed manner by researchers who, in the past two decades, have been enlightened by studying the issues reviewed here.

It is difficult to select a "last word" for a chapter of this nature, but I have decided to quote William McGuire, a highly respected social psychologist. In commenting on those who would find laboratory research to be unacceptable in terms of the treatment accorded to human subjects, McGuire had this memorable thought:

> We must also be concerned about an equally questionable ethical position epitomized by the words, "I have *not* run any subjects today." It seems to me all too simple to decide that it is safer to do no research. We must strictly censor our own work and find ways of maximizing gains and minimizing costs to some point at which we can ethically go ahead, perhaps inevitably with fear and trembling. But go on with our work we must, or else we must change our field. (1967, pp. 131-32)

6

CRITICISMS OF METHOD AND ALTERNATIVES TO DECEPTION IN THE STUDY OF OBEDIENCE

That the S will in an experiment carry out behaviors that appear destructive either to himself or others reflects more upon his willingness to trust the E and the experimental context than on what he would do outside of the experimental situation.

Orne and Holland (1968)

Orne observes that behavior is legitimized in the subject-experimenter relationship. He sees this only as getting in the way of establishing general truths, while in actuality, it is precisely an understanding of behavior within legitimized social relationships that the investigation seeks to attain. What Orne can construe only as an impediment is in fact a strategic research opportunity.

Stanley Milgram (1972)

It is not without irony that the obedience experiments have been a target for intense methodological criticism. Given the abundant ethical disagreements surrounding these studies, one might presume that people generally agree on what Milgram did in these experiments and what in fact was observed in them. This is not the case, however, for the methodological status of the obedience paradigm has, as with the ethical dimension, become a major controversial issue in its own right. When I speak of *methodological status* I am not referring to matters of research design, the number of subjects, control groups, statistical analyses, etc. The issue is more basic: *Given the experimental procedures used by Milgram, did he in fact accomplish his mission, that of investigating destructive obedience to authority?* Did his paradigm succeed in operationalizing the concept of harmful obedience? These are critical questions. The essential meaning of the research—the legitimacy of drawing inferences from the experiments, of generalizing to destructive obedience in other contexts—rests on the answers given to them.

The most incisive and influential methodological criticism was given by Martin Orne and Charles Holland in a symposium on the obedience experiments that appeared in a 1968 issue of the *International Journal of Psychiatry*. That Orne was the major author is significant in that Orne, himself, was (and is) a highly prominent specialist in the experimental analysis of social influence. His specific area of expertise is in the field of hypnosis, a phenomenon with obvious linkage to the problem of obedience.

More germane to our concern, however, is another facet of Orne's professional identity. In 1962, he had published an extraordinarily influential methodological essay concerning laboratory research with human subjects—"On the Social Psychology of the Psychological Experiment: With Particular Reference to Demand Characteristics and Their Implications." Orne and Holland's 1968 critique is essentially an application of the concept of "demand characteristics" to the obedience paradigm. In this chapter, we will examine their criticisms, Milgram's response, and the impact of their exchange upon subsequent investigators.

Although we have made, to this point, a rather sharp distinction between the ethical and methodological dimensions of the obedience research, it is actually the case that they interact. A fascinating illustration of this integration or fusion occurred when a number of investigators sought methodological alternatives to the paradigm used by Milgram. The general approach involved the use of *role playing*, a technique which had first been advocated in the heat of ethical debates on the use of deception. In this chapter, we shall review the application of role-playing techniques to be obedience problem—an illustration of one of the methodological strategies that resulted from the ethically oriented developments reviewed in the last chapter.

ORNE'S CONCEPTUALIZATION OF DEMAND CHARACTERISTICS

Orne's basic argument is that the subject should be viewed as an active, curious, and concerned individual, one for whom participation in a psychological experiment is an important venture. Rather than being a passive, inert recipient of the experimenter's instructions, the subject is more likely to be actively involved, concerned (usually at least) with being good or helpful, and, to attain these ends, motivated to interpret the experimenter's real purpose or hypothesis. A factor that plays a central role in Orne's critique of the obedience research is his idea that the subject comes to the experiment with certain presumptions or expectations. The subject can thus be viewed as adopting a specific *role*, which, through socialization, has been acquired without his necessarily having ever been in an experiment. What are some of these anticipations held by subjects?

Orne suggests that the subject is cognitively set to invest everything the experimenter says with importance, with a kind of halo, reflecting the legitimacy endowed by the fact that "this is a scientific experiment." Even if a specific activity might, to an outsider, seem trivial or bizarre, the fact that the experimenter, at least, is interested in it would, for a majority of subjects, lend it a modicum of significance. Orne includes, in his 1962 publication, reports of subjects engaging in incredulous pursuits of seemingly absurd behaviors, such as working on endless streams of addition problems on what appeared to be potentially thousands of sheets of paper. For the subject, perhaps it was a test of perseverance—surely the experimenter had a good reason for asking this.

Thus, subjects are predisposed to search for those cues which would convey the experimenter's hypothesis or essential research goal. If these cues are not explicit or obvious, which often would be the case in that the experimenter would not want subjects to be aware of the major influences being investigated, then subjects are likely to formulate their own interpretation. In any event—and this is the key point —the subjects' interpretation of these cues or "demand characteristics" may constitute an important—perhaps *the most important*—determinant of their subsequent behavior. Note that the demand characteristics of the experiment might very well depart from the experimenter's *stated* purpose of the research, particularly if this latter statement involved deception in one form or another.

Orne also portrays the experimental setting as one in which there is an extraordinary degree of *control* on the part of the experimenter. The subject is primed to trust the experimenter. Henry Riecken, in another classic formulation of this issue (1962), has also spoken to the expectations of subjects in this regard:

He also has some ideas about the limits of appropriate behavior . . . this experimenter-professor has responsibilities toward his students and is bound to protect as well as guide them. He is . . . trustworthy . . . rational, serious, and purposive . . . he is not lunatic, a prankster, or an idler . . . he will not knowingly risk the subject's life, steal, or physically attack him." (Pp. 28-29)

The demand-characteristic formulation has, in this context, particular importance when the research involves certain behaviors, for example, actions which involve punishment or harm—either to others or to oneself. Is it not likely that subjects would interpret things differently?

In an investigation of hypnosis, Orne and Evans (1965) observed that subjects would throw what was alleged to be fuming nitric acid at another individual, as well as pick up a poisonous snake and put their own hands into a jar of nitric acid. The experimenter did not, however, have to place subjects in a hypnotic trance to elicit these actions. Simply asking them to simulate being hypnotized—specifically, to try to fool a trained hypnotist into thinking they were deeply hypnotized—was sufficient to produce these acts of "destructiveness." That such behaviors could be produced in the "control" group—those asked to simulate receiving the experimental treatment, that is, being hypnotized—led Orne and Evans to this significant methodological conclusion:

> The burden of demonstrating the production of antisocial behavior by hypnotic techniques lies with the investigator, who must demonstrate that the so-called antisocial behavior does exceed that which is legitimized by the experimental situation, and that the behavior is perceived by the subject as truly dangerous or antisocial. It is our belief that it may not be possible to test the antisocial question in an experimental setting because of the problems of finding tasks which are not seen as legitimized by the experimental context. (1965, p. 199)

Thus, the subject's behavior in the laboratory does not inevitably "speak for itself." It must be interpreted, taking into account the determining role of the laboratory context itself. Of course, the issue of *generalizing beyond the laboratory* demands, to an acute degree, recognition of this contextual influence as well.

Orne and Holland (1968)

Orne and Holland applied the essential features of the demand-characteristic formulation to the obedience paradigm. In general, they argue that the obedience paradigm was a highly intricate, multifaceted scenario, which made it likely that subjects would make a variety of inferences during their participation, inferences that might depart radically from Milgram's own interpretation.

Their central criticism concerns what might be termed the *incongruity* factor. They view the experimenter's behavior as incongruous with (1) what subjects generally expect from an experimenter and (2) more specifically, Milgram's assertion that the subject was genuinely inflicting unbearable pain upon the learner. This point is absolutely critical—the entire foundation of the obedience research rests on the believability of the victim's increasingly mounting suffering. Orne and Holland, however, are skeptical:

> Incongruously the E sits by passively while the victim suffers, demanding that the experiment continue despite the victim's demands to be released and the possibility that his health may be endangered. This behavior of the E, which Milgram interprets as the demands of legitimate authority, can with equal plausibility be interpreted as a significant cue to the true state of affairs—namely that no one is actually being hurt. ... The incongruity between the relatively trivial experiment and the imperturbability of the E on the one hand, and the awesome shock generator able to present shocks designated as "Danger—Severe Shock" and the extremity of the victim's suffering on the other, should be sufficient to raise serious doubts in the minds of most Ss. (P. 287)

The similarity between this account of the obedience paradigm and Orne's critique of laboratory approaches to the study of hypnosis, mentioned earlier, should be apparent. The imperturbability of the experimenter, they argue, redefines the situation. The subject now realizes that it is, in actuality, an "as if" situation, that it is "safe" to shock the learner. Orne and Holland admit that an unscrupulous experimenter could, in fact, arrange for genuine harm to occur in the laboratory—just as a malevolent mechanic could arrange for one's rear axle to disintegrate or a sinister pharmacist could put poison in a nose drop bottle. They argue, however, that people ordinarily presume—that is, *trust*—that these things will not occur. Included in this category of non-occurrences would be an experimenter demanding that research subjects inflict tremendous voltage upon a screaming individual who has complained of a heart problem (see also Masserman, 1968).

Orne and Holland also suggest that research subjects are inclined *not* to reveal their awareness or interpretation to the experimenter. Should this redefinition of the situation depart radically from the experimenter's cover story or stated purpose, the revelation of this insight would only serve to embarrass the experimenter and ruin the entire study, outcomes that are not acceptable to either subject or experimenter. A "pact of ignorance" (Orne, 1962) thus tends to develop. The subject wants his participation to be valuable to the experimenter. The experimenter, in turn, does not wish to discard the data of the (in fact aware) subject. Both subject and experimenter thus have a stake in perpetuating the myth, namely that the subject has been naive in responding to the experimental manipulations.

Therefore, unless the experimenter makes an extraordinary effort, during postexperimental inquiry, to check on the precise effectiveness of the deceptions employed during the experiment, he or she is very likely not to learn of their inadequacies, but rather to presume, in subsequent discussion and interpretation, that the deceptions were successful. Regarding the obedience paradigm, Orne and Holland again are unimpressed:

> Because of the ingenuity of the deception, the reader is drawn to assume with Milgram that the Ss accepted the situation at face value. It is unfortunate that no data are presented to indicate whether this was in fact the case. Yet the extent to which the deception actually was accepted by the S determines how the results should be interpreted. (P. 285)

A test of the demand-characteristic thesis was reported in a doctoral dissertation by Holland (1968). In addition to including a condition comparable to Milgram's voice-feedback condition, Holland used two "control" conditions. One of these involved telling subjects, prior to their participation, that they were in the control group, that their experimenter was not going to know this, but that their job was "to play the role of a regular, naive subject, which meant that he had to figure out what the experiment was really all about" (p. 27). The purpose of this condition was to induce the kind of problem-solving set—some might say suspiciousness—that Orne had claimed was characteristic of research subjects in general. If these "sensitized" subjects behaved similarly to those in the standard paradigm, this would strengthen the argument that the original subjects were acting *as if* they had believed the experimenter's definition of the situation. Subjects in a third group were also led to believe that they were in a control group, but in this instance they were told that the real purpose of the study was to examine the effect of the learner's *anticipation* of receiving intense shocks—that, in actuality, the shocks were only *one tenth* of the voltage indicated on the generator. The purpose of this condition was to lower the hypothesized incongruity factor by making the experiment more believable. It was expected that subjects in this condition would be significantly more disobedient because the entire scenario would be more plausible to them. Given that they really believed they were inflicting at least some genuine punishment (less in absolute amount, but increasingly severe), Holland predicted that they would be significantly more defiant.

The results of this investigation were mixed. Obedience levels in all three of Holland's conditions were high. The percentages of subjects who were totally obedient (that is, to 450 volts) were as follows: Condition 1 (comparable to Milgram's 1963 condition)—70 percent; Condition 2—55 percent; Condition 3—80 percent. None of these figures differed statistically from Milgram's baseline figure of 65 percent. Holland emphasizes that the data from Condition 2 support the demand-characteristic interpretation, but acknowledges that the results of Condition 3 were not as predicted. Another finding, regarded as supporting the demand-characteristic thesis, was that a second, "blind" experimenter could not accurately guess, during post-experimental inquiry, to which condition the subjects had been assigned. Thus, subjects who were instructed to role-play were not detected, leading Holland to conclude that subjects in the original obedience paradigm could have been similarly aware (via their own reaction to the incongruity factor, etc.) and that this would not have been detected by Milgram.

There are many details to Holland's complex experiment that do not support his interpretation, such as, the results of Condition 3; the fact that of 20 subjects assessed as being low in suspiciousness (Condition 1) 14 obeyed to 450 volts; the fact that the role-playing subjects (Condition 2) generally disobeyed the experimenter earlier in the shock series than did subjects in the other conditions (or Milgram's 1963 variation). Holland, however, emphasizes the similarity in the obedient behavior of *all* of his subjects, particularly the similarity between supposedly naive subjects—those in Condition 1—and those who were clearly not naive (Conditions 2 and 3):

> it appears that the "naive" subjects of this study, those of Condition 1, were no more naive than those of other conditions. What directed their behavior did not fundamentally differ from what directed the behavior of simulating subjects; namely, the belief that the learner really was not in as much pain and danger as it seemed. Moreover, it is reasonable to assume that the basic source of this cognition was probably the same in all cases—the demand characteristics of the psychological experiment. (P. 65)[1]

On this rationale, Holland then denies the validity of generalizing from the obedience paradigm:

> Milgram's subjects were obedient, but they were obedient only in that they pushed levers. Death-camp executioners were obedient, but they were obedient in that they pushed levers knowing that in doing so they were committing murder. No real relationship may be drawn between these two cases unless it can be established that Milgram's subjects "knew" that they were shocking the learner as they had been told. This has not been established. (P. 71)

It should be noted that Orne and Holland do not claim that the behavior of *every* subject in Milgram's research was in response to perceived demand characteristics, although they clearly indicate that it was the major dynamic for a majority of subjects. How then do they explain the finding that as the proximity between the teacher and learner increases (in Experiments 1 through 4), obedience is seen to decrease? A strict application of the demand-characteristic thesis would seem inconsistent with differences in obedience across experimental variations, in that the basic paradigm should be incongruous regardless of the kind of changes introduced by Milgram. This is not the case, apparently, as Orne and Holland argue that demand characteristics also are responsive to situational variation:

> Apparently by using good actors in close proximity it is easier to convince Ss that the situation might be real. (P. 288)

Similarly, the reduced obedience rate in Bridgeport is explained by a greater perceived sense of the reality of the suffering. That is, the subjects' presumptions regarding the inherent safety of the laboratory are reduced when the research is removed from the university setting.[2]

It would seem, therefore, that although *obedience* to the experimenter's commands is interpreted by Orne and Holland as reflecting a kind of charade or "going along with the act" on the part of Milgram's subjects, *disobedience* is substantially a different matter. One disobeys because one does in fact believe that the shocks are real. Orne and Holland do not make this distinction, but it seems to be a reasonable implication of their position.

Milgram's Response to Orne and Holland

Orne and Holland's analysis, though essentially speculative in my view, is provocative because it is based upon an orthodox social-psychological perspective. The orientation of their analysis is conceptually—

and paradoxically—similar to that of Milgram's. Notice, for example, their emphasis upon the powerful role of the experimenter in influencing the subject's perception of events. Their highly situational view of behavior—that the context not only influences what subjects do but also what their behavior means—is certainly compatible with Milgram's own point of view. Also, Orne's reputation as an empirical scientist adds credibility to their argument. Their views cannot be understood in terms of different values or philosophical positions on the viability of an experimental analysis of social behavior. How, then, does Milgram respond to their methodological criticisms?

Milgram (1972) presents three kinds of arguments: (1) the responses of his subjects, (2) evidence from other investigations, and (3) a number of personal reactions to the demand-characteristic formulation itself. He indicates that when subjects were asked, in post-experimental ratings, to estimate how painful the shocks were to the learner, the most frequent response on a 14-point scale was 14 (extremely painful). In the survey obtained one year after their participation, subjects were asked how certain they were that painful shocks were being delivered. Approximately 60 percent indicated complete certainty, 25 percent expressed some doubts but indicated that they believed the learner was probably getting the shocks, and the remaining subjects expressed uncertainty or strong doubts. Milgram concludes that a clear majority of subjects accepted the stated reality of the paradigm. He notes that for some subjects, a verbal denial of the realism of the shocks could enhance self-esteem—"I pressed the shocks but knew all along that I wasn't really harming anyone." He suggests that while there were a number of reasons why it might have been in the subjects' best interest to deny the reality of the shocks, the vast majority failed to do so.[3]

As noted earlier, however, Orne is not persuaded by Milgram's reference to supportive verbal reports. Orne (1969) has suggested that the post-experimental phase of an experiment is itself laden with demand characteristics (for example, the "pact of ignorance"), and that the detection of true beliefs and awareness requires the most painstaking, increasingly directive kind of probing by an interviewer blind to the subject's condition or behavior—a procedure almost never employed, and clearly not used by Milgram.

Milgram also cites a number of investigations which, in his view, counter Orne and Holland's contention that subjects did not believe that genuine pain was experienced by the learner. The study by Ring et al. (1970), described in Chapter Five, was noted, particularly because in that investigation the behavior of the experimenter was far less detached and stoic than in Milgram's paradigm:

> Instead of remaining impassive throughout, the experimenter pretended to be somewhat surprised by the initial protests of the learner. He occasionally shook his head in apparent perplexity during these trials and, after trial 26, he mopped his forehead with a handkerchief. (Ring et al., 1970, p. 72)

This study, apparently conducted without awareness of Orne and Holland's critique, is particularly relevant to their argument concerning the "incongruity" of the experimenter's behavior. Ring et al. may have sensed intuitively the substance of Orne and Holland's argument, as they described their purpose in modifying the experimenter's behavior as one of enhancing "the verisimilitude of the situation" (p. 72). Thus, their study, in addition to having important implications regarding the ethics of the paradigm, takes on a supporting function in terms of its methodological status.

Milgram also refers to a doctoral dissertation by Kudirka (1965), in which subjects were instructed to ingest bitter, quinine-soaked crackers which elicited nausea and other related symptoms. Even with the experimenter absent from the laboratory, 14 of 19 subjects ate 36 of these crackers. Milgram's point is that compliance to the experimenter's authority was high in a circumstance which permitted no uncertainty regarding the unpleasant reality of the subject's experience. Milgram then cites Orne's demonstrations (1962) of the power of the experimenter to induce subjects to perform incredibly tedious tasks:

> He says that although these actions may appear stupid, subjects perform them because they occur within a psychological experiment. When Orne moves on to the obedience experiment, however, he shifts his argument. The power of the experimenter, which Orne so carefully demonstrated, suddenly evaporates. Whereas his subjects genuinely did carry out actions prescribed by the experimenter, Orne would have us believe that my subjects did not. This is, at best, twisted logic, and Orne really cannot have it both ways. On the one hand he asserts an extreme degree of control over the subject, and on the other hand he denies this control exists in the present experiment. It is far more logical to see the obedience experiment as climaxing a consistent line of research demonstrating the power of authority, a line that can be traced to Frank (1944), through Orne (1962b), and into the present research. (P. 149)

It is hard to be certain, of course, but Orne and Holland might respond by claiming that they were not denying that Milgram's subjects did in fact carry out actions, but were questioning the interpretation or meaning given to them. Their interpretation is, of course, far more benign than Milgram's.

Milgram also cites the Hofling et al. study, described in Chapter Four, as supporting the ecological validity (i.e., generalizability) of his laboratory findings. The Hofling et al. investigation is particularly relevant because one of Orne and Holland's specific recommendations regarding the experimental analysis of obedience was to "devise experiments that are not recognized as such by the Ss" (p. 292).

Milgram concludes his rebuttal by commenting upon Orne's general methodological approach. He notes that the demand-characteristic accusation is essentially *post hoc*, that it fails to predict, but serves, instead, only to champion an artifactual view of things. Acknowledging a degree of methodological refinement in Orne's approach, Milgram nevertheless expresses a kind of general resentment:

> There is no substance in things, only methodological wrinkles. This seems to me the history of the school of social psychology which Orne has assiduously cultivated. I do not believe that, in its present one-sided form, it constitutes a contribution to our understanding of human behavior. (P. 151)

Aronson, Brewer, and Carlsmith (1985)

Aronson, Brewer, and Carlsmith, in their chapter on methodology in the *Handbook of Social Psychology*, express reservations concerning the generalizability of the obedience experiments. Their position is related to the Orne and Holland criticism in its concern with the demand characteristics of Milgram's paradigm. However, they are not questioning the internal validity of the paradigm; they do not seriously doubt that subjects believed that the learner was being shocked. Rather, they are concerned with the fact that the role of authority in Milgram's experiment was enacted by the researcher. In their view, it is conceivable that attributes of the role of researcher or scientist, other than his authority, may have been influential. Thus, they hesitate to generalize Milgram's findings to other settings—to the Nazi situation for example—where the authority figures are, in possibly crucial ways, different from the specific embodiment of authority used by Milgram:

> One cannot be certain . . . whether it was the implicit authority of the scientist-researcher that was responsible for the degree of obedience from subjects or other aspects inextricably associated with his role in the experimental situation (e.g., the normative value of science, the potential

for negative personal evaluation of the subject, etc.). . . . Such ambiguities make us hesitate to assume that the processes underlying obedience in this experimental setting are the same as those operating in other authority situations, such as those of Nazi Germany. (P. 479)

This position is also presented in a discussion of Milgram's research in Aronson's influential text, *The Social Animal* (1984): "The subjects might reasonably assume . . . that no scientist would issue orders that would result in the death or injury of a human as part of his experiment. This was clearly not true in either the Eichmann or Calley example" (p. 42). (For a related position, see commentary on Patten, 1977b, in Chapter Seven).

Aronson's position, both here and in the *Handbook of Social Psychology*, is a particularly interesting one. He seems to want to have it both ways, so to speak. On the one hand, he is unequivocally supportive of the potential significance of the obedience experiments. He gives the research a considerable amount of space, characterizing the experiments as "dramatic," and "provocative." He relates the findings to the Nazi phenomenon, the My Lai massacre, and notes that replications (for example, Mantell, 1971; Kilham and Mann, 1974) have added an important measure of reliability to Milgram's original findings. Yet, he appears uneasy about the demand-characteristic issue. He cannot dismiss the possibility that Milgram's findings were, in an important way, contingent upon the perceived legitimacy of his setting. Thus, as one of social psychology's most respected methodologists, Aronson sees value in the demand-characteristic challenge. (Curiously, he does not cite the Orne and Holland commentary either in his text or in the *Handbook of Social Psychology*). Yet, as a most forceful proponent of the practical relevance of social psychology, Aronson does not conceal his admiration for the moral implications of Milgram's research.

The criticisms of Orne and Holland are intriguing. The force of their argument is weakened, in my view, by a lack of data. Their major citation is Holland's dissertation, but as discussed earlier, his investigation is hardly unequivocal support for the demand-characteristic conceptualization. Many of the illustrations of laboratory compliance in Orne's influential 1962 essay, the "nitric acid" scenario for example, are used as analogies to Milgram's study of obedience, but his study is qualitatively very different from those of Orne. For example, the experimenter explicitly tells the subjects that the learner will not suffer permanent harm. Thus, Milgram is, at the outset, straightforward about the issue of harm. It is the *temporal shift* in the obedience paradigm that is also unique. The agonizing conflict is never present at the start, so that the subject is not faced with an obvious "demand" or experimental hypothesis to discover. The gradual escalation of conflict is a point repeatedly emphasized by Milgram (cf. Gilbert, 1981, discussed in Chapter Two) in differentiating his paradigm from Orne's demonstrations of demand characteristics. It should be noted, however, there are data which speak, convincingly, to the potential importance of demand characteristics in creating ambiguity in the interpretation of research findings (see Miller, 1972a; Orne, 1969).

In my view, the central issue becomes one of characterizing the precise nature of the conflict or moral crisis that Milgram claims is being experienced by his subjects. On the one hand, it is hard to deny, totally, the assertion of Orne and Holland that the research laboratory is viewed by subjects as an inherently safe or benign environment. Yet, it seems to me that Milgram is challenging Orne and Holland on this very issue. As his experiment begins, everything is quite in order, but as things progress, Milgram is in fact creating an unethical role for the experimenter (cf. Schuler's criticism, noted in Chapter Five). That is, he is taking the experimenter's role—one of legitimate authority in the context of a scientific study of punishment and learning—and superimposing upon it a fundamentally unreasonable attitude regarding the possible harm being inflicted upon the learner. Thus, *by design, Milgram's paradigm is not inherently safe or benign*. The cries from the learner, ultimately reaching a frenzy of incessant pleas for release, would, without question, point to such a conclusion. Of course, this line of reasoning presumes that subjects *believed* in the authenticity of these cries.

At this point, one simply must decide whether Milgram's data warrant an acceptance of his claim that a credible scenario was created. Short of the in-depth probing for suspicion of deception advocated by Orne, Milgram's evidence strikes me as convincing. The reader may or may not agree at this point. Regardless, it should at least be agreed that Milgram was intentionally challenging the presumption (made by Orne) that the experimenter has the right to ask anything of the subject. From Milgram's point of view, the experimenter did *not* have the right to ask the subject to inflict increasingly severe pain on a vehemently protesting victim. The question was whether or not subjects would be able to recognize this moral violation on the part of the experimenter and act on this awareness. The results, according to Milgram, indicated considerable recognition of the experimenter's violation but, with exceptions in certain variations, a decided inability to act decisively in terms of defying the experimenter's orders. Orne and Holland, however, claim that this kind of moral conflict is, by definition, impossible to create in the context of a research laboratory.

RESEARCH BEARING ON ORNE AND HOLLAND'S CRITICISMS

Sheridan and King (1972)

Sheridan and King, after noting the criticisms of Orne and Holland, performed an experiment to "elicit obedience in a more authentic situation" (p. 165). To this end, they used a "cute, fluffy puppy" as the learner, and arranged the situation so that it was manifestly *undeniable* that this animal was receiving painful shocks. Their purpose was essentially to restructure the laboratory so that the criticisms of Orne and Holland would not apply, that is, there would be no "incongruity" in terms of the experimenter's behavior and no opportunity for subjects to define the situation as one in which real pain was not being delivered. The question, then, was simple: Would subjects obey an experimenter's orders to shock a protesting puppy?

The stated rationale of this experiment differed somewhat from that used by Milgram. The subjects were told that they were participating in a study of visual-discrimination learning in dogs, and that their role was to prevent an experimenter-bias effect by acting as a substitute (that is, intentionally naive) experimenter. It was arranged that the dog would make "errors" for which subjects would be required to deliver increasingly intense electric shocks to the grid floor of the animals' cage. Protests on the part of subjects were reacted to in a standard manner, using, if necessary, the identical four prods described by Milgram.

The results were interpreted as powerful confirmation of Milgram's original findings. Of thirteen males, 54 percent were maximally obedient; 100 percent of 13 females were maximally obedient.[4] Subjects also displayed various symptoms of anxiety or stress, such as "gesturally coaxing the puppy to escape the shock, pacing from foot to foot, puffing, and even weeping" (p. 166). There was also evidence that as the shocks increased in voltage, subjects tried to depress the shock lever as quickly as possible, that is, to reduce the shock duration.

Interestingly, the investigators observed that half of their disobedient subjects did not confront the experimenter, but attempted to deceive him by claiming that the dog had in fact learned the problem.

Milgram had observed a similar type of "deceit" in Experiment 7, in which the experimenter, absent from the laboratory, gave his orders by phone. Subjects were observed giving lower shocks than those specified by the experimenter. Sheridan and King concluded that "their willingness to distort the results of a 'scientific experiment' suggests that, for them, the authority of the E outweighs the prestige of science as a factor controlling their behavior" (p. 166).

It should also be noted that the investigators held extensive post-experimental debriefing sessions, including interactions between subjects and the puppy. In addition, when 45 students were asked, in a classroom setting, how much shock they would have delivered in an experiment of this kind, only 3 (6.6 percent) indicated that they would have gone beyond 300 volts. We see, once again, an extreme underestimation of the incidence of observed obedience.

Sheridan and King viewed their results as support for Milgram and inconsistent with the position of Orne and Holland:

> The findings are in consonance with the view that Milgram's findings may correctly be taken at face value. Ss are willing to follow repugnant commands, even when it is clear that the victim is truly receiving shocks. Milgram's findings have proven remarkably robust in the face of a variety of procedural variations, and the impact of his findings cannot be mitigated by appeal to the notion that Ss are merely "playing games with" and "outguessing" the E. (P. 166)

When I describe this study to my classes, there is invariably an outcry in behalf of the puppy! There is, indeed, an ethical concern over subjecting the dog to distress. The fact that the animal is being shocked clearly wins few friends for the investigators, notwithstanding the informational value of their research.

The study would seem germane to Orne and Holland's criticisms. This depends, of course, upon a presumed endorsement by subjects of a norm which dictates that the animal should not be shocked. This is not established explicitly by Sheridan and King, but the fact that students in the "estimated behavior" condition produced a low shock rate is suggestive, at least, that subjects do not privately identify with the experimenter's means of accomplishing this research.

A crucial issue is the perceived suffering of the animal. The subjects in this experiment, unlike those of Milgram, were not informed that the "learner" would suffer no permanent injury. The investigators noted behaviors such as foot flexion, occasional barks, running, and, at the higher voltage levels, continuous barking and howling. These certainly seem to qualify as analogies to the increasingly severe protests used by Milgram, although there are no post-experimental data to provide a check on subjects' perceptions of the animal's suffering.

Conceivably one could apply the Orne and Holland construction to this study and question whether subjects *in fact* believed that they were harming the animal, particularly at the higher voltage levels. I personally do not question the study on this basis. The prospect of administering punishment to laboratory animals is a highly visible (if not universally approved of) form of scientific activity, and to use Orne and Holland's reasoning, one seriously doubts whether subjects come to the laboratory with the expectation that this setting is a safe or benign environment *for animals*. In conclusion, although this study is obviously limited in its scope, involving relatively few subjects and no objective post-experimental data, it addresses, in a quite imaginative manner, some of the essential features of the Orne and Holland argument.

Penner et al. (1973)

Louis Penner and his colleagues investigated the role of *experimenter competence* on obedience. Their study was based on Orne and Holland's hypothesis that obedience in Milgram's laboratory was an artifact—that is, that subjects saw through the deception because of their prevailing belief that an experimenter would not be involved in actions which would result in pain and suffering in an unwilling victim. Penner et al. arranged things so that subjects could not hold to such an assumption. The victim in this study, as in so many others, was a white rat.

Subjects were recruited (allegedly) for a study of reactions to the stress involved in administering shock to a laboratory animal. The task was to respond as quickly as possible to a signal light under one of two conditions, "harmer" and "saver." If a trial indicated that the subject was in the "harmer" role, the rat would be shocked if the subject's reaction time was faster than that of another subject (nearby) who, for that trial, was the "saver." If the saver's reaction time was faster, however, the rat would not be shocked. Subjects were in direct view of a caged laboratory rat who was in fact given electric shocks, mild in absolute voltage but sufficient to elicit clearly observable reactions. The rat was shocked on 30 percent of the trials, regardless of the subject's reaction time on the button. Each subject responded to 40 trials, on half of which they were in the roles of harmer and saver.

Penner et al. assumed that subjects would not want the rat to be shocked, and thus would be motivated to press the button faster when in the saver condition. However, they were instructed, formally, to respond as fast as possible in both the harmer and saver conditions. Thus, *obedience to the experimenter's instructions would consist of highly similar reaction times in both conditions.* Defiance would consist of slower reaction times in the harmer condition. By calculating a "harmer minus saver" reaction-time difference, each subject's relative obedience could be assessed.

The major variable was *experimenter competence*. To test Orne and Holland's thesis regarding the benign nature of the laboratory environment, Penner et al. introduced, in one condition, an experimenter who behaved as if he lacked experience—he arrived late, acted confused about procedural details, etc. At a mid-point in the trial sequence in both conditions, the rat was apparently killed (actually went into a harmless convulsion determined by the experimenter). The experimenter, in this incompetent guise, became upset and expressed uncertainty as to how to proceed. In the "competent" condition, the experimenter behaved in a thoroughly "in charge" manner.

A major interest was in comparing the behavior of subjects after the rat was apparently killed with their behavior on the prior trials. The "death" of the animal was intended to represent a challenge to the subjects' expectations of a "safe, trustworthy laboratory," as Orne and Holland had portrayed Milgram's research setting. A new animal was brought in for the second set of trials. Penner et al. predicted that obedience would be lower following the "incident."

The competence of the experimenter was a powerful variable. Subjects were significantly less obedient to the instructions of an incompetent experimenter. There was also an increase in defiance following the "kill" incident, but this was observed only in the competent-experimenter condition. Thus, Penner et al.'s predictions were essentially confirmed.

Penner et al. concluded that their findings support at least one theme in Orne and Holland's critique:

> The results of this study provided fairly straightforward support of the hypothesis that the obedience usually observed in the "Milgram" situation is, to a large degree, a function of the explicit and implicit guarantees that nothing can really "go wrong." When these guarantees were attenuated . . . disobedience . . . increased rather dramatically. (Pp. 243-44)

The investigators suggest that an incompetent experimenter lacks what French and Raven (1959) have termed "expert social power," and thus elicits less compliance with his instructions. Also, it is more difficult for subjects to attribute responsibility for the victim's fate to an incompetent experimenter, hence they assume more personal responsibility for the victim's welfare.

Penner et al. note, however, that this study does *not* support Orne and Holland's position that demand characteristics are the prevailing dynamic in Milgram's paradigm. This is because there was no doubt, in the present study, that there was a real victim receiving genuine punishment—a perception which, Orne and Holland argue, was not held by Milgram's subjects. Yet, this study, in suggesting the importance of the subjects' belief in the competence of the authority, does limit the generality of Milgram's findings "to those situations where there is little ambiguity concerning the competence of the individual giving orders to aggress" (p. 244).

The Penner et al. experiment is an imaginative investigation. It uses a novel measure of obedience, and demonstrates that rather extreme manifestations of experimenter incompetence must be used to reduce obedience. Even under these circumstances, however, *subjects still remained in the situation and continued to witness an animal receiving pain*, although under somewhat longer latencies. This study is, of course, similar to the Sheridan and King experiment—subjects were instructed to administer pain to a live animal and indeed, they inflicted it. I suspect that Orne and Holland would counter by claiming that the use of animals as victims changed the psychological context. This may be true, yet Sheridan and King, and Penner et al., provide evidence that subjects clearly did not want to harm the animals. Thus, it is likely that these investigations instilled a conflict in subjects—not wanting to harm, and not wanting to defy the experimenter—which was, in Milgram's view, a fundamental psychological dynamic operating in the obedience paradigm. It should be noted, in conclusion, that the results of Penner et al.'s investigation are consistent with Milgram's Experiment 13, in which obedience was substantially diminished when a "peer" of the subject played the role of the experimenter.

Meeus and Raaijmakers (1985)

Meeus and Raaijmakers have conducted a recent investigation on the obedience problem at the University of Utrecht. Their research, entitled "Administrative Obedience: Carrying Out Orders to Exert

Psychological-Administrative Violence," is of interest on a number of grounds, but its relevance to the demand-characteristic criticism of Orne and Holland is of primary concern for our present discussion.

They note two problems with Milgram's paradigm. First, the voltage designations may be ambiguous to subjects. The experimenter states that "the shocks may be painful, but they are not dangerous," yet the labels on the generator would seem to indicate danger. For example, at 375 volts, the label reads "Danger: Severe Shock." When the learner ultimately stops responding altogether, this, also, may strike subjects as inconsistent with the experimenter's assurances regarding "no danger." Thus, the investigators pose an interesting question: Is Milgram dealing with obedience to inflict painful shocks or shocks that are both *painful and dangerous*? This is important, because it implies that the subjects may not know precisely what they are doing to the learner. Yet, the significance of the research depends upon a clear understanding of the subjects' phenomenological point of view—we must know what *they* think they are doing.

Meeus and Raaijmakers are inclined to define obedience as limited to the delivery of painful shocks, that is, not shocks which are dangerous or lethal. They note that there are probably sufficient cues to support the subjects' trust in the experimenter and to indicate that the learner is not harmed or dead—at least there is sufficient *ambiguity* in the situation for subjects to rely upon the experimenter. They cite research by Mixon, to be reviewed later in this chapter, indicating that if subjects really believe harm to have occurred, they will stop shocking the learner. They also note Milgram's Experiment 15 (two experimenters—contradictory commands) as evidence that subjects will disobey if they are given sufficiently alarming information regarding potential harm to the learner.

The fact that harm or fatal injury are ruled out by these investigators does not in any way minimize the significance of Milgram's research in their view. Their purpose is to *clarify* the events occurring in Milgram's paradigm. From their perspective, the agonizing screams of a protesting learner are more than sufficient justification for disobeying the experimenter's orders even if permanent harm or death are not construed as a likely outcome by most subjects.

The second issue raised by this research concerns the "content validity" of the response itself, that is, shocking the learner. The investigators wish to use a different kind of behavior—"In modern society the use of physical force is no longer the predominant mode for resolving conflicts . . . power is not primarily wielded by way of physical force" (p. 7). I think they are being somewhat narrow here, for reports of physical torture, terrorism, and genocide occurring in various areas of world conflict—South America, Africa, the Middle East, and Northern Ireland to name just four—are readily available in any daily newspaper. However, their interest in using a different index of obedience is understandable and methodologically valuable in terms of assessing the generality of obedience. Certainly on a more mundane level, Milgram's perspective on obedience to authority should be applicable to activities that do not involve the administration of physical punishment.

Meeus and Raaijmakers set up an interesting scenario. The subject was placed in the role of someone who is instructed to purposely disturb another individual who has come to the laboratory to apply for a job.[5] The stated purpose was to help the experimenter investigate the relationship between psychological stress and test achievement. Three conditions were used—a base line, and two variations analogous to those in which Milgram observed a sharp reduction in obedience, an experimenter-absent condition, and a peers-rebel condition.

In the baseline condition, the procedure was similar in important respects to that of Milgram's paradigm. The key difference was the response itself. The subject was instructed to administer "stress remarks" (such as "if you continue like this, you will fail the test") over an intercom, while giving a multiple-choice test to an applicant who was (subjects were told) applying for a civil service position. Subjects were instructed to administer a total of 15 negative remarks. The applicant, actually a confederate, was programmed to respond after each remark, starting with mild protests ("surely my answer wasn't wrong, was it") and culminating in vehement accusations toward the subject. If the subject refused to administer the stress remark, the experimenter went through a series of four prods, identical to those used by Milgram.

Among the many details of the procedure, one should be emphasized. Before the experiment actually started, it was arranged that subjects would overhear the experimenter assure the applicant that the experiment was not connected with the job application and would not interfere in any way with the applicant's chances of obtaining the job. In this conversation, the experimenter was, by design, dishonest with the applicant in two respects. First, he did not inform him that the subject would be directing stress remarks to make him anxious. Second, although he assured the applicant that there would be no adverse consequences, the actual subjects had been explicitly told that this would occur. The applicant in fact made a total of ten errors which resulted in his "failure" to pass the test, and hence to obtain the desired job. Thus, subjects were aware, from the start, that the experimenter had been dishonest with the applicant.[6]

Obedience in this condition was extremely high as 22 of 24 subjects (92 percent) made all of the required stress remarks. The mean number of remarks was 14.81 out of a possible 15.00. In a Milgram-type control condition, in which subjects were free to administer as many in the series of 15 remarks as they wished, no subject administered all 15 remarks. The average was 6.75, with 12 of 15 subjects administering 8 or fewer remarks. Post-experimental questionnaires revealed that subjects (number not reported), "considered it irresponsible and unfair to deal with the applicant in this manner. The subjects also intensely disliked making the stress remarks and were convinced that the applicant's test achievements had been very negatively affected by the stress remarks" (p. 20). Despite these professed attitudes, there was virtually no opposition to the experimenter during the study itself. Unlike the agitation characterizing Milgram's subjects, the predominant mood in this study was that of aloofness.

Meeus and Raaijmakers also asked subjects to attribute responsibility for the "definite harm to the applicant." For subjects in the baseline (non-control condition), the average responsibility attributed to the experimenter was 45 percent, to themselves, 33 percent, and to the applicant, 22 percent, leading the investigators to conclude that the subjects "are in what Milgram coined as the 'agentic state' " (p. 22). (This is the central theoretical concept in Milgram's 1974 model of obedience, which is reviewed in Chapter Eight, pp. 222 and 227.)

The "experimenter absent" and "two peers rebel" conditions were virtually identical to the corresponding variations in Milgram's research, with the exception of the use of stress remarks instead of shocks. Obedience was markedly reduced—to levels of 36.4 percent for "experimenter absent," and 15.8 percent for "two peers rebel." The interpretation of the investigators is similar to that given by Milgram: In "experimenter absent," the subjects are forced to be more responsive to the applicant's protests; the physical absence of the experimenter reduces the likelihood of an "agentic shift" response. In "two peers rebel," modeling of defiance is the purported dynamic: "none of the subjects is disobedient before the confederates start protesting . . . while 9 out of 16 are disobedient at the same time as the confederates" (p. 26).

The conclusion reached by Meeus and Raaijmakers bears significantly on the Orne and Holland thesis: "Even when subjects realize they are causing permanent harm to an innocent victim by exerting psychological-administrative violence, obedience is extreme" (p. 27). The investigators were careful in assessing their subjects' reactions. They report that 80 percent or more were genuinely convinced of the reality of the situation.

Much of their discussion centers on the fact that obedience in their baseline condition was significantly *higher* than that observed by Milgram. The fact that the subject agrees to be in this experiment, *knowing from the outset that it may negatively affect the applicant*, creates a sense of commitment that probably exceeds that in Milgram's paradigm. Also, the applicant, in this research, is genuinely motivated to continue—that is, he is (apparently) trying to obtain a job. Despite his protests, he does not "want out" of the experiment as does Milgram's learner. Thus, the conflict experienced by subjects in this study is less, and this also contributes to the high obedience rate. Finally, Meeus and Raaijmakers suggest that the threshold for inflicting "psychological-administrative" punishment may be lower. It is a more remote kind of behavior—its impact on the applicant is relatively abstract in comparison to the vivid effects of electric shock.

This study is impressive in that despite radical changes in its "surface characteristics"—the purpose of the study, the nature of the punishment, etc.—it provides a convincing conceptual replication of Milgram's paradigm. Not only is obedience demonstrated, but defiance also occurs in the predicted variations. The investigators' central thesis, that subjects committed what they knew to be "real harm," is an important issue in view of Orne and Holland's critique. From this point of view, I find their investigation to be a major contribution to the obedience literature. A more extensive interpretation of their subjects' "cool" stance during the punishment phase would be of interest, as well as data concerning the attribution of responsibility—these are not reported for any condition other than the base line.

I find it interesting that these investigators are concerned with a clarification of the nature of the behavior actually investigated in Milgram's paradigm. Whether or not they are correct in inferring that Milgram's subjects were convinced that the learner was not being seriously harmed is, of course, debatable. What Meeus and Raaijmakers succeed, unquestionably, in doing, however, is to make a very convincing case for the substantive importance of Milgram's findings *even if his subjects did not think they were permanently harming the learner* (*or worse*). In this sense, Orne and Holland could be viewed at least as partially correct, in that one might conclude that Milgram's subjects were basically trusting the experimenter's word on the ultimate welfare of the learner. Still, on the basis of the findings of this experiment, the implication is that subjects are extremely willing to inflict serious, irrevocable punishment (not necessarily in terms of physical injury) upon a person who is explicitly protesting such actions. This may be a reasonable interpretation of what Milgram was demonstrating, and thus it may not be necessary to assume that Milgram was demonstrating a willingness on the part of his subjects to permanently harm or kill the learner.

THE ORNE AND HOLLAND CRITICISMS: AN APPRAISAL

I have difficulty in accepting the proposition that obedience in Milgram's paradigm was essentially an artifact. It seems quite reasonable to conclude, rather, that it did in fact constitute a genuine episode of harming upon authoritative orders. I agree with Milgram's (1972) position that the kind of hierarchical structure observed in his research setting is similar to social arrangements in other contexts—that, at least in principle, phenomena which occur in the laboratory should be generalizable to other contexts that share significant psychological features with the laboratory. It is also not clear to me that subjects invariably have, as Orne and Holland suggest, vivid and accessible expectations about what can and cannot occur in psychological experiments. In the case of Milgram's research, it is likely that some subjects may have been *unclear* as to what, precisely, was happening, but for Orne and Holland to argue, with certainty, that Milgram's subjects were cognizant of all of the realities of the situation and were simply acting on behalf of sympathies with the experimenter's purposes, strikes me as unwarranted.

Nevertheless, I view the Orne and Holland essay as valuable in terms of forcing the issue regarding the paradigm's generalizability. Although I find Milgram's own account to be quite convincing, I think we are fortunate to have access to the research reviewed in this chapter, research which might not have been performed were it not for the impact of Orne and Holland's criticisms. The cumulative impression, after considering the research of Sheridan and King, Penner et al., and Meeus and Raaijmakers, as well as some of the replications noted in Chapters Three and Four (such as Hofling et al., Milgram's Experiment 10) is that the generalizability of the obedience paradigm has withstood a number of critical tests.

ROLE PLAYING: A METHODOLOGICAL ALTERNATIVE?

As indicated in the previous chapter, the ethical controversy sparked by Baumrind's (1964) initial reaction to Milgram's experiments occurred at a time when laboratory research in general was beginning to receive penetrating analyses regarding its methodological as well as ethical limitations. In a singularly influential article, Herbert Kelman (1967) argued against what he viewed as the unrestrained and largely unmonitored use of deception. One of his recommendations was that methodological alternatives to the use of deception be considered, specifically the procedure of role playing. In this technique or general approach,[7] subjects would be given the same treatment or manipulation but without deception. The subject would thus know, for example, that the "other person" was an accomplice of the experimenter, that the "shocks" were not real, etc. The subject might be asked to play the role of a deceived individual but would not actually be deceived.

The ethical superiority of role playing resided in two of its features. First, the subject would not be deceived. For some, this would constitute a virtue in its own right. Because the role-playing format would be activated immediately upon the subject's entrance into the study, a kind of enriched informed consent would be achieved. A second envisioned result of role playing would be that the entire moral atmosphere of the research would be enhanced. Viewing the subject as an object to be manipulated would be minimized, and the experimenter could be more open and disclosing to the subject. The quality of the experimenter—subject relationship would be more collegial and trusting.

There were significant developments following Kelman's recommendations. Experiments were performed which compared role playing with techniques involving deception, with mixed results. Several reviewers concluded that the prospect for role playing as an alternative methodology were poor (see Freedman, 1969; Miller, 1972b). Not only were the empirical comparisons less than encouraging, but the very need for a comparison (using deception) obviously negated the ethical advantage. Still, the role playing issue has become another zone of controversy, with various commentators taking highly polarized positions on its merits. A symposium on the technique, involving many of the complex issues raised in the decade following Kelman's article, appeared in a 1977 issue of *Personality and Social Psychology Bulletin* (Hendrick et al., 1977).

It was inevitable that the "grand meeting" between role playing and Milgram's obedience paradigm would take place. Given that every critique of the use of deception made explicit—at times seemingly exhaustive—reference to the obedience experiments, it became obvious that role playing, in order to make its case, would have to be shown capable of producing meaningful data when applied to the problem of obedience to authority. Let us examine now the major research efforts which have addressed this issue.

Milgram (1965)

As noted in Chapter Two, Milgram gave considerable attention to the question of "predicted" obedience. His findings—the marked underestimation of obedience—may be viewed as the first role-playing study pertaining to the obedience paradigm. Of course they present, dramatically, a discrepancy between hypothetical or imagined behavior and the actual responses of involved subjects.

The underestimation of obedience, noted by Milgram (1965b) as well as other studies (Miller et al., 1974), is an extremely well-publicized finding. In social psychology texts, for example, the underestimation effect is almost invariably coupled with the findings obtained from experimental subjects. As noted in Chapter Two, the fact that people underestimate, to such an extraordinary degree, Milgram's findings provides rather compelling evidence for the value of his research—clearly, we would be "in the dark" on the obedience problem were it not for the type of experimental analyses conducted by Milgram and others.

It must be noted, however, that the results obtained using role playing may reflect the *specific cognitive state* of the subject. In the case of Milgram's procedure, subjects were given a *verbal description* of the paradigm. They were not actually involved—physically as well as psychologically—in a re-enactment of the obedience experiment. I mention this because, as will become apparent, a number of role-playing enthusiasts are *not* convinced that the technique of asking subjects to predict behavior—their own or that of others—after giving them a verbal transcript of a particular research scenario is in fact a genuine test of role playing.

Before examining other findings, it may be appropriate to recapitulate the interpretation given by Milgram to the underestimation of obedience:

There is a clear consensus that the only behavior consistent with social values and individual conscience is to defy the experimenter at some point before the completion of the command series. Yet there is a marked discrepancy between this value judgment and the actual performance of subjects in the laboratory. (1965c, p. 130)

O'Leary, Willis, and Tomich (1970)

O'Leary et al. conducted the first major experimental analysis of obedience using a role-playing methodology. They noted that the obedience experiment had been viewed as "the epitome of an experiment in which deception is unethical (Baumrind, 1964), and at the same time is considered as a valuable experiment that could not have been carried out without using a deceptive technique" (p. 88). Their rationale was based on Kelman's (1967) discussion of the ethical problems raised by the use of deception, specifically its incompatibility with the value of "informed consent."

Subjects participated in a simulation of Milgram's (1963) baseline experiment (learner in adjacent room, pounding on wall heard at 300-volt level). The role-playing procedure was introduced when the subject first arrived. Subjects were told to read the method section of Milgram's 1963 article. This information described all the basic features of the obedience paradigm, that is, the shock generator, the purpose of the experiment as stated to subjects, the fixed draw to assign teacher and learner roles, and so on. (The method section is found in Milgram, 1963, pp. 372-374.) They were told that the purpose of the study was to investigate the "behavior of individuals informed as to what is being studied and how it is being studied" (p. 89). It was emphasized that it was their behavior, in the role of "teacher," that was under study and that the learner was not actually going to be shocked. Each subject was instructed to behave as if he had not been informed. Minor departures from Milgram's procedure included the use of college students (males) as subjects, and features of the learner's "electric chair." A simulated shock generator, similar to that used by Milgram, was used in this study.

The results were remarkably like those reported by Milgram. An obedience rate of 70 percent was obtained, in comparison to Milgram's 65 percent. Asked to estimate the pain of the learner, their subjects yielded a mean rating of 12.86 (on a 14-point scale), in comparison to Milgram's figure of 13.42. Regarding signs of tension, O'Leary et al. reported that the profound symptoms cited by Milgram—sweating, digging fingernails into flesh—were not in evidence. However, "nervous activity" was shown by many subjects, in two instances almost requiring a termination of the experiment.

The investigators were, understandably, encouraged: "*The similarity of the action data is so high . . . that Milgram would very likely have reached the same conclusions using the data in the present study*" (pp. 92-93). (Milgram did not refer to this study in his 1974 text.) The investigators viewed the absence of extreme tension in conjunction with the high obedience rate as a distinct advantage for their role-playing technique—"Milgram was primarily interested in action [that is, actual shock-lever behavior] and so were we" (p. 93).

The findings of this study are interesting. They suggest that a more active role-playing strategy can, in principle, yield convincing data. It is obvious, of course, that one could not evaluate the findings of this study without having recourse to the data of Milgram's original investigation. In this respect, it would have been informative had O'Leary et al. actually replicated the deception version in addition to their role-playing variation. Of course, this design may have violated the ethical standards of these investigators.

The similarity in the results of the role-playing and deception versions of the obedience paradigm, while provocative and encouraging from an ethical point of view, does not necessarily mean that the psychological determinants of the behaviors were the same in both techniques. O'Leary et al.'s subjects knew that the entire scenario was, in a critical sense, unreal—Milgram's subjects did not have this cognition (discounting Orne and Holland's thesis). It is possible that both groups *performed similarly but for different reasons.* In this context, the marked reduction in the emotionality of their subjects was not viewed as significant by O'Leary et al., but the extreme tension of subjects, as indicative of moral conflict, was to assume a fundamental role in Milgram's subsequent interpretation of his findings.

Geller (1978)

In a scholarly, intricate investigation of role playing and obedience, Daniel Geller (1978) re-enacted three of Milgram's variations—the base line, experimenter-absent (Experiment 7), and victim's limited contract (Experiment 9). Like O'Leary et al., Geller was meticulous in assuring all subjects that the experiment was "not real," noting that "participants were simply asked to suspend reality and pretend that the situation was real even though they knew it was not; they were asked not to be a typical subject, but to be themselves in another situation" (p. 225).

Geller also obtained several measures of each subject's "involvement" in his role playing (for example, an external judge's rating; the subject's score on a role playing ability scale). He was addressing a common criticism of role playing, that it lacks vividness and emotional impact, by acknowledging that subjects could reasonably be expected to differ in their degree of involvement. The most successful role-playing experiment would be one in which highly involved persons were doing the role playing, and this degree of involvement could, in principle, be objectively assessed.

Geller's prediction was interesting. For subjects who were relatively *low* in involvement, their attention would presumably focus on the fact that the shocks were not real. Obedience for these subjects should be high in all conditions, in that obeying the experimenter's instructions would be the simplest course of action. For subjects *high* in involvement, however, their primary attention would be on the authority of the experimenter. These subjects, being able to suspend the *as if* nature of the experiment, would, as with Milgram's subjects, be primarily attentive to the hierarchical aspect of their role. For these subjects obedience should decrease in the experimenter-absent condition. This result, which is, of course, what Milgram observed, would not be expected to occur for the non-involved subjects.

Geller's findings were very supportive of his line of reasoning. In terms of the three experimental conditions, there were no significant differences between Geller's results and those reported by Milgram concerning the percentage of maximum obedience: Base line: Milgram —65 percent, Geller—51 percent; Experimenter Absent: Milgram— 22.5 percent, Geller—33.3 percent; Limited Contract: Milgram—40 percent, Geller—50 percent. The average maximum shock levels were also highly similar to those observed in Milgram's research.

Regarding the variable of subject involvement, the data were again as predicted. Only those subjects categorized as relatively high in role-playing involvement displayed a reduced obedience in the experimenter-absent condition. In Geller's view, this was the crucial condition because it was known, from Milgram's original data, that obedience should be strongly reduced in this variation. A wide range of manifestations of tension and conflict was observed. These were expressed more strongly by subjects rated as highly involved in their role playing. Individuals who defied the authority at some point were more likely to report having been tense.

In summary, Geller's results are impressive. Similar to O'Leary et al., Geller expressed confidence regarding the methodological virtues of role playing:

Since the methods used in this simulation were rigorous and well-controlled, there is no a priori reason not to accept the findings. In highly involving situations like obedience, role playing may be an effective and successful experimental method if participant involvement is taken into account. (P. 233)

Geller's discussion, however, is unusual in some respects. He appears to view deception itself as a kind of simulation—a simulation of "the real world." He thus objects to the fact that role playing is traditionally criticized because of its simulation aspect, when in his view deception is but another form of simulation methodology. He notes that "role playing methods should be evaluated by comparison to some nonsimulating method (a criterion that has not even been applied to most deception studies)" (p. 233). In effect, Geller implies that ideally it should not be necessary to assess the success of role playing by comparing it to a deception study as the criterion. Yet, because his study, like many others, makes its entire case on a meticulous comparison with Milgram's original findings, his argument loses considerable force.

Geller is surprisingly equivocal regarding the ethical advantage of his procedure. Unquestionably he is convinced of the ethical superiority of not deceiving the subject—the gain in "informed consent" is crucial here. However, he is concerned that the intense involvement experienced by some individuals, particularly those who would be considered ideal from the point of view of this study, may expose them to unacceptable levels of stress.[8] He is apparently convinced of the involvement potential of role playing to the extent that he is hesitant regarding its ultimate ethical advantage. Clearly, however, role playing has fewer *ethical disadvantages* than deception methods, and this is perhaps Geller's most significant conclusion.

Geller used Milgram's shock generator in his research, and put subjects through as close a facsimile of the original paradigm as might realistically be achieved. It is striking to contrast his findings, as well as those of O'Leary et al., with the "expected obedience" results reported by Milgram and others (see Chapter Two). When subjects are asked to reflect on a verbal description of the obedience paradigm, they seem dominated by the thought that "not shocking the learner" is the desirable thing to do, that defying the experimenter is what they or others *should* do in such an experiment. However, when actually embedded in a "live" enactment of the obedience experiment, subjects seem primarily oriented to the influence of the experimenter. Research in social cognition and human judgment supports the general proposition that behavior is often strongly influenced by the salience or vividness of a particular cue or stimulus (Nisbett and Ross, 1980; Taylor and Fiske, 1978). Perhaps the salience of authority is simply not accessed by individuals when reading a relatively pallid verbal account of the method section of an article, even Milgram's article!

There are potential limitations to role playing—even in successful experiments such as those of O'Leary et al. and Geller—which will be considered at the end of this chapter. Regardless of one's stand on role-playing procedures—on its epistemological status as a source of meaningful data—it should be understood that the term "role playing" refers to a variety of techniques. Those who advocate the more active, involved form of role playing are quite justified in divorcing their approach from the "estimated behavior" procedure used by Milgram and others.

Mixon (1972, 1979)

Don Mixon was an early proponent of role playing, endorsing both its ethical advantages and its substantive value as an analytical methodology. In the first of two experiments, he conducted what he termed an "active role playing" version of the 1963 Milgram baseline study. In fact, this study was relatively "passive," as subjects were asked to imagine the presence of the experimenter and learner (both played by Mixon himself), and to indicate on a paper diagram of the shock generator their response to the experimenter's orders. Relative to the estimated-behavior technique, however, Mixon's approach was more active. Using several groups of college students, Mixon reported rates ranging from 40 percent to 100 percent in terms of maximum obedience, and also a high incidence of expressions of tension and conflict (such as nervous laughter). Thus, Mixon was one of the first investigators to report obedience data, comparable to those of Milgram, using role playing procedures (1972, 1976, 1977).

Mixon clearly understood the significance of the "underestimation" noted by Milgram: "If Milgram's experimental situation is in fact an example of the rule 'refuse to obey an experimenter's command to seriously harm another,' the conduct of obedient subjects can be understood as transgressions of that rule" (1979, p. 165). According to Mixon, Milgram has taken this approach, using the discrepancy between estimated and obtained obedience as "evidence of the power of the situation to make people behave badly. The presumed discrepancy gives the study much of its drama and power" (p. 165). What is Mixon's objection here? Why does he speak of a "presumed" discrepancy between estimated and obtained obedience?

Mixon points out that there were actually two obedience experiments—the *real* experiment, namely Milgram's intention to investigate harmful obedience, and the experiment *as described to the subjects*, namely a scientific study of punishment and learning. Mixon suspects that Milgram's obedience "estimators" were responding to the "real" experiment, and, for this reason, unanimously denied that they would obey to the higher shock levels. Thus, the estimated-behavior procedure (as described in Chapter Two) was, in Mixon's view, an inappropriate verbal base line with which to compare the experiment as described to the subjects themselves. More generally, Mixon argues that the underestimation of obedience was a function of the specific verbal description given to Milgram's estimators. Other descriptions might have elicited quite different data patterns.

Before describing Mixon's second experiment, it should be noted that Mixon strongly endorses Orne's (1962) general conception regarding the perception of the laboratory held by subjects. Although Mixon does not cite the Orne and Holland reference in any of his papers, his views are, in many respects, compatible with their criticism. He asserts that the strong interpretation given to Milgram's findings presumes that subjects in fact believed that they were harming the learner. Mixon, from comments made by subjects in his first study, concludes that the experimenter's behavior is of particular significance for subjects. He then states what we have referred to earlier as the "incongruity" thesis, that subjects in Milgram's paradigm had reasonable cause to doubt that the learner was actually receiving unbearable punishment.

In his second investigation, Mixon presented groups of subjects with different verbal descriptions of the obedience paradigm. His major interest was the effect of telling subjects that safeguards had broken down and that there could be no certainty that the learner was not being seriously harmed. Four of the conditions involved descriptions of the obedience paradigm that were essentially similar to those used in Mixon's first study, and which explicitly avoided any reference to Milgram's real interest in destructive obedience. Rates of estimated obedience ranged from 40 percent to 80 percent. Thus, even in a passive role-playing context, Mixon's subjects produced data radically deviating from the underestimation pattern reported by Milgram, in that they were similar to Milgram's observed obedience rates. In a fifth condition, Mixon excluded a reference to the verbal warnings on the shock generator, and obtained an obedience estimate of 90 percent. Mixon's interpretation is that because it was even more reasonable in this condition for subjects to presume that no harm would befall the learner, the estimate of obedience was virtually at a maximum rate.

In three conditions, cues were inserted in the verbal scripts which suggested the likelihood of actual harm. One script, for example, simply avoided the experimenter's assurance that no permanent harm would be experienced by the learner. Here, the estimated rate of obedience was 0 percent.

Mixon's conclusions are diverse. First, the judgments of non-active role players, that is estimators or predictors of obedience, depend critically on the specific scene described for them. Details, perhaps seemingly unimportant, can strongly influence the estimations. The extreme underestimation of obedience reported by Milgram and others may be "script specific" and not indicate a cognitive inability to visualize the power of authority. In this sense, Milgram's approach (and that used by others as well) may have been an unfair test of role playing.

Because Mixon was able to obtain estimates of total obedience, as well as total defiance, simply by varying verbal descriptions of the experiment, he concludes that Milgram's actual setting was ambiguous. It was interpreted by some subjects as involving illegitimate authority —an experimenter ordering that an innocent subject be harmed. It was interpreted by others as legitimate authority—an experimenter ordering that pain *but not harm* be administered. What *should* subjects have done, in Mixon's view?

> They should turn on the experimenter and refuse to cooperate further until he makes clear precisely what is going on. But I hardly can condemn them for failing, because with all our vaunted individualism it seems that in some circumstances we have no rule directing us to defy authorities when the legitimacy of their command is dubious. (1979, p. 172)

Mixon's position, basically similar to that of Orne and Holland, is that Milgram was not justified in labeling the behavior of his obedient subjects as "shockingly immoral." He does not completely dismiss the findings because, as noted in the above quotation, he acknowledges that subjects could have, at least, been uncertain as to what was happening to the learner. From his role-playing data, however, he infers that had subjects been absolutely convinced that the learner's welfare was in jeopardy, they would have disobeyed the experimenter. In effect, Mixon seems satisfied with Milgram's explanation of *defiance*, but not of obedience.

As with many of Milgram's critics, Mixon is an articulate scholar whose views are worth studying in detail. Whether or not in agreement with them, the reader will know that he or she has been in a methodological battle! In my view, the strengths of Mixon's contributions are (1) his evidence supporting the potential for active role-playing techniques to produce interesting and potentially valuable findings and (2) the importance of specifying the precise content of verbal scripts in passive role-playing (i.e. prediction or estimation) studies. I also find interesting his raising the possibility that subjects who defied the experimenter may, in some important respects, have had a different perception of the intrinsic nature of the experiment from that of subjects who continued to obey the experimenter. On this latter point, however, I do not feel that Mixon has made a convincing case.

My reservations are largely based on what I view to be Mixon's reliance upon Orne's thesis regarding the inevitably benign context of the laboratory. The empirical research reviewed earlier in this chapter, as well as a number of experiments cited elsewhere—for example, the Hofling et al. nurse study and the Shanab and Yahya study on obedience in children—do not, in my opinion, justify this perspective, as rational or intuitively compelling as it may seem to be.

One illustration of an apparent inconsistency in Mixon's analysis should be noted. In terms of his hypothesis that subjects will be obedient as long as they remain convinced that no lasting harm is being perpetrated, he cites Milgram's pilot research in which it was noted that subjects "went blithely to the end of the board, seemingly indifferent to the verbal designations" (Milgram, 1965b, p. 61, cited by Mixon, 1979, p. 169). Milgram reported having to introduce feedback from the learner to elicit (at least some) defiance (see Chapter Three). Mixon infers that Milgram's pilot subjects obeyed *because they did not believe they were actually harming the learner*. That is, the lack of feedback from the learner was, itself, evidence that the learner was safe. However, in the actual paradigm, Milgram made considerable use of feedback (pounding, agonized screams, etc.), yet Mixon denies their validity, using the Orne thesis that the experimental context, for example, the behavior of the experimenter, defines the learner's protests as non-indicative of genuine harm. Thus, Mixon seems to be saying that Milgram's pilot subjects obeyed because they did not hear protests, but his experimental subjects obeyed because they did not believe the veracity of the protests. This seems to be an inconsistent line of reasoning.

It should be mentioned, in conclusion, that in reading Mixon, one senses that he objects to Milgram's research on *ethical* as well as methodological grounds. Thus, while recognizing the methodological contributions that Mixon has made, the possibility that he has an ethical bias which infuses his general perspective on the work must at least be entertained. Note, for example, Mixon's view on the debriefing used by Milgram:

> The "debriefing" included an account of the "real" definition of the situation and an interpretation of subject conduct. But because their conduct was not understood, their behavior was carefully explained to them in a way that made what they had just done appear worse than in fact it was: a gratuitous burden for subjects, and experimenter. (1979, p. 175)

Mixon's position has, itself, become an object of controversy. Critics of the obedience research invariably embrace Mixon's analysis. Consider the view of Rom Harré, whose ethical criticisms were noted in Chapter Five:

> The mystery of the Milgram experiment—how it was possible for otherwise kindly citizens to perform these exceedingly dangerous and cruel actions, was resolved eventually by Mixon's classic reworking of the Milgram study . . . Mixon, in a brilliant exercise in the scenario method, was able to manipulate the interpretations and beliefs which the subjects brought to the experiment (1979, pp. 104-5).

Similarly, in a paper advocating the use of role playing as not only a more ethical alternative but a superior methodology to deception techniques, Forward, Canter, and Kirsch (1976) gave the strongest possible interpretation to the value of Mixon's approach:

> By exploring and specifying the particular meanings attributed to variations in the role/rule context of "legitimate authority in experiments," and by being able to produce and observe the whole range of possible obedience responses, Mixon is better able to claim that he has an adequate conceptualization and description of obedience in this particular social context. . . . By use of exploratory role-enactment techniques, Mixon was able to discover that subjects in Milgram's experiment never intended to cause harm to the apparent learner. (P. 600)

However, Mixon's views tend not to be well received by those who endorse Milgram's research. J. Richard Eiser, in his text *Cognitive*

Social Psychology (1980), after describing Mixon's conceptualization and evidence, expressed some methodological reservations of his own:

> The descriptions of procedure are probably the vaguest and flimsiest of those in any of the studies I have read while writing this book. . . . One simply cannot tell whether Mixon's various scripts were adequate simulations of any of Milgram's conditions, and Mixon does not put their adequacy directly to the test himself by running them under Milgram-type deception procedures to compare the results. (P. 255)

Joel Cooper (1976), in a balanced review of the role-playing/deception controversy, recognized the value of role playing, but expressed what is perhaps the most commonly voiced reservation:

> The role enactor, from the relatively detached position of the "pretend," cannot predict which aspects of the situation he or she will be paying *attention* to when the real time comes. One of Mixon's (1972) role players, pretending to be in Milgram's (1963) obedience study, may believe that he or she would not pass the 150-volt mark in response to the experimenter's demand. This is an honest guess for, when reading the script used by Milgram (or even watching the film of his experiment), the individual may focus on the potential pain and damage to the learner. But when involved in the actual situation, the participant may actually pay attention to other features, such as the authority figure standing over him or her, or the dispassive manner in which the participant is instructed to continue. (P. 608)

CONCLUSIONS

The paradox noted at the beginning of this chapter should now be even more apparent. We have seen in Chapter Five that the obedience research raised to an unprecedented degree a concern with the ethics of social research. The primary basis of these criticisms was the extreme tension and stress evidenced by many of Milgram's subjects, both during the experiment and after it—that is, when having to live with the "insights" gained in realizing the implications of their actions. It is thus paradoxical, to understate the matter, that the primary methodological criticism is that a majority of subjects could not imagine that the learner was in any sort of dire circumstances. Milgram, himself, noted this paradox:

> To be sure, I could certainly improve my image with D. Baumrind (1964) and others who have criticized the experiment because of the tension it induced, constructing a defense on Orne's interpretation, but this would be utterly false, for the conflict *was* present, intensely experienced, and cannot be wished or theorized away. (Milgram, in Miller, 1972a, p. 140)

After reviewing the research described in this chapter, one should be in a position to evaluate Milgram's claim.

My own view is that the weight of evidence argues against the Orne and Holland thesis, certainly against what might be construed as the *strong* version of their argument—that subjects saw through the deceptions of the obedience paradigm and acted out the role of deceived subjects, all of this prompted by their adherence to demand characteristics which, among other things, defined the laboratory as an intrinsically benign setting. On the basis of the *research evidence*, I think there are sufficient data concerning both the *degree of obedience* and the *expressions of conflict* to indicate that many subjects faced the prospect of a peer being genuinely devastated in the role of "learner." I think it is clear that one does *not* have to presume that Milgram's subjects were certain that they were irreversibly harming the learner in order to be impressed by the generalizability of Milgram's findings. Larry Coutts, in the 1977 symposium on role playing (Hendrick et al., 1977), articulated this point of view:

> Whereas Mixon contends that Milgram's interpretation necessarily "rests on the belief that subjects were given clear and overwhelming evidence of harmful consequences" . . . I suggest that the potential ambiguity of the situation in no way removes the subjects' actions from the realm of destructive obedience. That is, if an individual is confronted with a situation in which he is uncertain as to whether or not his actions are injurious to another, and in order to resolve this conflict he submits to a definition of the situation proposed by a third party, then we may speak, at least in the present context, of destructive obedience to authority. (P. 520)

This characterization would, I think, be sufficient for Milgram's basic conceptualization of obedience, although as we have seen, he generally seems to argue for an even stronger interpretation.

The role-playing developments are of considerable interest. We have several instances in which an active role-playing procedure produced rates of obedience comparable to those observed in the original baseline experiment. Clearly, these studies differ very significantly from the implications of Milgram's "expected obedience" data and other findings based on "passive" role-playing techniques. Furthermore, the underestimation of obedience certainly could reflect the specific verbal translation of the paradigm given to subjects. This is not to suggest that the passive role-playing procedure is unimportant or without the value commonly ascribed to it. Asking subjects "what would you do if . . . ?" is extremely relevant, because it is this kind of *cognitive rehearsal* or imagery that might occur frequently in everyday life. Thus, we observe an action—or hear about someone's behavior more indirectly—and in trying to understand it, we consider what we might have done in the same situation. It remains true, however, that this type of mental exercise is, in possibly crucial aspects, different from being directly involved in a scenario in an active, dramaturgical sense. The fact that active role playing did yield markedly higher rates of obedience is therefore intriguing.

On this latter point, I confess that I am still unsure of precisely how much significance to attach to the findings of the active role-playing experiments. The fact that each of the investigators based his strongest case on a comparison to Milgram's original research cannot be ignored. Without the original, deception-based experiments, what position would we be in regarding the role-playing data? Geller and Mixon have argued that the deception-based original should, in fact, not be the standard of comparison because it, too, is a simulation of the primary criterion, that is, naturally occurring destructive obedience. Regardless of the merits of this argument—I, for one, remain unconvinced—these investigators nevertheless proceed to make the comparison! The fact that the comparison is flattering to role playing is a plus—the fact that the comparison has to be made at all is a negative.

I indicated in an earlier examination of role playing that because active role players may be able to produce behaviors similar to those of deceived subjects does not automatically indicate that the causes or determinants of role-played behavior are the same as those of deceived subjects (Miller, 1972b). That is, surface comparability in behaviors does not necessarily imply an identicality in the processes mediating the behaviors. Geller, in his approach to "involvement," and Mixon argue that the processes are, in fact, comparable, but this, at least in my view, seems highly debatable. An even less complimentary view is that role-playing procedures increase the likelihood that demand characteristics will influence behavior.[9] This is because the role-playing "mind set," despite the noble intentions on the part of most subjects, may detract from the immediacy of events. The role player has a kind of cognitive flexibility, a natural curiosity prompted by the "as if" or "let's pretend" definition of the research setting. Consider, in this context, the "Candid Camera" television program. Was it not the fact that the observer knew that the behavior was natural and spontaneous, that is, *candid*, that gave this program its fascination? Certainly deception was at the heart of the "candid camera."

We must recognize, however, that one of the most important consequences of the obedience research has been the growing awareness that methodological considerations are not necessarily the deciding issue.[10] There is serious doubt whether institutional review boards at many universities would currently sanction research using Milgram's original paradigm. Some have viewed this general development very negatively (see, Festinger, 1980, p. 249), while others, of course, would applaud it (Baumrind, 1985). Regardless of one's position, the active role-playing findings are encouraging for those who take a negative stance regarding the ethics of the Milgram paradigm but who nevertheless wish to investigate obedience to authority. I believe that given the diverse procedures reviewed not only in this chapter, but in Chapters Four and Five as well, we have a far more enlightened understanding of the nature of Milgram's experimental findings.

We asked, at the start of this chapter, whether or not Milgram had succeeded, *methodologically*, in investigating destructive obedience to authority. Did his research paradigm capture, in a convincing manner, the obedience phenomenon? An affirmative answer would encourage efforts to apply Milgram's findings to analyses of phenomena associated with obedience outside of research contexts, that is, in the world of authority, bureaucracies, social hierarchies, political and military chains of command, etc. A negative answer would relegate Milgram's findings to the status of laboratory artifact—provocative, perhaps, but without sufficient substantive credibility to warrant serious generalizations beyond the research context itself.

As I have indicated in several places, I am personally impressed with the accumulated research evidence testifying to the validity of Milgram's findings. I would thus answer the above question with an unequivocal "yes." I emphasize the value of the *cumulative* evidence reviewed in this chapter and the two previous chapters as well—research with children, with animals as the victim, using responses other than inflicting electric shock, in settings other than research laboratories, with oneself as the victim rather than someone else. This list is, I think, impressive testimony regarding the methodological status of the obedience paradigm.

Douglas Mook (1983) has written, in my view, one of the most informative analyses of the problems associated with generalizing from laboratory experiments. As have countless other methodologists, Mook uses Milgram's research to present a number of major arguments. He notes, for example, that people frequently object to the "artificiality" of laboratory experiments. How can they be useful, when they seem so bizarre, so "unlike life?" Regarding the obedience paradigm, Mook asks:

> Soldiers in the jungles of Viet Nam, concentration camp guards on the fields of Eastern Europe—what resemblance do their environments bear to a sterile room with a shock generator and an intercom, presided over by a white-coated scientist? As a setting, Milgram's surely is a prototype of an "unnatural one." (P. 385)

He cites the views of Michael Argyle, a prominent British social psychologist: "When a subject steps inside a psychological laboratory he steps out of culture, and all the normal rules and conventions are temporarily discarded and replaced by the single rule of laboratory culture —do what the experimenter says, no matter how absurd or unethical it may be" (Argyle, 1969, p. 20).

Mook's reaction is quite different:

> What Milgram has shown is how easily we can "step out of culture" in just the way Argyle describes—and how, once out of culture, we proceed to violate its "normal rules and conventions" in ways that are a revelation to us when they occur. Remember, by the way, that most of the people Milgram interviewed grossly underestimated the amount of compliance that would occur *in that laboratory setting.* (P. 386)

Another critical reaction results from an attempt to list the similarities and differences between the laboratory setting and the (purportedly analogous) natural one—the more differences, the more invalid or ungeneralizable the experiment. Baumrind's original (1964) criticism, though primarily ethical in its focus, was an early illustration of this methodological objection as well. Kantowitz and Roediger (1984), in their recent text *Experimental Psychology*, illustrate this kind of reaction:

> One element lacking in Milgram's situation that typically exists in similar real-world situations is the power of the person who is commanding (the experimenter, in this case) to harm the subject if the subject fails to obey orders. The subject could always simply get up and walk out of the experiment, never to see the experimenter again. So when considering Milgram's results, we should bear in mind that a powerful source of obedience in the real world was lacking in this situation. (Pp. 373-74)

Instead of seeing the cup half empty, however, Mook sees it as half full (and perhaps more):

> Now the lack of punishment is, to be sure, a major difference between
> Milgram's lab and the jungle war or concentration camp setting. But
> what happened? An astonishing two thirds obeyed anyway. The force
> of the experimenter's authority was sufficient to induce normal decent
> adults to inflict pain on another human being, even though they could
> have refused without risk. Surely the absence of power to punish, though
> a distinct difference between Milgram's setting and the others, only adds
> to the drama of what he saw. (P. 386)

As we will see in Chapter Eight, Milgram was to reconsider in some
detail the "psychology of leaving the experimental situation."

Mook, however, does acknowledge the importance of recognizing
potentially important differences. Regarding Orne's thesis that subjects may have construed the laboratory as an inherently "safe" place,
he notes, "Camp guards and jungle fighters do not have this cognitive
escape hatch available to them. If Milgram's subjects did say 'It must
not be dangerous,' then his conclusion—people are surprisingly willing to inflict danger under orders—is in fact weakened" (p. 386).

Mook's major conclusion is that one should not attempt to calcu-
late the generalizability of a laboratory experiment in terms of a "final
count" regarding its surface resemblances and departures from non-
laboratory analogues. Every major issue that is raised, such as the experimenter's inability to punish the subject's viewing the learner as
safe and secure, must be considered and pursued to a satisfactory resolution regarding its significance.

Chapter Seven will consider another manifestation of the "generalization problem" concerning Milgram's obedience experiments. Its
focus will not be on the findings of experimental research, nor on the
epistemological controversies surrounding such issues as role playing
and deception. We will be dealing with very sober issues, with the emotional imagery in such phrases as "man's inhumanity toward man,"
and "I was only following orders." Douglas Mook has noted, "Ultimately, what makes research findings of interest is that they help us
understand everyday life. That understanding, however, comes from
theory or the analysis of mechanism; it is not a matter of 'generalizing' the findings themselves" (p. 386).

What have the obedience experiments taught us in regard to "everyday life," even the "everyday life" of the Holocaust?

7

GENOCIDE FROM THE
PERSPECTIVE OF THE OBEDIENCE
EXPERIMENTS

I just said to myself, my God, what is this? What's happening here? How could people do this to other people?

> —Dr. Leon Bass, one of the first American soldiers to
> arrive at the Buchenwald death camp in 1945.

The annihilation of six million Jews, carried out by the German state under Adolf Hitler during World War II, has resisted understanding. The question persists: How could it have happened?

> —Dr. Lucy Dawidowicz, in the Preface to
> *The War Against the Jews: 1933-1945.*

The extermination of 6 million Jewish men, women, and children by the Nazis, a policy of genocide referred to as the Holocaust, constitutes the most vexing challenge for intellectual analysis. In representing the epitome of humankind's capacity for mass murder, the Holocaust demands and yet seems to defy understanding. The literature, from a host of disciplines in the social sciences and humanities, is seemingly endless. Thousands of volumes, research articles, and conceptual essays have been directed at the most simply stated of questions—Why did it happen? How could it have happened? Might it happen again?

The Milgram experiments have provided, in the view of numerous scholars, a compelling analysis of one very crucial feature of the Holocaust, the willingness of people to obey orders to harm other individuals.[1] In this context, the obedience experiments have assumed a *moral relevance* quite apart from their impact on more traditional social-scientific grounds. We observed in Chapter Six that the legitimacy of making generalizations from these experiments was a topic of considerable controversy and research interest. Regardless of formal methodological considerations, however, it must be recognized that many students of the Holocaust have, with unbounded confidence and passion, embraced the obedience experiments. Milgram's research has been seen as containing profound insights regarding human nature, in particular the propensity of human beings to fail significant tests of conscience and moral decision making.

Not all, of course, share these sentiments. The emotionalism so readily evoked in a consideration of the obedience experiments may be attributed in part to the intrinsically arousing aspects of the Holocaust itself. The enormity of the Holocaust seems to render any effort to explain it controversial. The very act of attempting to reduce the Holocaust to more manageable intellectual dimensions may be viewed as presumptuous, as an ill-fated venture to comprehend that which is ultimately unknowable.

The purpose of the present chapter is to examine the relevance of the obedience experiments to an understanding of the Holocaust. What specific associations have been made in linking Milgram's research to the Holocaust? How have various analysts perceived these associations? What have been the arguments *against* the value of the obedience research in informing us about the Holocaust? What kinds of political and historical events, other than the Holocaust, have been related to the obedience experiments? Hundreds (perhaps many more) of commentaries have been addressed to questions of this nature. I have attempted to select a number of well-developed positions representing different points of view for inclusion in this discussion.

Although the issues to be examined are diverse and seem to lack the basis for a coherent framework, there is a pivotal concept that permeates much of the literature to be reviewed. I refer, specifically, to what might be termed as the "normality thesis" versus the "pathology thesis." We saw, in Chapter Two, a powerful inclination for people to make an internal or personality-based attribution to the behavior of the "teacher." The subject who obeyed to 450 volts was viewed in negative, almost pathological terms. Milgram's causal perception of the subject's behavior was, of course, far more situational, or external.

We are also concerned in the present chapter with the manner in which events are perceived or given meaning. Many analysts of the Holocaust and other instances of genocide have taken strongly polarized positions on whether the behaviors at issue should be viewed essentially in terms of the *personalities* of those involved or primarily in terms of external or *situational* forces. Not surprisingly, one's explanatory bias on this matter will often determine the nature of the reception given to Milgram's research. A contest between personal and situational explanations is not, of course, necessarily appropriate or ultimately productive—a more precise inquiry might concern the *relative* importance of personal *and* situational influences. Yet, most arguments are readily categorized in terms of one basic causal perspective or the other. The house of intellectual discourse is rarely large enough for those with radically different perceptions of the Holocaust. The thesis that "*anyone* could, in specific conditions, engage in genocidal obedience" is extremely offensive to many people. Conversely, the assertion that "only pathologically disturbed personalities could have been directly involved in the Holocaust" strikes many as simplistic and possibly dangerous in its naivete.

ON GENERALIZING TO THE HOLOCAUST—POSITIVE VIEWS

Milgram

It is appropriate to begin with Milgram's position on the larger significance of his research. We have made numerous references in previous chapters to his basic position—that he was *not* attempting to create a mirror image of the Holocaust in his laboratory, but was intent on capturing a central dynamic of the Holocaust, namely obedience, in a controlled experimental environment. His success in this venture was, in his view, a result of creating a genuine moral conflict for his subjects. He rarely spoke of his research in such terms as "simulation," "analogy," or "model." He was convinced that he had witnessed a vital reality:

> The essence of obedience, as a psychological process, can be captured by studying the simple situation in which a man is told by a legitimate authority to act against a third individual. This situation confronted both our experimental subject and the German subject and evoked in each a set of parallel psychological adjustments. (1974, p. 177)

Milgram wrote his 1974 book *Obedience to Authority* during the final agonizing years of the Vietnam War. He quotes at length from an interview by Mike Wallace with a participant in the My Lai massacre, an individual who acknowledged his role in shooting infants and unarmed civilians:

Q. Again—men, women, and children?
A. Men, women, and children.
Q. And babies?
A. And babies. And so we started shooting them . . .
Q. Why did you do it?
A. Why did I do it? Because I felt like I was ordered to do it, and it seemed like that, at the time I felt like I was doing the right thing, because, like I said, I lost buddies. (1974, p. 185)

Milgram is not hesitant to generalize from such atrocities on the basis of his research on obedience, "In the Vietnam war, the massacre at My Lai revealed with special clarity the problem to which this book has addressed itself" (p. 183).

He views the My Lai massacre, the disclosures at the trial of Eichmann, and other examples of genocide as intimately related to the dilemma posed in his laboratory. People, Milgram states, are often obsessed with carrying out their jobs—they become dominated by "an administrative rather than a moral outlook" (p. 186). They are willing, in principle, to allocate responsibility to someone "higher" in command. He emphasizes the role of the mission itself, its noble purpose: "In the experiment, science is served by the act of shocking the victim against his will; in Germany, the destruction of the Jews was represented as a "hygienic" process against "jewish vermin" (p. 187) (Hilberg, 1961).

He speaks to the role of "silence" in the process of destructive obedience, "In Nazi Germany, even among those most closely identified with the 'final solution,' it was considered an act of discourtesy to talk about the killings. . . . Subjects in the experiment most frequently experience their objections as embarrassing" (p. 187).

In the preface to the French translation of his book (1979), Milgram describes another episode of mass death, the events at Jonestown, Guyana in 1978. More than 900 people died, many by their own hand, by drinking poison upon the urging of their leader, the Reverend Jim Jones. Milgram observes that the most typical explanation, for instance, in media accounts, was psychiatric—the people, as well as their leader, were fundamentally deranged. Acknowledging that Jones, himself, may have been psychotic in holding to illusions of persecution, Milgram sees the larger event in social-psychological terms, with strong parallels to the obedience experiments:

More important than the characterological deficiencies of the cultists was their immersion in an authoritarian group life, the isolation of the group from the larger society, and the virtual control of the informational field by their leader ... something else underlies our reaction of shock to this tragedy—the general sense that we have confronted inexplicable madness: namely, Reverend Jim Jones lacked legitimacy in the eyes of the larger world. National governments, we acknowledge, have the right to determine policy, and even when such policies are misguided and lead to the needless destruction of thousands of people, we do not regard those who execute the commands of the government to be "pathological," but as merely performing their duty. The difference in our reaction is not dependent so much on the deeds carried out, but on the perceived legitimacy of those who command such actions. The link between an event such as Jonestown and the experiments described in this book lies in the extraordinary degree of compliance to authority manifested in both situations. (1979, pp. 2-3)

In this context, Milgram describes, in some detail, the research of Kudirka (noted in Chapter Six), showing that people will obey orders to engage in behaviors which involve harming (temporarily) *themselves*. We noted, in Chapter Four, a study by Martin et al. which speaks to a similar finding.

In closing this section, we quote from Milgram's epilogue, where he gives his most encompassing interpretation regarding the meaning of the obedience experiments:

The behavior revealed in the experiments reported here is normal human behavior but revealed under conditions that show with particular clarity the danger to human survival inherent in our make-up. And what is it we have seen? Not aggresson, for there is no anger, vindictiveness, or hatred in those who shocked the victim. Men do become angry; they do act hatefully and explode in rage against others. But not here. Something far more dangerous is revealed: the capacity for man to abandon his humanity, indeed, the inevitability that he does so, as he merges his unique personality into larger institutional structures. This is a fatal flaw nature has designed into us, and which in the long run gives our species only a modest chance of survival. (1974, p. 188)

Milgram's conclusion is strikingly reminiscent of Hannah Arendt's "banality of evil" thesis developed in her coverage of the trial of Adolf Eichmann in Jerusalem:

It would have been comforting indeed to believe that Eichmann was a monster, even though if he had been Israel's case against him would have collapsed or, at the very least, lost all interest. Surely, one can hardly call upon the whole world and gather correspondents from the four corners of the earth in order to display Bluebeard in the dock. The trouble with Eichmann was precisely that so many were like him, and that the many were neither perverted nor sadistic, that they were, and still are, terribly and terrifyingly normal. (1963, p. 276)

Roger Brown (1985) has provided a particularly informative discussion of the Eichmann case in conjunction with the obedience research. He reports that Eichmann was found sane by a number of psychiatrists, that his family life following his escape from the Nuremberg trials to Buenos Aires was characterized as ideal. Prior to his role in the Final Solution, he had actually expressed pro-Zionist sentiments. For a time in Vienna he had a Jewish mistress and a Jewish half-cousin whom he protected. In essence, Eichmann's biography was remarkably free of psychopathology:

> Eichmann seemed so ordinary, so like bureaucrats everywhere. The things he cared most about, the events he remembered best, all concerned his own career, not the fate of the Jewish people. The things he felt ashamed of, the things that gave him anguish, were trifling breaches of German etiquette. For example, he once invited senior officers to join him for a glass of wine when that was not his prerogative. What he felt proud of was his strict adherence to duty in transporting Jews and his efficiency in the job. What he regarded as a temptation successfully resisted was the occasional sentiment of pity for individual victims. Perhaps Hannah Arendt and all those who have agreed with her about Eichmann were too credulous; the man was, after all, on trial for his life. Yet she made the startling claim that "in certain circumstances the most ordinary decent person can become a criminal." That should not be so if monstrous deeds presuppose a monstrous character. However, the most famous series of experiments in social psychology, Stanley Milgram's (1974) experiments on obedience to malevolent authority, confirm Arendt's prophetic claim. (Pp. 2-3)

Arendt's perception was ultimately to evoke a degree of controversy and outrage very similar to that experienced by Milgram. Neither reached conclusions that would be easily accepted, at least on first hearing.

The views of Milgram and Arendt illustrate what I have referred to as the "normality thesis." The basic argument is that people who would not ordinarily be described as unusual, deviant, sick, mentally ill, or pathological are capable of committing acts of unrestrained violence and evil. In defining the discipline of social psychology, Elliot Aronson has, in his text *The Social Animal*, elaborated upon the idea that "people who do crazy things are not necessarily crazy." He states, eloquently, what I refer to as the "normality thesis:"

The social psychologist studies social situations that affect people's behavior. Occasionally, these natural situations become focused into pressures so great that they cause people to behave in ways easily classifiable
as abnormal. (When I say "people" I mean very large numbers of people). To my mind, it does not increase our understanding of human behavior to classify these people as psychotic. It is much more useful to
try to understand the nature of the situation and the processes that were
operating to produce the behavior. (1984, pp. 8-9)

Note that this thesis does *not* suggest that people who *are* pathological may not also engage in genocide or destructive obedience. The
"normality thesis" does not necessarily imply a moral justification or
rationalization for acts of evil, nor does it legitimize "blaming the
devil." It is situational in its focus, but recognizes that situations are
the product of people. The "normality thesis" simply denies the proposition that doers of evil are necessarily "different" from the rest of
us in terms of basic psychological functioning.

Robert Jay Lifton, a psychiatrist who achieved initial eminence
for his interviews with the survivors of the atomic bombing of Japan
(1967), has expressed a version of the normality thesis in a recent analysis of the threat of nuclear war. Among his primary concerns is what
he views as a dangerous phenomenon of compliance. In the face of
overwhelming threat, people appear to take solace by leaving things
to leaders or experts:

In this stance of waiting for the bomb, then, we encounter various com-
binations of resignation, cynicism, and yearning—along with large numbers of people, some of them very talented, going about tasks that contribute to this potential holocaust. And here I confess that my perception
of the danger of our situation has been intensified by recent research on
Nazi doctors. There one could observe (in a very different kind of situation, to be sure) how very ordinary men and women who were in no way
inherently demonic could engage in demonic pursuits; how professionals
with pride in their professions could lend themselves to mass murder;
how in fact the killing process itself depended upon an alliance between
political leaders putting forward particular policies and professionals
making available not only technical skills but intellectual and "moral"
justifications. (Lifton and Falk, 1982, p. 12).

Regardless of the simplicity or eloquence of its formulation, the
"normality thesis" is not, as we have already remarked, intuitively
compelling, while its formidable antagonist, the "pathology thesis,"
has rarely lacked for enthusiasts.

We will now examine a number of analyses of the linkage between the obedience experiments and the Holocaust.[2] As in previous chapters, it is convenient to categorize specific positions as basically positive or negative regarding the hypothesized linkage, and we begin with analyses which have taken a positive view on this matter.

Sabini and Silver (1980): Destroying the Innocent with a Clear Conscience

These writers—social psychologists and former students of Milgram —have expressed the most extensive view of the conceptual relationship between the obedience experiments and the Holocaust. They begin by commenting upon a major Holocaust event, that of *Kristallnacht*. This involved a widespread attack on Jews, their property, and their synagogues in November, 1938, following the killing of a German official by a 17-year-old Polish Jew. This event seemed prototypical— violence, anti-Semitism, unrestrained hostility directed at innocents. Yet, the authors argue that Kristallnacht was *not* symptomatic of the Holocaust, that the Holocaust cannot be explained simply in terms of an extended series of acts of violence and prejudice:

> The German state annihilated approximately six million Jews. At the rate of 100 per day this would have required nearly 200 years. Mob violence rests on the wrong psychological basis, on violent emotion. People can be manipulated into fury, but fury cannot be maintained for 200 years. . . . Thorough, comprehensive, exhaustive murder required the replacement of the mob with a bureaucracy, the replacement of shared rage with obedience to authority. (Pp. 329-330)

Sabini and Silver refer to Hannah Arendt's depiction of Adolf Eichmann, a high-ranking Nazi who supervised the deportation of Jews to various concentration camps during the most intense phase of the Holocaust. Arendt's thesis, that Eichmann was notable in lacking the kind of motives, passions, or hostilities one might have expected, is interpreted by Sabini and Silver as evidence that focus on individuality—i.e., sadism, psychopathology, prejudicial attitudes—must be questioned as the appropriate orientation for understanding the genocide of the Holocaust:

> It is not the angry rioter we must understand but Eichmann, the colorless bureaucrat, replicated two million times in those who assembled the trains, dispatched the supplies, manufactured the poison gas, filed the paper work, sent out the death notices, guarded the prisoners, pointed

left and right, supervised the loading-unloading of the vans, disposed of the ashes, and performed the countless other tasks that also constituted the Holocaust. (P. 330)

Orders for these activities had to be issued and obeyed. It is this perspective which leads Sabini and Silver to Milgram's research on obedience. At the Nuremberg trials, the officials of the Nazi regime claimed that they were following orders, that on this basis they were not guilty of war crimes. Eichmann gave a similar account. But were these merely excuses? Sabini and Silver argue that we can be appropriately critical of "following orders" as a *justification* for genocidal behavior, but that it is reasonable to consider that the psychological processes underlying the phenomenon of obedience may provide an explanation for the Nazis' replies.

Sabini and Silver take the strongest possible view regarding the implications of the obedience experiments:

> Subjects in the experiment *did* continue to shock even though the person they were shocking demanded to be released and withdrew his consent, even though the person they were shocking had ceased responding and might have been unconscious or even dead. Subjects in the experiment were induced to act in ways that we simply would not expect ordinary citizens of no obvious deficit of conscience to act. (P. 333)

This interpretation enables Sabini and Silver to use the obedience experiments as a laboratory model of the Holocaust. The strategy of their analysis is to present numerous parallels between the obedience experiments and specific features of the Holocaust—similar, essentially, to Milgram's interpretive approach. They mention Experiment 18, in which 37 of 40 subjects performed subsidiary tasks while another peer shocked the learner. This is related to the idea that the Holocaust "industry" required countless subsidiary tasks, that is, not just primary killing, but support functions of almost endless variety. The Bridgeport variation and Experiment 9, where the agreed-upon contract with the victim is broken, are seen by Sabini and Silver as indicating that people will persist in bestowing legitimacy upon institutions which, on the surface, would seem to lack credibility.

Moral Responsibility

Sabini and Silver address themselves to one of the most difficult but pressing issues involved in the obedience phenomenon, that of responsibility. They are among the very few analysts with a primarily social-scientific perspective who have done so. They state that many of Milgram's subjects continued to obey because they did not feel responsible. Sabini and Silver argue that these subjects were, in fact, responsible, morally, for their behavior, but confused *technical* responsibility (that is, the experimenter's accountability for the conduct of the experiment itself) and *moral* responsibility. Bureaucracies facilitate this confusion, and, in this context, the authors make a particularly pointed equation between the obedience research and the Holocaust:

> Eichmann and Milgram's subjects lost the right to be unconcerned with the moral implications of their actions just when the German state and the experimenter's demands became immoral. Milgram's obedient subjects and Hitler's murderers ought to have seen that these institutions were no longer legitimate, could no longer claim their loyalty, and could no longer settle for them the question of moral responsibility. Milgram's subjects, insofar as they accepted the experimenter's explicit or implicit claim to accept responsibility, failed to see what is, from a distance, so obvious. (P. 336)

Sabini and Silver point out that the subject in the obedience experiment and the typical German bureaucrat could readily see themselves as "good" persons, as people trying to do a good job—trying to be a good subject, to help the researcher, to help the Third Reich, to support their families, etc. The evil these people made possible may not have been intended. Often, in fact, the actions were personally abhorrent. It was easy, therefore, for these individuals to feel innocent, to perceive themselves as lacking in responsibility. Yet, Sabini and Silver indicate that the lack of evil intent was not germane to the attribution of responsibility. People are morally responsible for the actions they cause, or help to cause, as long as they are able to see a connection between their behavior and its consequences.

Thus, a person can truthfully say that he or she did not intend to harm a victim but did so because he or she was ordered to do it. This individual may be thinking very clearly on the matter of intent, but is erring in suggesting that the fact of orders being issued absolves one of moral responsibility. Sabini and Silver contend that bureaucracies effectively allow people to *feel* that they are not personally responsible for the end product. As in Gilbert's (1981) analysis, noted in Chapter Two, the authors emphasize the "entrapment" aspect of the obedience paradigm and draw a parallel to the slow, barely perceptible increase in activities ultimately resulting in the Holocaust. This complicates the individual's task of moral decision making, for as easy as it is to say that "a line must be drawn," it is far more difficult to know when and where, precisely, that line should have been drawn—perhaps Hitler will stop persecuting the Jews; perhaps the learner will stop making errors.

The Issue of Brutality

Parallels between the Holocaust and the obedience experiments seem challenged by the zeal and brutality of the Nazi SS which are highlighted in every account of the concentration camps—behaviors which contrast sharply with the anguish and conflict shown by many of Milgram's subjects. At first glance, this discrepancy suggests different psychological processes—internal or personality factors in the personnel operating the concentration camps, as opposed to external or circumstantial pressures in the obedience experiments.

Sabini and Silver do not accept this distinction. They point out that concentration camp personnel often experienced severe distress in carrying out the extermination activities. They quote a number of scholars on this important point (such as, Musmanno, 1961; Steiner, 1967). Kren and Rappoport (1980), in a particularly impressive analysis of the Holocaust, confirm Sabini and Silver's position:

> Many of the killers turned to heavy drinking or drugs or arranged transfers to different units. Others, such as General Nebe's chauffeur, committed suicide; still others, such as SS General von dem Bach-Zelewski, suffered nervous breakdowns requiring hospital treatment. During a tour of the "front," Himmler himself became ill to the point of collapse after watching two hundred Jews being killed at Minsk. One witness to this scene claimed that as a consequence of his experience, Himmler set in motion plans to find new methods of killing which would be less disturbing to the killers. (P. 59)

This is evidence supporting the "normality thesis." The SS, regardless of whether they were rabid anti-Semites prior to their camp actions, were normal in manifesting stress reactions.

The brutality shown by the SS is also viewed by Sabini and Silver as powerfully influenced by the situation of the camp itself. There is evidence that the SS were selected on the basis of *not* having the kind of personality disorders that would lead to uncontrolled violence. In this context, Sabini and Silver present an extended analysis of the prison simulation study of Zimbardo (1973). The major finding here was the intense brutality of the guards and the extreme stress reactions experienced by some of the prisoners—all under a role-playing context in which well-adjusted volunteers had been randomly assigned to guard and prisoner roles. It was necessary to terminate the experiment after six days, far sooner than anticipated.

Zimbardo's experiment differed radically from Milgram's paradigm —it lasted longer and did not involve explicit instructions to inflict harm. A key message in this experiment is, however, very similar to that of Milgram's research: *Certain social conditions, when viewed as legitimizing in their larger purpose, can induce participants to engage in relatively extreme acts of harming.* There was no need to pre-select individuals who would be likely to manifest extreme aggression or hostility—the setting, itself, sufficed. The extermination camps were, conceivably, settings of this nature.

In conclusion Sabini and Silver take an unequivocal position on what I have called the "normality thesis." Their basic analytical strategy is to show that ordinary people performed acts in laboratory contexts that bear highly significant analogous relationships to various scenes of the Holocaust. Their goal is to make the Holocaust more comprehensible. Humankind wants desperately to understand the Holocaust for many reasons, one of these being what may sound like a cliche—that if we do not understand how it happened, there is no reason to think that it could not recur. Sabini and Silver suggest that the Milgram experiments—and related social-psychological research, e.g. by Asch, Sherif, and Zimbardo—provide insights that can make the Holocaust more comprehensible. This is a thesis that cannot be "proven," in a statistical sense, of course. It rests on plausibility, on the subjective sense of informational "gain" or "control" that one experiences in this kind of analysis. The work of Sabini and Silver is, in my view, the best-developed expansion of the "normality thesis." However, it is appropriate to examine the opinions of other scholars, especially those who, unlike Sabini and Silver, are not social psychologists, and who bring different conceptual orientations or backgrounds to this general problem.

Hans Askenasy (1978)

A half-Jewish son of a Frankfurt attorney, Hans Askenasy spent his adolescence under Nazi rule. Later a Marine pilot and recipient of a Ph.D. in clinical psychology from UCLA, Askenasy asks a stark question in the title of his provocative, highly impassioned book—"Are we all Nazis?"

Askenasy describes, in detail, psychological profiles of key Nazi leaders of the SS—Hess, Eichmann, Heydrich, Himmler, and others.

He concludes that these were not monsters in any usual sense of that term:

> All were family men with children . . . they were above all ordinary—banal, in Hannah Arendt's term. And banal were their almost inconceivable crimes, if measured in causal and motivational terms. None of them basically hated their victims. None was sadistic. None psychotic. None insane. None of course was criminal by the laws of his society. None, for that matter, apparently ever personally killed any of their victims. Normal, ordinary men. (P. 34)

This psychodiagnostic impression of the Nazi hierarchy was not to be shared by several other investigators who have also taken a clinical approach to this question, an issue to be discussed later in this chapter. Yet, Askenasy's citations are impressively diverse: Dr. Douglas Kelley, a psychiatrist at the Nuremberg trial; Bruno Bettelheim, a psychiatrist who had been a prisoner in one of the early concentration camps, and Dr. Ella Lingens-Reiner, an former inmate at Auschwitz.

His appraisal of the obedience studies is unreservedly positive:

> Stanley Milgram . . . asked himself a similar question. He designed and carried out a series of experiments concerning man's inhumanity to man. His findings must be among the most important in the history of psychological research. (P. 37)

> From our study of the Nazis we have found that they were essentially normal, ordinary men—as normal and ordinary as those good citizens who walked the streets in New Haven and answered Milgram's advertisements. And so we now know that those Nazis and these Americans—which is to say you and I—for all our superficial differences such as time and place, are, psychologically speaking, interchangeable. (P. 49)

Askenasy thus endorses the "normality thesis." His book is a scathing critique of human nature. Using the Holocaust and the Milgram experiments as a cornerstone, he adopts a radically situationist position—situational forces are vastly more influential than personality factors in terms of accounting for our potential for destructive behavior. Askenasy seems, in fact, to replace what he views as traditional—and naive—conceptions of psychopathology with a doctrine of "social abnormality," resting essentially upon the capacity of human beings to relinquish moral responsibility for the welfare of others under certain circumstances. These circumstances have recurred numerous times and have resulted in the deaths of millions. Askenasy surmises that a nuclear holocaust will be yet another episode, avoidable in principle

but, given the facts of history, likely to happen. Askenasy is pessimistic.

Max Rosenbaum (1983)

Max Rosenbaum, a psychoanalytically oriented clinical psychologist, has edited an important volume entitled *Compliant Behavior*:
Beyond Obedience to Authority. In his own chapter, he features the
linkage between Milgram's research and the Holocaust. Noting the importance of establishing real-world contexts for laboratory findings,
Rosenbaum chooses Arendt's profile of Eichmann:

> The picture Arendt presents of Eichmann, then, is of an individual undis-
> tinguished by either intelligence or imagination, but obedient to figures
> of authority. As such, his behavior bears some striking resemblances to
> that of Milgram's experimental subjects: the abdication of personal re-
> sponsibility, an increased attention to technical and procedural concerns,
> and the acceptance of an authority's definition of the situation—in short,
> the picture of an individual in an agentic state. (P. 36)

Rosenbaum emphasizes that in both the Eichmann case and the
obedience research, the power of a legitimate authority was anticipated
by those lower in the hierarchy, a rationale for the required actions
was provided by the authorities, and there was a sense in which human
institutions (for example science, the state) were presented as transcending the control of individuals.

He concludes with a warning quite similar in its implications to
that of Hans Askenasy:

> Obedience to authority and compliance at the expense of personal eth-
> ics is unique to no one age or nation. It is an issue every society must
> face. We in the United States, chastened by the disclosures of American
> conduct in Southeast Asia—the murder of civilians at My Lai, the secret
> bombing of hamlets, and the disclosure of widespread political sabotage
> and corruption—are finally learning this truth. Anyone concerned with
> personal ethics, social morality, and the very survival of mankind must
> examine these questions anew. (P. 45)

Israel Charny (1982)

Israel Charny, a psychotherapist, is one of a number of recent
scholars of genocide who have adopted the "normality thesis." In re-
counting origins of the Holocaust, he refers to the euthanasia program
—the murdering of the mentally ill, retarded children, and other non-

Jewish undesirables—which is viewed as an important precursor to the "final solution" instituted in 1942. That the euthanasia programs were administered by pediatricians and psychiatrists—people who, presumably, were well educated and compassionate—is one of many examples used by Charny to document his basic theme, that "genociders are not generally distinguishable as 'sicker' than most other people" (p. 10).

Charny views the obedience experiments as a scientific confirmation of his basic formulation. Noting the ethical controversy surrounding Milgram's work, he defends the experiments on the basis of their implications:

> The Milgram experiment is not brutal so much as it forces all of us to realize that someday we must gain control over our violence. In this sense, the assaulting quality of the Milgram experiment is really a valuable attack on the denial and indifference of all of us. Whatever upset follows facing the truth, we must eventually face up to the fact that so many of us are, in fact, available to be genociders or their assistants. (P. 16)

Charny cites a number of other widely cited research programs—the Zimbardo et al. prison study (1973), Rosenhan's (1973) study on pseudo-patients in mental hospitals—to illustrate the dehumanization processes that are readily induced by situations which place normal people into roles of divergent power. Particularly disconcerting is the ease with which people fall into roles that are defined for them by others. If these "others" are malevolent, those operating under their influence become capable of immoral acts, even though these same individuals would never engage in such actions on their own.

In his conclusion, Charny (pp. 340-41) takes a position very similar to that of Hans Askenasy. That is, although we are referring to genocide as within the capability of normal people, what we are actually dealing with is abnormality on the highest level. In effect, the behavior of Milgram's obedient subjects is indeed abnormal:

> Genocidal evil is normal (common) in history and normal (readily available) in our human potential; but it is, by every sane standard, distinctly abnormal (undesirable). I think that seeing genocide as the ultimate expression of a disturbed balance between strength and weakness—an extreme form of pseudostrength that is as psychotic as the maddest form of mental weakness and incompetence—may open the door to a solution to the conceptual dilemma in psychology that we have not known how to call this very abnormal (evil) and antilife act what it really is, profoundly abnormal. (Pp. 340-341)

In the writings of Askenasy, Rosenbaum, and Charny, one observes perhaps the ultimate in terms of generalizations from the obedience research. These authors view Milgram's research as a symptom of moral decay, as an indictment against human nature itself. I have said that each of these analysts adopts the "normality thesis," but they in fact proceed to condemn this form of normality. It is of interest in that although each of these writers is a clinician by professional training, they display an unusually sympathetic attitude toward an intrinsically social-psychological perspective. I suspect that this is attributable, at least in part, to the impact of the obedience experiments.

Henry Dicks (1972)

Henry Dicks, a British psychiatrist, interviewed eight convicted Nazis who had participated directly in the mass extermination of Jews and other victims. His analysis, presented in *Licensed Mass Murder: A Socio-Psychological Study of some SS Killers*, is an integration of psychoanalytic conceptions, cultural observations, and historical perspective. Dicks does not break the issue down simply to a choice between personality and circumstances, but his conclusions seem clearly on the side of the "normality thesis:"

> Two commonly encountered thought-stereotypes about the Nazis will, surely, already have been weakened or eliminated by my interview reports. The first is that these SS killers were "insane" or uncontrollable people, in any generally understood clinical sense. This makes the assessment of their "temporary" systematic, murderous activity all the more baffling and psychologically important. The second widely believed idea—that Hitler's terror and extermination activities were exclusively and narrowly focused on Jews and thus a murderous exaggeration of anti-Semitism alone—is also found to be untenable. (P. 230)

Dicks views the ideology of the Third Reich as insane—the dream of a world of supermen, genetically purified of every imaginable alien trait—but the grip that this ideology was ultimately to have on the millions who became instrumental in the Holocaust was essentially a matter of loyalty and obedience. Dicks presented what may have been the earliest citation, and clear endorsement, of the obedience experiments by a major Holocaust analyst:

> Milgram's subjects, "Like the armchair moralists who would have advocated disobedience in the name of moral principle," knew and felt just as keenly what they *ought* to have done, but could not implement these

values in action and found themselves continuing with the experiment despite inner protest. (P. 261)

Milgram's experiment has neatly exposed the "all too human" propensity to conformity and obedience to group authority, and even managed to measure it in graduated voltage terms. His work has also pointed towards some of the same ego defences subsequently used as justifications by his "ordinary" subjects as my SS men, following their group ethos, employed in their legal defences and as enduring rationalizations. (P. 263)

John Steiner (1980)

John Steiner, a sociologist, interviewed several hundred SS officers. His chapter, which will be viewed by some readers as astonishingly non-judgmental, is highly enthusiastic regarding the obedience experiments. In a section entitled "The imperatives of compliance," Steiner notes:

Although most people seem to be guided by a conscience, this does not necessarily deter them from inflicting pain or participating in cruel acts if these are authorized. . . . This has been demonstrated by members of the SS in death camps, killing units, and the like. More recently the Milgram and Zimbardo studies have shown that otherwise normal individuals will commit cruel acts against innocent persons when authorized to do so. (P. 247)

Steiner cites Dicks' 1972 research, pointing to further parallels between the SS and Milgram's subjects—the devaluation of the victim, the adoption of a "helpless cog" attitude in explaining their behavior.

The methodology of interviewing former SS personnel and drawing conclusions about the psychological processes operative during their experiences in the Holocaust is not without its difficulties. The biases of the interviewer are one obvious source of ambiguity in this respect. Nevertheless, this kind of data must be given at least a fair hearing among the mosaic of information that constitutes efforts to explain the Holocaust. That people like Steiner and Dicks find the Milgram studies meaningful is relevant for understanding the impact of the obedience experiments. One might have thought that the realism of their interview experience might have relegated any laboratory experiment—performed by a non-clinically oriented investigator—to the realm of the trivial or artificial. Instead, both Steiner and Dicks use Milgram's research to add scientific legitimacy to the "normality thesis" they present from a remarkably different data source.

Herbert Kelman (1973)

Herbert Kelman, social psychologist and ethicist, might at first be considered as one of the arch-critics of the obedience research. His anti-deception position and advocacy of role-playing methodologies are in conflict with many aspects of the obedience experiments. Ironically, however, Kelman's own research has been intimately involved with the obedience problem. This concern derives from his influential analyses of violence and genocide.

Kelman's most influential work in this area was published in 1973 in conjunction with his receiving the Kurt Lewin award from the Society for the Psychological Study of Social Issues. Entitled "Violence without moral restraint: Reflections on the dehumanization of victims and victimizers," this article addresses the problem of sanctioned massacres—actions of destruction directed at non-hostile targets within the context of a governmental or military policy. He is speaking, of course, of the Holocaust, but also of the My Lai massacre, the massacre of the Armenians, the purges in the Soviet Union, atrocities in Africa, the atomic bombing of Japan, terrorist activity in Ireland, in the Middle East, and so on.

Kelman believes that genocide occurs, psychologically, because of a "loss of restraint." Because of certain prevailing conditions, the individual experiences a collapse or weakening of normally operative inhibitions. Three key "prevailing conditions" are described: dehumanization, routinization, and authorization. The first of these deals with the perception of the target: because of stereotyping, propaganda, brainwashing, etc., one can reach a point of thinking about another person or a group as less than human. Moral restraints against killing such individuals are then more readily overcome.

The processes of routinization and authorization are more directly linked to the obedience experiments. Routinization involves the individual's adaptation to a role in which the moral ramifications of one's duty or task are effectively bypassed. Many commentators have noted this feature in the obedience paradigm. Authorization, of primary concern to this discussion, involves the loss of a crucial restraint, namely a sense of personal responsibility:

> Behaviorally, authorization obviates the necessity of making judgments or choices. Not only do normal moral principles become inoperative, but—particularly when the actions are explicitly ordered—a different kind of morality, linked to the duty to obey superior orders, tends to take over. (P. 39)

Kelman's analysis is a pronounced endorsement of the "normality thesis"—anyone could, in principle, experience a loss of restraint and, as a result, be capable of unimagined atrocities. To prevent sanctioned massacres, Kelman suggests that we must question the normalization and legitimization of violence and the sanctioned definition of victim categories, such as, "It's ok to bomb the Vietnamese." For our purposes, however, his most compelling recommendation deals with obedience:

> The relationship of wide segments of the population to political authorities is governed by unquestioning obedience and by ideologies that support it. This habit is built into the structure of authority situations more generally, even in nonpolitical contexts, as Milgram's . . . provocative experiments have demonstrated. To counteract this habit, it will be necessary to create the conditions for developing a sense of personal agency in wide segments of the society. . . . As more people develop a sense of personal agency, they will acquire the capacity to take personal responsibility for their actions even when these are ordered by superior authorities. (P. 52)

Writing during the agonizing closing phases of the Vietnam War, Kelman points repeatedly to what he views as moral atrocities committed by the United States in this conflict, such as the My Lai massacre. Kelman's perspective was undoubtedly shaped by his having emigrated from Nazi Germany and having lost relatives and friends in the Holocaust.

Kelman and Lawrence (1972) surveyed public opinion regarding the trial and conviction of Lieutenant William Calley, who was accused of ordering the massacre at My Lai. A major finding was the large number of people who endorsed the prospect of their own obedience to a command to shoot villagers.[3] Kelman and Lawrence saw distinct parallels to the obedience experiments:

> The relevance of Milgram's paradigm to the Calley case (and vice versa) is apparent from his statement of the general question to which his research is addressed: "How does a man behave when he is told by a legitimate authority to act against a third individual?" . . . The key to people's reaction to the authority situation in the Milgram experiment as well as in My Lai seems to be the allocation of responsibility. (P. 178)

Recognizing that their survey was essentially a record of attitudes and perceptions of individuals, not behaviors per se, Kelman and Lawrence were dismayed at what they viewed to be a pervasive mindset toward obeying authorities in morally unacceptable contexts.[4] They were encouraged by exceptions to the rule:

> In the Milgram experiments not all of the subjects remained submissive
> to the experimenter; at My Lai not all of the men followed Calley's
> orders to shoot the captured civilians. Those who resist in these situa-
> tions have somehow managed to maintain the framework of personal
> causation that applies in "normal" situations. Perhaps they have never
> made the radical shift in perception of the situation described by Mil-
> gram. (P. 181)

In a related investigation, Cockerham and Cohen (1980) concluded after surveying 672 United States Army paratroopers that
"there is enough ambiguity and disagreement among American soldiers
on the matter of compliance to immoral and illegal orders in combat,
that it remains quite possible for an incident such as My Lai to occur
again" (p. 1272). (In this context, see also Shalala, 1974).

In using the obedience experiments to illuminate the findings of
their survey research, Kelman and Lawrence exhibit yet another manifestation of the relevance of Milgram's research to the problem of
genocide.

Barrington Moore (1978)

Barrington Moore, a political scientist, discusses the obedience research in his influential book *Injustice: The Social Bases of Obedience
and Revolt*. His primary interest is in disobedience. For example, he
cites Milgram's extended portrait of Gretchen Brandt (1974, pp. 84-
85) who had grown up in Nazi Germany and was one of the disobedient subjects in Experiment 8. He elaborates on the significance of
"rebellious peers" variation (Experiment 17):

> Pure moral autonomy in the form of lone resistance to an apparently
> benign authority is very rare. With support from peers, on the other
> hand, the same kind of resistance increases enormously. These facts cor-
> respond to what it is possible to observe in the real world and shed much
> light on why it happens. (P. 97)

Moore characterizes the basic paradigm as one in which the subject enters a benign setting (a scientific study), assured that the shocks
will do no permanent damage. He does not, however, minimize the
significance of the research, as do Orne and Holland. Rather, he views
the situation as one in which it is very difficult to disobey, "The more
one thinks about the situation with the very unfair advantage of hindsight, the more surprising it becomes that disobedience did occur at
all, and even more that it occurred on such a large scale. Evidently
empathy under the right conditions can break through some very
powerful obstacles" (p. 98).

Moore suggests that it may be a misreading of Milgram's basic contribution to assume that human beings have an inherent tendency to obey authority. If one focuses on the conditions that reduced obedience—close proximity to the learner, observation of rebellious peers—this "inherent tendency" is not in evidence. In stressing the situational variability of Milgram's data, Moore is voicing one of Milgram's own points of emphasis, and he is one of very few commentators to have done so.

Moore's analysis may best be regarded as a confirmation of Milgram's theoretical perspective, an issue to be reviewed in the next chapter. He does not speak directly to the issue of genocide or of the Holocaust. Rather, he presents a scholarly treatise on the more general problem of personal freedom. The obedience experiments are instructive, in Moore's view, because they:

> Indicate that there are just about as many ways to dissolve an oppressive social atmosphere that stifles moral autonomy as there are ways to create such an atmosphere. Purely human capacities and their technical manipulation appear to be about neutral. The obstacles to moral autonomy come rather from the fact that the opportunities to control this atmosphere are unequally distributed in hierarchically organized societies. (P. 100)

Moore's perspective, quite different from others reviewed in this chapter, demonstrates the impact of the obedience experiments in terms of conceptions of political status and power.

Jerome Frank (1982)

It is, for many, impossible to think of the Holocaust without ultimately considering the prospect of nuclear war. Indeed, the term "holocaust" in contemporary life is primarily used with the adjective "nuclear" preceding it. In an analysis of the bureaucratic features of the North American Aerospace Defense Command (NORAD), specifically the complex decision-making structure involved in responding to a nuclear attack, Daniel Ford (1985) has pointed to the role of obedience to authority:

> How well the NORAD staff and the civilian decision-makers are prepared to respond to the confusion and appalling uncertainty that may accompany an actual or apparent attack is difficult to determine. "Our people don't shock very easy, because they are so trained and disciplined on the crews—they have certain steps that they must perform, and they don't sit around and think about how many babies are going to die if they do something wrong," General Wagoner said. "They might do that

at a coffee break, but when they're back sitting at the consoles and an event happens, it is just like an orchestra when the conductor says 'Go' —they all have their individual acts to perform." (P. 78)

Jerome Frank, the psychiatrist and anti-nuclear activist, makes explicit reference to the obedience experiments in his book *Sanity and Survival in the Nuclear Age* (1982). His focus is a familiar one, namely the crucial dynamic involved in a person's willingness to allocate responsibility to a higher authority. Frank's conclusions are strikingly similar to Ford's description of the decision-making process at NORAD:

> Nuclear weapons are fired by a team against distant victims. The experiments suggest these conditions should elicit ready obedience, so it is not surprising that when the commander of a Polaris submarine was asked how it felt to be the man whose act could unleash the submarine's destructive power, he replied: "I've never given it any thought. But, if we ever have to hit, we'll hit. And there won't be a second's hesitation." (P. 84)

Serge Moscovici (1985)

Serge Moscovici, the eminent French social psychologist, has written the chapter on "Social Influence and Conformity" for the revised *Handbook of Social Psychology* (Aronson, Brewer, and Carlsmith, 1985). On substantive grounds, Moscovici is unequivocal in praising the experiments. Using such terms as "famous," "elegant," and "impressive" to describe Milgram's research, Moscovici interprets the experiments as extremely pertinent to the issue of genocide. In this context, he makes an interesting contrast between the obedience research and the experiments of Latané and Darley (1970) dealing with altruism:

> The most up-to-date and impressive investigation of obedience is presented in Milgram's famous experiments. In their research on bystanders, Latané and Darley (1970) have opened up the investigation of apathy. I might illustrate the contrast between these two sets of studies by an analogy drawn from a historical event some of us have experienced personally: the holocaust. Milgram raises and tries to answer the following question: How could German soldiers and officers agree without protest to commit actions that are so contrary to morality and human rights? Conversely, Latané and Darley attempt to elucidate the following question: How can people stand by passively without reacting to a situation that is detrimental to them or to someone else? (P. 383)

Moscovici's personal involvement with the Holocaust lends a special poignance to his conviction regarding the significance of Milgram's findings. His pronouncement on the ethics of the obedience experiments is found in this short, but very impassioned statement:

> Milgram's experiments have aroused a flood of virtuous protests and insinuations on ethical grounds, and the Pontius Pilates are well represented among us. Unfortunately, they present us with the mirror of a truth about our social nature that we are loathe to face squarely and that only those who have known the horrors of war and the horrors of peace in concentration camps find trifling. (P. 378)

Social Psychology Texts and the Generalizability of the Obedience Experiments

The obedience research has, as its home base, the discipline of social psychology. It is reasonable to ask how this field has treated the purported linkage between the obedience experiments and real-world events of genocide and destructiveness. One index of this treatment is the reception given to Milgram's experiments in textbooks. The following excerpts illustrate a consensus of opinion:

> To say that the results obtained by Milgram ... are disturbing is a gross understatement. The parallels between the behavior of subjects in these studies of obedience and atrocities directed against civilians during time of war are too clear to require further comment. (Baron and Byrne, 1984, p. 276)

> It is tempting to presume that Eichmann and the Auschwitz camp commanders were uncivilized monsters. But after a hard day's work, the Auschwitz commanders would relax, listening to Beethoven and Schubert. Eichmann himself has been described as bland, outwardly indistinguishable from common people with ordinary jobs (Arendt, 1963). And so it was in the obedience research. Milgram's conclusion makes it harder to attribute the Holocaust to unique character traits in the German people. (Myers, 1983, p. 240)

> Although the most common examples of blind faith in following orders occur in emergency or wartime situations, there is nowhere a more striking and, we think, more terrifying example of how blindly people follow orders than in the demonstrations of Stanley Milgram. (Worchel and Cooper, 1983, p. 446-447)

> When thousands of Germans obeyed orders to send Jews to the gas chambers, were they simply acting in the way people normally act? Or was this behavior an example of some pathology in their own individual personalities, or in the German people as a whole? Stanley Milgram

(1963) believed that their actions reflected a normal human tendency to obey the orders of legitimate authorities, even when it means hurting innocent people. (Sears, Freedman, and Peplau, 1985, p. 42)

How much they apply to real-life situations has been questioned (Baumrind, 1964), but parallels to real-life incidents of extreme obedience, such as the massacre of civilians at My Lai during the Vietnam War by American soldiers and the unquestioning acceptance of poison by members of Jim Jones' cult at Jonestown are unmistakable. (Baum, Fisher, and Singer, 1985, p. 310)

In real-world situations where prods or similar devices are used to keep people at tasks that are personally abhorrent, Milgram's findings may well be applicable. (Deaux and Wrightsman, 1984, p. 318)

Citations similar to the above are to be found in numerous other texts in social psychology, as well as in books dealing specifically with social influence (e.g., Cialdini, 1985; Wheeler, et al., 1978).

I have described in this section a number of reactions to Milgram's research dealing specifically with the generalizations which have been made to the Holocaust and other manifestations of genocide and social destructiveness. Numerous additional sources could have been included—the analyses of Helen Fein (1979) on genocide; of Drekmeier (1971), Hampden-Turner (1971), and Sanford and Comstock (1971) on the atrocities in Vietnam; of Neal Osherow (1984) and Hugo Zee (1983) on the events at Jonestown, Guyana. Textbooks in introductory psychology and sociology almost invariably give relatively extensive coverage to the obedience experiments and draw inferences regarding their significance similar to those reviewed here.

In scanning the diverse coverage of the obedience research, I have occasionally found, in addition to relatively extensive treatments of the kind referred to in this chapter, brief comments made in passing, for example, the view of Herbert Simon, the Nobel laureate. In reviewing the progress of behavioral and social sciences for the journal *Science*, Simon makes this reference to Milgram's research:

I must register my personal view that we learned more than enough about human psychology (that is, about ourselves) from these experiments to justify the possible (and largely conjectural) damage, in the form of guilt feelings, that might have been inflicted on the subjects who obeyed the experimenter's instructions. We learned, for example, that events like the Holocaust are explainable without attributing to the German culture any psychological characteristics that are not widely shared by other cultures, including our own. (1980, p. 73)

We have seen, to this point, a remarkable consensus regarding the generalizability of the obedience experiments. Clearly they are viewed by many commentators from a diversity of disciplines and orientations as convincing and meaningful to an understanding of the Holocaust, and of other instances of what is often referred to as "social evil."

It is appropriate to note in this context a recent analysis by Robert Jay Lifton (1985) of Josef Mengele, the infamous Nazi doctor of Auschwitz. Although he does not deal specifically with the obedience research, Lifton makes several observations relevant to the normality thesis. First, people like Mengele who attained positions of true authority in the death-camp industry of the Third Reich were probably *not* normal or average from a psychiatric point of view. Lifton concludes that Mengele was schizoid in his basic personality and that he had delusions of omnipotence and was capable of genuinely sadistic behavior. However, Lifton also argues that Auschwitz provided a unique setting in which Mengele could express these character deficiencies; had there been no Auschwitz or Holocaust, Mengele may very well have led a relatively unremarkable life as a physician:

> Mengele possessed unusually intense destructive potential, but there were no apparent signs of aberrant behavior prior to the Nazis and Auschwitz. Without Auschwitz, he would probably have kept his destructive potential under control. As a wise former inmate physician told me, "In ordinary times, Mengele could have been a slightly sadistic German professor." It was the coming together of the man and the place, the "fit" between the two, that created the Auschwitz Mengele. (P. 16)

This is an instructive refinement or expansion of the normality thesis. Lifton is suggesting that the extraordinary environment of a place like Auschwitz activated a form of psychopathology that, in other contexts, may well have remained relatively dormant.

Lifton contributes another insight concerning the nature of evil. Endorsing Hannah Arendt's thesis on Eichmann, Lifton raises, in my view, an extremely important point:

> Hannah Arendt gave currency to a concept of the banality of evil in her portrayal of Adolf Eichmann as a rather unremarkable bureaucrat who killed by meeting schedules and quotas. She is surely correct in her claim that an ordinary person is capable of extreme evil. But over the course of committing evil acts, an ordinary person becomes something different. In a process I call "doubling," a new self takes shape that adapts to the evil environment, and the evil acts become part of that self. At this point, the person and his behavior are anything but banal. (P. 16)

The normality thesis, as discussed in this book, focuses upon the personality of an individual who commits acts of destructive obedience. However, it is not inconsistent with this thesis to say that a person may be quite normal or typical in the *beginning phase* of a scenario of destructive obedience, only to develop ultimately a personality which bears the scars of his actions. Lifton's point, that a person's behavior can alter his personality—his attitudes, his perceptions of others and of himself—is both reasonable and consistent with a considerable amount of psychological research. The forms of behavior pathology observed in Zimbardo's prison-simulation study, noted earlier in this section, are, in an experimental context, illustrative of the kind of changes to which Lifton is referring.

We will be concerned, at the close of this chapter, with the question of why so many analysts of the kind cited here have championed the "normality thesis." It is appropriate at this point, however, to consider the other side of this issue—perspectives which argue *against* generalizations based on the obedience experiments and, in particular, against the "normality thesis."

AGAINST GENERALIZING TO THE HOLOCAUST

There are a number of reasons for arguing *against* the kind of strong interpretations noted above regarding the implications of Milgram's research. All of the arguments against the methodological validity of the paradigm are pertinent to this issue—for example, Baumrind's (1964) argument concerning the high base line of obedience one might expect to occur in a laboratory (see Chapter Five) and Orne and Holland's position concerning subjects' presumptions about the intrinsic safety of the laboratory context (see Chapter Six). Rather than simply repeat the views of those with ethical and methodological reservations, however, it would be more informative to consider positions that argue for a *different thesis* regarding the cause of the Holocaust. The most clearly developed line of reasoning is that of the political scientist Michael Selzer and his colleague Florence Miale, a clinical psychologist.

Miale and Selzer (1975): *The Nuremberg Mind*

In their book *The Nuremberg Mind: The Psychology of the Nazi Leaders* (1975), Miale and Selzer present a different view of the obedience problem from those we have considered previously. Their book presents the Rorschach test responses of 16 major Nazi officials—

Hermann Goering, Rudolf Hess, Alfred Rosenberg, Albert Speer, among others. Included in an appendix is the Rorschach test protocol of Adolf Eichmann. The tests were administered by G. Gilbert, an American German-speaking clinical psychologist who had gained access to the prison staff at Nuremberg in 1945, prior to the trials. According to Gilbert, who wrote a forward for this volume, he had continuous and unrestricted interaction with all of the prisoners. A psychiatrist, Douglas Kelley, was also involved in the Rorschach testing.

Miale and Selzer ask, in their opening chapter, these questions: "Were *all* the Nazi leaders, then, normal people? Or were only some of them relatively normal, while others were psychotic or psychopathic? Or, finally, could it be that none of them resembled what might reasonably be considered as a normal personality?" (Pp. 14-15).

After more than two hundred pages of detailed Rorschach interpretation, they conclude, "The answer can be stated briefly and decisively. The Nazis were not psychologically normal or healthy individuals" (p. 287).

Miale and Selzer state that as a group the Nuremberg War Criminals (NWC) were characterized by depression, violence, a concern with status, and a rejection of responsibility. The major diagnostic category was psychopathy: "The term 'psychopath' generally refers to people who engage in antisocial activity with apparent absence of guilt, and who seem capable of no real feeling for, or loyalty to, other human beings, and no real commitment to principles or ideals" (p. 278).

How do Miale and Selzer respond to the obedience experiments? First, they comment on the implications of Milgram's own conclusions:

> Eichmann and his fellows, then, were right; and so is Hannah Arendt. The most vicious act in human history is not to be explained by the viciousness of the human beings who perpetrated it. Rather, the largest slaughter of human beings in history is to be accounted for by a mechanism that has its origins in the human struggle for survival. Obedience rather than aggression is what made the ghastly tragedy possible. Moreover, under the conditions which prevailed in Nazi Germany, any of us decent normal people could have behaved as the most bestial Nazi did. This, at least, is what Milgram would have us believe. But are the conclusions which he draws from the results of his experiments warranted? (P. 10)

Miale and Selzer answer their question with an unqualified "no." Their strategy is to emphasize *individual differences*, personality factors which differentiated obedient from defiant subjects. They select a passage from Milgram's theoretical analysis (to be reviewed in Chap-

ter Eight), which is important for their thesis: "Residues of selfhood
. . . keep personal values alive in the subject and lead to strain which,
if sufficiently powerful, can result in disobedience" (Milgram, 1974,
p. 155—Cited in Miale and Selzer, p. 10).

For Miale and Selzer, then, obedient subjects are those who have,
in Milgram's language, failed to keep their personal values alive. But
they extend this line of reasoning:

> It could be argued that the disobedient subjects did not merely keep
> their personal values alive, as Milgram suggests, but that *they actually
> had different values to start with.* . . . Is it not possible that the disobe-
> dient subjects disobeyed because they were more moral, more averse to
> inflicting pain on other human beings, than the obedient subjects? (P. 10)

This is an important question. There clearly *are* individual differences in many of Milgram's variations, as noted in Chapters One and
Three, and these have never been clearly explained. It is possible that
people do in fact differ in their moral development—Miale and Selzer
cite Kohlberg's data on this issue (which will be examined in Chapter
Eight)—and, as a result, are more or less able to defy the experimenter.

But how do Miale and Selzer deal with the *situational* dimension
of obedience? For example, in Experiment 11, where the subject
selected the intensity of shock to be administered, the results indicated extremely low levels of punishment. Milgram interpreted this
finding as revealing the true influence of the experimenter's commands in the other variations. When these commands were absent, the
subject did not shock the learner, implying that when the subject did
shock the learner, it was *because* of the commands.

Miale and Selzer assume, however, that obedient subjects were
more aggressive and violent by nature. The authoritative commands of
the experimenter, in their view, gave license to these particular individuals to vent their aggressive drives. Why, then, did not the aggres-
sive-prone individuals involved in Experiment 11 harm the learner?
According to these authors, without the releasing or sanctioning influence of the authority, "the potential obedient's aggressive drives
are once again brought under the control of the superego, with the
result that he behaves in much the same way as the potential disobedient" (p. 11).

Thus, for Miale and Selzer, it is never an issue of obedience per se.
Rather, the experimenter's commands legitimize the expression of
acts that the aggressive *type* of individual is motivated to display.
Presumably if the act is not overtly displayed, the individual is sup-

pressing the urge on the basis of various perceived fears or anxieties. Miale and Selzer account for the intense expressions of tension and arousal in similarly intrapsychic terms, again resorting to essentially psychoanalytic doctrine. The tension reflects a conflict *not* between the subject's humane feelings and the experimenter's ruthless demands, but rather between the subject's aggressive impulses and his or her own superego-driven restraints on their behavioral realization.

Miale and Selzer defend their view of Milgram's findings in this manner:

> The social lesson to be learned from this is not that in a wicked world decent people will act in a wicked way but that in a wicked world people with a penchant for wickedness will freely indulge it, justifying themselves (when called upon to do so) on the ground that they were merely obeying orders. (P. 11)

To this point, Miale and Selzer do not explicitly deny the generality of Milgram's results. They are offering an alternative *interpretation* of the behaviors observed in his laboratory. They note, in this regard, that Milgram's failure to obtain pre-experimental measures on his subjects' moral development prevents an assessment of the validity of his situational hypothesis.

Miale and Selzer then proceed to a more direct challenge to the generalizability of the obedience paradigm. They view Milgram's use of a "mild and likable middle-aged man" as the victim—or learner—as totally inappropriate, given the nature of the real victims of the Holocaust—people who had been vilified as "sinister, dangerous, hateful, and altogether less than human" (p. 12). Miale and Selzer argue that the use of a likable peer as victim biased the results in favor of Milgram's interpretation. That is, because no one would have personal reasons to aggress against such an innocent person, the fact that they do so suggests that their behavior is to be construed as obedience (after all). This argument seems completely inconsistent with their previous intrapsychic aggression formulation. Here they appear to be agreeing that Milgram was studying obedience, but because of the nature of his "victim," it was completely devoid of significant generality to the Holocaust:

> For his experiments to have approximated conditions in Nazi Germany, Milgram would have had to have had members of, shall we say, the Ku Klux Klan as teachers and a black person as learner. He did not do so, of course, and we must conclude, therefore, that his experiments are almost as irrelevant to an understanding of the Nazi phenomenon in

Germany as his interpretation of the results of those experiments is in-
conclusive. (P. 13)

Miale and Selzer conclude their discussion of Milgram's research
by associating it with the banality-of-evil position of Arendt and the
view of Douglas Kelley,[5] a psychiatrist who had a major role in anal-
yzing the NWCs but did not adopt a "psychopathology thesis" regarding the causes of their behaviors. All of these contributions are, in
their view, untenable.

Selzer, in an article published in the *New York Times Magazine*
(1977), also defends the "psychopathology thesis" regarding the behavior of the Nazis in the Holocaust. In this instance, the issue involves psychiatric interpretations of drawings made by Adolf Eichmann prior to his trial in Jerusalem in 1960 (he was subsequently
hanged). The title of the article reveals Selzer's position—"The Murderous Mind." The drawings—the House-Tree-Person and Bender-
Gestalt tests—are, in his view, of significance in contributing to the
debate "over one of the most profound questions raised by the Holocaust" (p. 36), whether the Nazi officials were intrinsically evil or,
rather, normal individuals caught in an evil situation.

Selzer obtained psychiatric interpretations that testified to Eichmann's psychopathology: "In the view of five psychologists who
analyzed Eichmann's drawings without knowing they were his work,
the sketches reveal a man who was "sadistic and violent in his hostility," "cut off from his own feelings and fantasies," anxious for approval, and probably paranoid" (p. 36).

Taking a position similar to that of Miale and Selzer's 1975 book,
Selzer criticizes the obedience experiments on numerous grounds—
that Milgram ignores personality factors, that in his focus on behavior
Milgram is unable to explain what kind of people his subjects were,
or why they behaved as they did. Raising a hypothetical scenario involving Milgram's paradigm, Selzer asks his reader to imagine that a
group of murderers and rapists had participated in the role of "teacher." Would they have disobeyed the experimenter, as they had disobeyed the rules of society (presumably because of their social-patho-
logical personalities), and thus have treated the learner with compassion? Or would they have taken advantage of the situation and inflicted
the most severe shocks? Selzer surmises that Milgram would have predicted disobedience:

> We may infer from Milgram's argument that such people, habitually
> disobedient, would not have given the helpless victim severe electric

shocks. To me it seems more plausible, however, to believe they would have seized this opportunity to indulge their proclivities for violence and would gleefully have given what they thought were fatal jolts. (P. 136)

I should point out that while I agree that the murderers would be likely to obey the experimenter and shock the victim, I cannot find, as Selzer suggests, any clear rationale stated by Milgram for predicting defiance because of the "habitual disobedience" of such individuals. It is worth repeating perhaps that the "normality thesis" does not preclude the possibility that certain types of individuals may be more likely than others to engage in destructive obedience or, in fact, to obtain enjoyment from such activities. Furthermore, the "normality thesis" does not deny that there are evil people.

Selzer's conclusion is perhaps the most succinct expression of what I have termed the "psychopathology thesis:"

> The gathering chaos of German life after World War I provided a handful of psychopaths with the opportunity to rally to their banner a large proportion of the psychopathic population of Germany. It was from among these people that Hitler recruited the men and women who devised and implemented the enormities perpetrated by the Third Reich (P. 140)

A further illustration of Selzer's position (1983) is found in his interview with Albert Speer, a high-ranking member of Hitler's inner circle who had spent 20 years in prison following the Nuremberg trials. Although Speer has been often portrayed as one of the most lucid and non-defensive of the Nazi hierarchy in terms of not manifesting the "I was following orders" rationale, Selzer's interpretation of Speer is virtually one of complete pathology. He challenges, for example, Speer's rather positive public image: "Speer was not activated by any authentic moral anguish but merely by the pretense of remorse which —in part because of the crudity of his moral reasoning—he believed was genuine" (p. 225).

The position taken by Miale and Selzer (1975) (also Selzer, 1973, 1983) represents a particularly extreme statement of the "psychopathology thesis." Before commenting on several issues raised in their analyses, I wish simply to point out that their thesis is one with intuitive appeal for many people. We saw in Chapter Two that there is a pervasive bias toward attributing undesirable personality characteristics to people who obey orders to harm others, particularly when the person doing the attributing would not, in his or her own mind, be capable of such actions. Most people think of the Nazi SS in terms that portray them as vicious, sadistic, and pathological. Few indeed would agree with Kren and Rappoport's assertion that "the overwhelming majority of SS men, leaders as well as rank and file, would have easily passed all the psychiatric tests ordinarily given to American army recruits or Kansas City policemen" (1980, p. 70). Certainly Miale and Selzer would not endorse such a position.

In terms of their criticism of Milgram's experiments, I have reservations. Their initial point about the importance of personality factors is well taken. We really do not have a solid basis to account for the individual differences in obedience which are an important feature of Milgram's results. Also, their argument concerning the "likable" victim is uncontested. Milgram did not use a member of a victimized or stereotyped category as the learner, and as Miale and Selzer (and Baumrind as well) note, this differentiates his paradigm from the reality of Nazi Germany. Milgram (1961b, p. 488) in fact intended to investigate this issue—what he termed "propaganda concerning the victim"—but he did not obtain data pertinent to this significant question.

My own view, noted in Chapter Six, is that Milgram's paradigm does not suffer, in principle, in lacking one or more specific features that comprised the authentic nature of the Holocaust. *If* one agrees that he succeeded in investigating destructive obedience with an admittedly likable peer of the teacher as victim, two conclusions seem warranted. One is that this kind of obedience would have been even more pronounced had the victim been dehumanized (see Bandura, et al., 1975). The second point is the realization that it is not necessary to have a dehumanized victim in order to demonstrate destructive obedience to authority.

The most glaring weakness of Miale and Selzer's analysis is that they virtually ignore the *programmatic* nature of Milgram's experiments—the 18 variations and the powerful impact of these different scenarios on the behavior of his subjects. It seems to me impossible to maintain an individual-difference or personality formulation, which is the heart of their position, as an account of the different behaviors Milgram observed *across conditions*. Assuming that each variation involved approximately the same representation or sampling of personality types, it seems implausible to maintain that personality factors explain the findings in the different experimental settings. Milgram's perspective—and that of most social psychologists and many other social scientists as well—is that most individuals have within them a relatively wide repertoire of potential behaviors, which in certain conditions might yield acts of great altruism and benevolence but, in other circumstances, acts of brutality and evil. Thus, were Joe Smith assigned to Experiment 18, the probability is extremely high that he would have been a non-intervening bystander to another peer shocking the learner to 450 volts, while if he had been assigned to Experiment 17, the probability is equally high that he would have defied the experimenter at a relatively early stage in the shock sequence. I believe this to be one of Milgram's major arguments, and I do not see that Miale and Selzer come to terms with it.

The interpretation given by Miale and Selzer to the available psychiatric test data obtained from the Nazi hierarchy has also not gone unchallenged (e.g., Rychlak, 1977). Molly Harrower (1976b) reports an intriguing historical perspective on this issue. She notes that in 1947, 10 Rorschach experts were sent copies of the Nazi Rorschach records and asked to comment on them:

> Although all of us agreed to respond, not one of us followed through. I was vice chairman of the committee that initiated this project, so my own failure to participate was particularly puzzling to me. Over the years, I have come to believe that our reason for not commenting on the test results was that they did not show what we expected to see, and what the pressure of public opinion demanded that we see—that these men were demented creatures, as different from normal people as a scorpion is different from a puppy. What we saw was a wide range of personalities, from severely disturbed neurotics to the superbly well-adjusted. But only Douglas Kelley, the Nuremberg psychiatrist who interviewed the Nazis, said aloud in 1946 "that such personalities are not unique or insane (and) could be duplicated in any country of the world today." (P. 76)

Harrower includes a short reference to the obedience experiments: "Recent studies by psychologist Stanley Milgram of the City University of New York come closer to showing how readily people can be induced to commit acts against an innocent individual" (p. 76).

Richard Rubenstein (1976), a rabbi and theologian, is highly critical of Miale and Selzer's approach as well as their conclusions. He argues that because Miale and Selzer knew the Rorschach tests were obtained from Nazi officials, this created an inevitable source of interpretive bias. Rubenstein notes that the dedication in Miale and Selzer's book—"To the victims living and dead"—implied a revenge motive that also clouded their analytic contribution:

One must further ask whether bookish vengeance disguised as psychological research is an appropriate memorial to the victims. It is tempting to portray the Nazis as demons or perverts, for such a view protects our illusions about ourselves. To see the Nazis as more or less ordinary men is neither to excuse their deeds nor minimize the threat they pose. On the contrary, it is to recognize how fragile are the bonds of civility and decency that keep any kind of human community from utter collapse. (P. 84)

Like Harrower, Rubenstein includes in his critique an emphatic endorsement of Milgram's research and its implications regarding the "normality thesis."

The most sophisticated review of the research in this area has been conducted by two clinical psychologists, Gerald Borofsky and Don Brand (1980). They find no fault, in principle, with the Rorschach interpretations. However, they have a number of reservations regarding methodology. They note, for example, that the NWCs were not in fact a representative sample of Nazis, but were unusually successful, high-level administrators. The Rorschach records of many lower-level Nazis—which are in fact available—would have constituted a more instructive sample. Borofsky and Brand are unusually sensitive in their critique. Expressing sympathy and admiration for those who have engaged in this research effort, they note the extraordinary methodological obstacles to such inquiry, as well as the emotional stress involved in the entire subject matter. Their conclusions, however, are important to note:

When the scientific method is applied to studying the psychological functioning of the NWCs, the results to date are such that no major differences between the psychological functioning of the NWCs and the psychological functioning of other comparison groups have yet been demonstrated. (P. 398)

Borofsky and Brand note the "normality thesis" implied in the position of Hannah Arendt and the obedience experiments. They do not explicitly praise or criticize the obedience research, but suggest that part of the controversy stemming from the work of both Arendt and Milgram was that neither built a scientific argument based on data obtained directly from NWCs or other Nazis. From a clinical perspective, therefore, they seem to imply that the Rorschach information would, in terms of dealing *directly* with the perpetrators of the Holocaust, be superior to the obedience experiments. Their major thesis is that despite the understandable and irresistible temptation for people

—behavioral scientists among them—to invest the Nazis with psycho-pathology, the scientific credibility of such a presumption must be firmly established:

> In the face of such limited understanding about such psychologically and humanly important issues, it is a characteristic human reaction to become anxious and disquieted. In the face of such disquietude, it is a predictably human reaction to attempt to reduce our dysphoria by "ex-plaining" that the Nuremberg War Criminals were vicious psychopaths or psychotic killers, and therefore were irreconcilably different from us. Such "explanations" may temporarily reduce our anxieties regard-ing the extent of our ignorance, however, they open the door to dogma-tic and absolute views—views that are not testable by the scientific meth-od with its capacity for making an empirical, if undramatic, test of real-ity. (P. 401)

Methodologically Based Criticisms

The "psychopathology thesis," as we have seen, presents a rather distinct alternative to Milgram's conception of destructive obedience. Those holding to such a position deny the explanatory value—that is, the generalizability—of the obedience experiments because it is rela-tively certain that few, if any, of Milgram's subjects were seriously disturbed in terms of their basic mental functioning. From this per-spective, Milgram may well have been investigating obedience—even harmful obedience—but it was an intrinsically *different kind* of obe-dience than that which was instrumental in the execution of the Holo-caust (and presumably other instances of genocide and atrocities), specifically in that *different kinds of people* were obeying the orders.

Another basis for criticizing the generalizability of the obedience research to the Holocaust is to focus on the paradigm itself, to ques-tion whether Milgram was, in fact, investigating destructive obedience to authority. This, of course, was the essence of Orne and Holland's position, described in Chapter Six. Several commentators have voiced reservations about the significance of the obedience experiments, large-ly in terms of the kinds of issues raised by Orne and Holland.

Erich Fromm (1973)

In his influential book *The Anatomy of Human Destructiveness*, Erich Fromm presents a somewhat ambivalent view of the obedience experiments. He is impressed by the technical accomplishment as well as, I think, the sheer impact of Milgram's research. However, Fromm is skeptical of generalizing to the Holocaust or the My Lai massacre:

I do not think this experiment permits any conclusion with regard to most situations in real life. The psychologist was not only an authority to whom one owes obedience, but a representative of *Science* and one of the most prestigious institutions of higher education in the United States. Considering that science is widely regarded as the highest value in contemporary industrial society, it is very difficult for the average person to believe that what science commands could be wrong or immoral. If the Lord had not told Abraham not to kill his son, Abraham would have done it, like millions of parents who practiced child sacrifice in history. For the believer, neither God nor his modern equivalent, Science, can command anything that is wrong. (P. 74)

Fromm's perspective is thus essentially comparable to that of Orne and Holland. Although we have had reason to question the validity of this line of reasoning (see Chapter Six), Fromm's articulation of the argument is, I think, interesting and thought-provoking.

Fromm is, however, particularly interested in the extreme discomfort displayed by many of Milgram's subjects. He attaches considerable significance to this evidence of emotional conflict, suggesting that symptoms of anxiety and tension indicated that the subjects were not sadistic or cruel in terms of their basic personality. Curiously he seems to imply that this kind of psychological pain or guilt reduces the significance of the subjects' behavior. Fromm indicates that he would have welcomed more precise data from Milgram concerning the frequencies of subjects who did or did not express severe emotional distress and the behaviors associated with these levels of emotionality. He appears skeptical of Milgram's presumption that the subjects were inherently benevolent toward the learner:

Have we learned "not to harm other people?" That may be what children are told in Sunday school. In the realistic school of life, however, they learn that they must seek their own advantage even if other people are harmed. It seems that on this score the conflict is not as sharp as Milgram assumes. (P. 75)

Although expressing, somewhat hesitantly, an appreciation for the efforts of social psychologists to engage in rigorous experimental research, Fromm's basic allegiance is clearly to the study of more patently realistic phenomena. He characterizes the laboratory context as inherently fictional and infused with pressures, on subjects, to comply with the researcher's definitions or purpose.

Steven Patten (1977b)

Steven Patten, an English philosopher, has written two major analyses of the obedience research. His ethical criticism (1977a) was outlined in Chapter Five. He has also written a methodological criticism (1977b). As an essential endorsement of Orne and Holland's position, Patten's views would have been appropriately cited in Chapter Six. However, he makes a number of observations specifically regarding the generalization of Milgram's findings to the Holocaust, and I have chosen to present his views in the present discussion.

Patten first lists a variety of aspects of Milgram's procedure that he feels weaken its purported validity. Most of these restate Orne and Holland's position—for example, the incongruous aspect of the experimenter's detached manner in juxtaposition with a screaming victim—to the effect that subjects were likely to see through the rather transparent deceptions used by Milgram. Patten is particularly doubtful regarding the validity of the subjects' post-experimental survey responses, specifically on the question asking whether subjects believed that the learner was receiving painful shocks. He notes, for example, that subjects who had defied the experimenter and then read the description of the research sent by Milgram would have been motivated to *claim* (fallaciously) that they believed in the genuineness of the shocks in order to think highly of themselves as the heroic defiant person defined in the account given to them.

After quoting Milgram's conclusions, that the experiments display man's capacity to abandon his humanity, and indicate the "fatal flaw that nature has designed into us," Patten is unwilling to accept such grim pronouncements:

> Pretty strong stuff, and unequivocally universal in scope. Claims about human nature, the man in the street, and what *we* will do are notoriously loose; none the less the confident assertions of Milgram suggest that at least he means to propose that the *vast majority* of human beings are inclined or disposed to be obedient . . . (P. 434)

Patten suggests that in using *volunteers* as subjects, Milgram was dealing with people who were far more likely to be submissive to the experimenter than would a truly random sample of the population.[6] This argument is similar to the "psychopathology thesis" in suggesting that all of Milgram's subjects were characterized by the "trait" of being a volunteer for a research project. Patten does not, however, consider the relevance of this hypothesis when considering a number of experimental variations in which obedience was sharply reduced.

Patten concludes his critique with an interesting commentary on the nature of authority itself. He distinguishes between *command* authority and *expert-command* authority—the former illustrated by policemen and, presumably, commanders in the Third Reich and in Vietnam—the latter by professors, piano teachers, and physicians.

Obedience to those in command authority reflects culturally defined rules granting such individuals the right to exert orders; obedience to those in expert-command authority reflects a respect for the individuals' expertise, competence, trustworthiness, and so on. Patten equates the role of experimenter with expert-command authority; hence generalizations to behaviors performed under conditions of "command" authority are unwarranted:

> The kind of obedience in the world about us which rightly exercises Milgram's indignation results from command authority and not expert-command authority. . . . The frustration in considering Eichmanns and Calleys comes from the fact that they are held in check by the commands of their superiors simply because . . . they are legally defined as subordinate, and not because those commanding are thought to have some special expertise. So, what follows? Generally, that the way someone behaves before a person he acknowledges to be an expert-command authority cannot tell us how he will respond to a command authority. Specific to Milgram's experiments, the obedience[7] which we are temporarily (and generously) assuming might be found in some of the subjects toward the person who has expert-command authority in the experiments, cannot tell us anything about the likelihood of Calley/Eichmann obedience in the population at large. Simply put, there is nothing at all contradictory in the idea of the absolute anarchist being completely trusting and obedient toward his doctor, his lawyer, his piano teacher, or the person who instructs him in the making of bombs. (Pp. 438-439)

Thus, Patten is in effect excusing Milgram's obedient subjects by implying that it is legitimate to obey expert-command authorities. Noting Milgram's own position on the functional value of authority in many instances (see Chapter Eight), Patten goes on to suggest that research subjects are simply in one of an almost endless array of settings in social life in which the "person in charge" must be given the respect and trust inherent in that position. It would be unreasonable to expect people to challenge the legitimacy of every authority in these settings—a chaotic breakdown in normal social functioning would result. But how, then, should one be able to know the difference—what will enable one to defy truly illegitimate authorities, that is, those who do not merit our respect and trust and who issue immoral orders by the sheer power of their command authority?

> The way out of this dilemma is to see that Milgram's model of authority does not fit the facts. This will remind one in turn that the mastery of wit, wile and intelligence is not what is needed to avoid being a Calley or an Eichmann in this world, so much as those Socratic skills of self-mastery, courage and moral stubbornness. (P. 439)

Thus, Patten presumes that when a truly evil order is given, it will be recognized and resisted by those who have the moral strength to do so—in essence, the "psychopathology thesis" in slight redress! Patten does not, it should be noted, consider that Milgram's subjects should have been responsible, in principle, for detecting a shift in the legitimacy of the experimenter's behavior. I agree with his construction of the subject's role *on entry* into the experimental setting, but I question his assumption that the subject has a right to define every event in that setting, *from beginning to end*, as legitimate and moral simply because it occurs under the auspices of a presumably expert authority figure.

Tedeschi, Lindskold, and Rosenfeld (1985)

I noted earlier in this chapter that textbooks in social psychology typically present a particularly strong case for the generality of the obedience experiments. One citation should be noted, however, as an exception. Tedeschi, Lindskold, and Rosenfeld (1985) give a traditionally extensive account of Milgram's obedience paradigm, including photographs of the laboratory, and an extensive account of the Kelman and Lawrence (1972) survey on attitudes toward the Calley trial. Their account of the significance of the obedience research is, however, uniquely skeptical and curiously reserved, given the considerable space devoted to it:

> There is a tendency to exaggerate the degree of obedience obtained in Milgram's studies. We cannot draw a conclusion that the results demonstrate an "Eichmann effect." Adolph Eichmann was a German who claimed that he only obeyed orders by overseeing the extermination of Jews in concentration camps. The willingness of many Americans to give a dangerous level of shock to a total stranger suggests that they might act as executioners if ordered to do so by an authority. However, research has shown that subjects refused to give shocks unless they were reassured that the victim would suffer no harm (Mixon, 1972). Along with his prods, Milgram continually reassured subjects that the confederate would suffer no harm. (Pp. 211-12)

Thus, Tedeschi et al. endorse the Orne and Holland thesis and, as a result, caution their readers regarding the implications of the obedience experiments.

CONCLUSIONS

This chapter has examined the implications of the obedience experiments for contributing to an understanding of the Holocaust and, more generally, of the capability of human beings to harm others under orders. Clearly, this issue relates intimately to the material reviewed in Chapters Five and Six. If one views the research as providing crucial insights regarding the nature of genocide and the capacities of well-adjusted individuals to engage in evil, one is likely to take a positive ethical perspective—that is, that the knowledge gained is worth the ethical costs incurred. Conversely, if one takes the position that the obedience experiments are unconscionable on ethical grounds, it is difficult to hold to a view that they are laden with significant implications. Similarly, to the extent that one is sympathetic with Orne and Holland's "demand characteristic" argument, it is difficult to invest the obedience research with substantive value. If, however, one is convinced by Milgram's defense of his paradigm and by research bearing on methodological criticisms, then it becomes possible to see the work as having extraordinary significance and generality far beyond the confines of the experimental laboratory.

I have attempted to limit the foregoing discussion to commentaries that focus directly on the issue of the generality or larger meaning of the obedience experiments. I will not belabor the obvious by restating the controversies as well as sensitivities involved in generalizing a scientific research program to an event such as the Holocaust. My hope is that the basic issues have been addressed and clarified to an extent in this chapter.

A fair reading of the literature suggests, I think, that a majority of writers strongly endorse a linkage between the obedience experiments and psychological determinants of destructive obedience.[8] Textbooks in social psychology are one striking example. Their treatment of Milgram's research is often extensive, including pictures of victims of the Holocaust or of the My Lai massacre along with photographs of Milgram's laboratory and transcripts of the teacher's conflict with the insistent experimenter. Social psychologists, in their role as educators, make, in my view, as strong an inference from these experiments as it is possible to make. We have also seen, however, that scholars from a diversity of academic backgrounds have paid unparalleled tribute to the significant lessons of Milgram's research.

I have found it surprising to observe the popularity of what I have termed the "normality thesis." Many social scientists, including those with a psychiatric or clinical perspective, are very comfortable with this thesis, one which departs radically from the bias, noted in Chapter Two, toward perceiving destructive obedience in terms of pathology or undesirable personality traits as the primary causes of such behavior.

Michael Selzer has also inquired about this issue, namely the trend among analysts to be sympathetic with the line of reasoning advanced by Milgram, as well as Arendt and others. As might be anticipated, he is dismayed by what he views as its undeserved acceptance:

> An underlying reason may be that the liberal ideology which has, at least until recently, dominated our cultural thinking, prefers to view evil as a social disorder, actually as a social malfunctioning, rather than as a failure of moral restraint within the individual. When people behave in a wicked fashion, according to this view, it is because the vast machine we call society is out of kilter. (1973, p. 136)

Selzer views the acceptance of Milgram's work as antithetical to his own "pathology thesis" regarding the nature of obedience involved in the Holocaust. He implies that an endorsement of the obedience experiments provides a moral excuse for genocidal obedience and fails to recognize the "obvious" fact that acts of great evil are far more likely to be committed by evil people. He attributes the "victory" of the normality thesis to political ideologies "that are in vogue in academic circles today" (1983, p. 213). He apparently suggests that a liberal or politically "left" orientation promotes a situational bias regarding the perceived causes of antisocial behavior, and hence the pervasive enthusiasm for Milgram's research among academics.

Selzer may not be totally in error on this latter point. My own position, however, is that the ascendance of the normality thesis—what Selzer describes as "this tenet's rapid and almost unchallenged rise to the status of social science orthodoxy" (1983, p. 213)—reflects primarily the impact of the obedience experiments themselves. That is, Milgram's research, and the experimental literature supporting it (see Chapter 4), have provided a very powerful *data base*. With this kind of information available, it is difficult to argue convincingly that individual traits of hostility, sadism, or aggressiveness are the critical predictors of the behavior at issue. Milgram did not select his subjects on these psychological dimensions, and one cannot attribute the causes of the behaviors demonstrated in his laboratory to such personality deficiencies in his subjects. It must be "something else"—something about the nature of social hierarchies, of our readiness to adapt to social roles defined by people we have reason to trust or respect, of our capacity to define certain of our actions, at least to our own satisfaction, as the responsibility of others. Regardless, therefore, of the intuitive appeal of dispositional accounts, it is the *evidence* regarding the situational determination of obedience that has, in my view, altered the thinking of many individuals on this problem.

I am not a clinician and cannot speak instructively to the validity of Miale and Selzer's psychodiagnostic interpretation of the high-ranking Nazi officials. I am persuaded by the doubts that have been raised by others with psychiatric expertise. It is worth re-emphasizing, however, that *individual differences* were observed in many of the experimental variations, that in a given setting, all subjects did *not* behave identically. There are personality issues involved in the obedience paradigm that have not been clarified, and the research is incomplete on this score. This is not to say that *psychopathology* will ultimately be the relevant basis for accounting for this variability, but to the extent that Miale and Selzer are advocating that characterological factors be given a proper hearing, their position does have merit.

In this context, I think it may be too limiting to focus on the Nuremberg War Criminals as the point of reference for inferences made from the obedience research. Obedience was demonstrated by a vast number of individuals, many never to wear uniforms or to deal directly with victims of the Holocaust. It is not difficult to accept the prospect that at least some of the Nazi hierarchy—Hitler's status being virtually uncontested on this score—were mentally ill, but does the "pathology thesis" still pertain to the millions of acts of obedience performed by non-officials, by those who failed to intervene when observing obedience on the part of someone whom they could have reasonably challenged?

I would close this chapter with an eloquent conclusion reached by two Holocaust scholars, the historian George M. Kren and the social psychologist Leon Rappoport. Having noted the initial feelings of rage and disgust that accompany a study of the Holocaust, they describe what eventually becomes the fate of this kind of inquiry:

> What remains is a central, deadening sense of despair over the human species. Where can one find an affirmative meaning in life if human beings can do such things? Along with this despair there may also come a desperate new feeling of vulnerability attached to the fact that one *is* human. If one keeps at the Holocaust long enough, then sooner or later the ultimate personal truth begins to reveal itself: one knows, finally, that one might either do it, or be done to. If it could happen on such a massive scale elsewhere, then it can happen anywhere; it is all within the range of human possibility, and like it or not, Auschwitz expands the universe of consciousness no less than landings on the moon. (1980, p. 126)

8

MILGRAM'S THEORY OF OBEDIENCE: AN APPRAISAL

I cannot bring myself to render a judgment on Richard Nixon, or for that matter, Henry Kissinger. I worked intimately for both men. It's not for me—it's not in me—to render moral judgments on them. I must leave that to others, to history and to God.

Alexander M. Haig, Jr.

May I, Mr. President, if it's possible at all, implore you to do something else, to find a way, to find another way, another site? That place, Mr. President, is not your place. Your place is with the victims of the SS.

—Elie Wiesel, speaking at the White House
on April 19, 1985, asking President Reagan
not to visit a German cemetery containing
graves of Nazi SS officers.

In his 1974 book, *Obedience to Authority*, Milgram presents, for the first time, a major conceptual analysis of obedience. Occupying four chapters, his discussion is not aimed at accounting for the specific findings of the experimental variations, as he did in earlier interpretations (reviewed here in Chapters One and Three), but is, rather, a more broadly scaled theoretical conception of the nature of obedience—why it occurs, what psychological components are vital to its operation, and what processes are involved in attempting to disengage oneself from the influence of authority. In this chapter, the major outlines of Milgram's theory will be examined and evaluated in terms of their empirical support. We will also consider how other social scientists have appraised Milgram's theoretical account of obedience.

Milgram approaches the problem initially from an evolutionary point of view. He comments on the advantages of social structure in both animal (e.g., dominance hierarchies) and human contexts (e.g., social organization). He contrasts the functional value of coordinated social interaction with the chaos of a tumultuous crowd. In this context, he notes, "A potential for obedience is the prerequisite of such social organization, and because organization has enormous survival value for any species, such a capacity was bred into the organism through the extended operation of evolutionary processes" (pp. 124-25).

Milgram uses a combination of psychoanalytic and cybernetic concepts to derive a model of a hierarchical chain of command. A major assumption is that the individual who may usually be self-regulating or independent must, under certain conditions, suppress this kind of

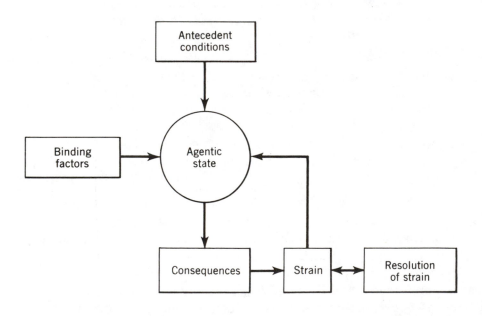

Figure 8.1. The Agentic Shift.
Source: p. 154 from *Obedience to Authority: An Experimental View*, by Stanley Milgram, Copyright © 1974 by Stanley Milgram. Reprinted by permission.

functioning in favor of control from higher-level sources. Milgram uses the example of pilots subjecting themselves, willingly of course, to air traffic controllers for the payoff of a coordinated landing system. Milgram is particularly concerned with the notion of *transition*. Thus, a person in one context may be virtually autonomous and yet in another be intricately involved in a complex network of social roles involving diverse power and obligations. He uses an example which should be familiar. A person's conscience, illustrative of a self-regulating feature of the autonomous person, might have to yield to other influences when this same individual is operating in a hierarchical social system.

Milgram then introduces the central concept of his theory, the *agentic shift*. This involves a change in one's self-perception, a type of cognitive reorientation induced when a person occupies a subordinate role or position in a defined system or organization. The most important characteristic of the agentic shift is that the individual "no longer views himself as responsible for his own actions but defines himself as an instrument for carrying out the wishes of others" (p. 134). A schematic model of Milgram's theory is shown in Figure 8.1.

Milgram next discusses three dimensions of the agentic state: The factors which promote an entry into this condition, the psychological consequences of being in the agentic state, and the forces operating to keep a person in this frame of mind.

ANTECEDENTS OF OBEDIENCE

Milgram identifies two categories of antecedent conditions, or background factors. One of these, the more generalized, has little connection with the obedience experiments per se or any other specific obedience scenario. Rather, it concerns the "socialization" of obedience. From early childhood, we internalize the virtues of obedience. The school, the family, the workplace, the church or synagogue, athletics—all of these institutions function, more or less explicitly, on the basis of obedience to authority.[1] The negative consequences of disobedience are often quite vivid and these, too, are remembered. Milgram emphasizes that in modern society the child learns to obey *impersonal* authorities. Mere indications of rank—dress, diploma, title, insignia—are often sufficient. The holder of authority can be a "perfect stranger" and suffer no loss of command. The rewards of obedience or, perhaps more accurately, of the deference shown to authority figures are, I think, elegantly if not subtly depicted in Figure 8.2.

"Nice touch, Jenkins. I like a man who salutes."

Figure 8.2. Drawing by Woodman; Copyright © 1979 *The New Yorker* Magazine, Inc. Reprinted by permission.

Thus, the average individual becomes extremely well versed in the act of obedience. Obedience is deeply ingrained, overlearned to such a degree that many of us are unwitting prey for those who might abuse our readiness to be influenced by apparently legitimate authorities (see Cialdini, 1985). If we *think* about our obedience at all, it is likely to occur after the fact, when in the light of hindsight we might whisper "I should have checked his credentials" or "How could I have been so gullible or submissive?"

Another set of antecedent conditions concerns obedience in more immediate, contextually specific terms. Most settings—a commercial airliner, a theater, a hospital, a barbershop, a strategic air-command base, a laboratory—have defined *roles*, often arranged in a hierarchical structure. The reader may be familiar with organizational charts or schematic diagrams of companies or governments, showing specific roles or job titles as boxes, with lines connecting such positions in both horizontal and vertical directions. Not all settings involve arrangements of this complexity, but the basic idea is always the same—positions of authority are clearly identifiable and there is usually one position of "highest authority," be it the owner of a small grocery or the president of the United States. Authority is built into the role, a matter of the role's very definition. All of this may be rather obvious, but Milgram is leading to a more subtle point, one that is important in terms of his research—people expect someone to be in charge, to constitute a legitimate authority. One should not, in Milgram's opinion, minimize the significance of this expectancy or presumption, held by all of us, that there is always an answer should we ask, "Who's in charge around here?" Of course, we rarely need even to ask.

Milgram adds that the successful enactment of authority requires the proper "look"—style may be more influential than substance, at least in the short term. Visual signs, such as the gray technician's coat worn by the experimenter, are another component in the mosaic of cues which signal the presence of authority. It is unlikely that these factors would even be consciously attended to by most people, although their absence might be acutely salient. A barber wearing a bathing suit might be more than a novelty—prospective customers might not risk their necks to such an unprofessional looking individual.

Milgram then presents a virtual "itemized list" of background factors relevant to the authority involved in the obedience paradigm. For example, there is a *commitment* on the part of the subject. Having volunteered to participate and having entered the laboratory, the subject is in a sense "locked" into what will transpire there. It is normative to play out the part, to see things through. This is how people usually behave in a variety of situations, even unpleasant ones. Milgram introduces a subtle but possibly crucial "etiquette" factor here, a dynamic which operates in many social settings, and which we will reconsider shortly in discussing the concept of *binding*. Milgram is concerned, in this context, with the subject's sense of propriety:

> The fact that this experiment is carried out in a laboratory has a good deal to do with the degree of obedience exacted. There is a feeling that the experimenter "owns" the space and that the subject must conduct himself fittingly, as if a guest in someone's house. (P. 140)

At first this sounds like Orne and Holland revisited—actually the argument is not totally irrelevant to their position—but Milgram is not challenging the generality of the laboratory. He is suggesting that the laboratory "belongs" to the experimenter, as the plane belongs to its pilot, the classroom to its instructor, the hospital to the physician, etc. We are socialized to behave according to the wishes of whoever is in charge in whatever place we happen to be—it is a rule that has been thoroughly mastered and that usually serves us well—but not always, as Milgram's research seems to inform us.

Milgram notes that the fact of the subject's *volunteering* to participate is significant—it adds to the psychology of commitment, implying that it would spoil the whole thing were the subject to quit. Such cognitions would be far less likely if there was coercion—if, for some reason the subject felt obligated to be in the experiment. Milgram states that in our society institutions often promote a sense of voluntary entry. If successful, this minimizes the need for direct surveillance. A person is less likely to continue to obey orders *on his or her own* if initially the orders are given "at gun point." In the obedience paradigm, therefore, there is an internalized basis for the subjects' obedience as well as an external one.

Another element to the background of obedience is what Milgram terms the "overarching ideology." This refers to a kind of cultural endowment of legitimacy or authenticity to certain institutions—to the military, the church, medicine, science, big business, government. Obedience is facilitated in these contexts. We have been taught to respect and to trust these institutions, perhaps even to fear them. Obedience could be achieved in the absence of such background factors—Milgram's Bridgeport variation is a case in point—but certainly it is often facilitated or "energized" in these sacred places. The individual sees his or her performance as serving desirable, culturally sanctioned ends—of patriotism, of national security, of redemption in the after-life, of contributing to scientific knowledge, etc. In a related argument, Kren and Rappoport (1980) describe, in their analysis of the Holocaust, the manner in which major institutions in Nazi Germany —science, the courts, religion—not only failed to protect innocent civilians (as they would ordinarily be expected to do) but were transformed in many instances to accomplish the genocidal policies of the state. The institutions have a "larger than life" quality and it is difficult for the average person to challenge whatever transpires in their domains.

The obedience experiments are characterized by all of these background factors—an authoritative-looking experimenter, his dress, the equipment, the sounds, the generalized mystique of the laboratory, all of these cues integrated quickly by a subject who enters the setting with a basic expectation that influence will indeed be exercised, and that it is all quite proper for this to occur.

THE AGENTIC STATE

As noted earlier, the primary consequence of the agentic shift is that the individual attributes responsibility for his or her actions to the person in authority. Milgram thus views the defense at Nuremberg (and countless other places)—I was following orders, I was doing my duty—as an honest assertion, at least in the mind of the person uttering the words, and not necessarily an "alibi concocted for the moment" (p. 146). Milgram breathes life into such terms as "loyalty," "duty," "honor," "discipline." These terms have moral significance, Milgram states, in that they suggest that obedience under orders can, by its very *form*, assume moral virtue.

In a recent, highly publicized trial, General William C. Westmoreland charged that CBS had libeled him by presenting a documentary indicating that he had falsified enemy troop strength during the Vietnam War. That is, he had purposely underestimated what he knew to be formidably high numbers of enemy troops in order to maintain morale on the U.S. side. Westmoreland finally dropped his libel suit before the jury had an opportunity to render a verdict. A key witness for the defense (that is, CBS) was a retired Army colonel, Gains B. Hawkins, who was in charge of estimating enemy strength in South Vietnam. He testified that Westmoreland had "imposed a 'dishonest' ceiling on reports of that strength because higher figures were 'politically unacceptable'" (*New York Times*, February 13, 1985). In the following account of Hawkins' testimony, one can observe, quite dramatically I think, Milgram's concept of the agentic state:

> Colonel Hawkins said he told General Davidson and Colonel Morris: "If you want a different figure you need to change to the rules of the game. You just give me what figure you think it ought to be and I'll carry it out for you. And this was the beginning of the reduction of our figures. I abdicated my position as order of battle chief."
> Q. Do you have any animus or ill-will towards General Westmoreland?
> A. No, sir, none whatsoever.
> Q. Do you have any animus or ill-will to the United States army?
> Colonel Hawkins drew himself up, and almost shouted the answer.
> A. No, sir, I carried out these orders as a loyal officer in the United States Army, sir.
> (*New York Times*, February 13, 1985, p. 10).

In Milgram's view, the restraints or inhibitions against certain acts can be effectively short-circuited by the location of the individual in a hierarchical system. Matters of conscience are no longer the controlling force in a person's behavior. The individual becomes preoccupied with duty, with the tasks at hand—a focus similar to that described by Kelman's concept of *routinization* (see Chapter Seven).

An illustration of this point is seen in a July 31, 1985 interview in *USA Today* with Paul Tibbets, the pilot of the B-29 that dropped an atomic bomb on Hiroshima:

> USA Today: How did you get involved in the mission to drop a bomb on Hiroshima?
>
> Tibbets: I was called into the office of the commanding general of the 2nd Air Force. He said, "This is your assignment," and I saluted him and said, "Yes, sir." . . .
>
> USA Today: What were your thoughts when you dropped it?
>
> Tibbets: I had no thoughts, except what I'm supposed to do. I had an airplane full of people, and I had a couple airplanes with me. We had to get them out of the way of the bomb blast. The next thing we had to do was prepare ourselves for the shock wave that would be coming up. We did all of these things routinely. There was no problem. We had practiced and practiced.

Milgram uses the concept of "tuning" to describe the individual's sense of priorities. Once one is in the agentic state, information from the authority is more salient than that from one's peer or a person lower in the bureaucratic chain. Cues from the experimenter are attended to more closely than those from the learner. Milgram sees this as another adaptive feature of obedience. The boss can fire you, promote you—it makes sense to listen diligently to what he or she is saying, more so than to a peer who may be speaking to you simultaneously. The "bottom line" is that the basic enterprise can work to the distinct disadvantage of a victim in the system, a person without status, without an advocate who can effectively challenge the authority.

Another psychological consequence of the agentic shift, according to Milgram, is that the individual accepts the authority's definition of the situation:

> An act viewed in one perspective may seem heinous; the same action viewed in another seems fully warranted. *There is a propensity for people to accept definitions of action provided by legitimate authority. . . .* It is this ideological abrogation to the authority that constitutes the principal cognitive basis of obedience. If, after all, the world or the situation is as the authority defines it, a certain set of actions follows logically. (P. 145)

BINDING FACTORS

What keeps the person in an agentic state? The actions performed under the auspices of authority may well be alien to the individual's personal values. Why doesn't the person simply leave the situation, particularly if there are no dire consequences to such an exit?

The answer is that it is not that "simple" to leave. Rationally, logically, it is easy to imagine getting up and walking out of the experiment. Realistically, it is more difficult. It involves "making a scene." Everything that has transpired, from volunteering to participate to pressing the last shock level, is put in jeopardy. We noted, in Chapters Six and Seven, that several analysts of the obedience paradigm pointed to the lack of consequences attendant upon disobeying the experimenter, and that this feature differentiated the paradigm from one of defiance in the real world of military orders, for example. Yet, Milgram contends that there *are* sufficiently unpleasant consequences involved in the act of defiance, even in the seemingly innocuous context of a psychological experiment, to keep people from leaving their seat:

> The subject fears that if he breaks off, he will appear arrogant, untoward, and rude. Such emotions, although they appear small in scope alongside the violence being done to the learner, nonetheless help bind the subject into obedience . . . The entire prospect of turning against the experimental authority, with its attendant disruption of a well-defined social situation, is an embarrassment that many people are unable to face up to. (Pp. 150-51)

Obedience thus can seem to be the lesser of two evils.

Milgram suggests an interesting "thought experiment" to clarify this issue of embarrassment. Imagine that you confront someone who has an authoritative role in your life—your major professor, priest, physician, college president, etc. Instead of greeting this person by his title—"Good morning, Doctor—(Rabbi, Father, Professor, Sir, Dean), try instead to substitute the person's first name or, for the truly courageous, the person's nickname—"Suzie," "Charlie," "Freddy," etc. The innocence of this endeavor should be as quickly recognized as is the utter impossibility of actually doing it! Students in my social psychology class might say that they would do it, but tend to agree with my prediction that they would readily justify their "deviance" by claiming that it was a "class project" for Dr. Miller—perhaps another instance of the agentic state.

The point is that there are subtle but yet powerful social norms or rules that operate to maintain an ongoing scenario, that serve to preserve a person's definition of the situation. Out of context, these rules—one shouldn't be impolite to a researcher even if his behavior seems brutal—may seem silly. Following them in the name of etiquette would appear out of the question. In context, however, they are influential. They *bind* the individual into the hierarchical structure of his or her relationship with authority. In Chapter Two, we examined the phenomenon of people's underestimation of the obedience actually observed in Milgram's baseline (1963) experiment. Milgram suggests (p. 210) that one likely basis for this underestimation is that people fail to appreciate the role of binding factors. They fail to appreciate the significance of the structural relationship involving the subject and the experimenter—the momentum of the social occasion of "the experiment," the subject's concerns regarding decorum, politeness, respect, etc. Milgram regards these components as important in understanding the realities of the phenomenon of obedience. Those who are asked to predict someone's behavior are, as we have noted, far more likely to focus on the *personality* of the individual, an issue far removed from Milgram's primary theoretical interest.

Milgram closes with a brief note on the role of anxiety. The paradigm, as we have seen, tends to evoke anxiety based on the conflict experienced by subjects. The contemplation of defiance creates its own form of anxiety, however, as the subject finds himself or herself thinking about doing a very "unnatural" thing, namely defying an authority figure. Abandoning the thought of defiance reduces such anxiety, hence another force which effectively binds the person to the agentic state.

STRAIN AND DISOBEDIENCE

Focusing upon the high incidence and intensity of expressions of tension in his subjects, Milgram elaborates on the concept of *strain*. He saw this strain as indicative of the conflict between the states of autonomy and agency, and of the *weakness* of authority. That is, in the experiment, many subjects do not enter a state of complete agency. The immersion in the role of "teacher" is far less complete, Milgram states, than might occur in obedience observed in naturally occurring totalitarian regimes, for example those of Stalin and Hitler. The subject has some very good reasons for being sensitive to the pain and protest from the learner. There is evidence suggesting that we are normally responsive to the emotional distress of others (see Berger, 1962; Baron, 1977). Subjects find themselves doing something they have never done before—harming another person against his or her will, a person who has not done anything to the subject.

A facilitator for obedience is anything that will reduce the salience or immediacy of the association between the subject's behavior and the pain experienced by the learner. Milgram uses the term *buffer* to describe this function. Buffers act to reduce strain. The shock generator, itself, is a buffer. It is precise, impersonal, so easy to press the levers—as compared, for example, with engaging in direct physical violence (Experiment 4, as contrasted with Experiments 1, 2, and 3). Milgram suggests that "distance, time, and physical barriers neutralize the moral sense" (p. 157).

In reading Milgram's theoretical account, one senses that the obedience paradigm has an intrinsic momentum or dynamism that promotes obedience on the part of the subject. The authority of the experimenter, the ease with which subjects enter a state of at least partial agency, the buffers, the binding factors—all of these work in the direction of the subject's continuing to shock the learner. Subjects are able, furthermore, to reduce their strain by a variety of avoidance or denial mechanisms.

Yet disobedience was certainly possible in this paradigm. A considerable amount of it was observed in certain experimental variations. Milgram states that for many it is actually painful to disobey. Unlike the obedient subject who can allocate responsibility to the experimenter, the defiant subject must accept responsibility for ruining the experiment:

> The price of disobedience is a gnawing sense that one has been faithless. Even though he has chosen the morally correct action, the subject remains troubled by the disruption of the social order he brought about, and cannot fully dispel the feeling that he deserted a cause to which he had pledged support. (P. 164)

The reference to the defiant subject's "morally correct action" is a clear acknowledgment of Milgram's own evaluation of the behavioral options available to subjects in his paradigm.

AN ALTERNATIVE THEORY: IS AGGRESSION THE KEY?

Milgram restates the aggression argument, which essentially is the rationale given by Miale and Selzer (described in Chapter Seven). The behavior of shocking the learner reflects aggression: "in shocking the learner, he is satisfying instinctually rooted destructive tendencies"

(p. 166). Thus, the experiment permits a socially acceptable expression of impulses which, though present in most people, are normally restrained.

Milgram refutes this argument completely. He refers to data from Experiment 11—subjects choose their own shock level—as the key empirical evidence bearing on the aggression formulation. Also, some of the role-permutation variations permitted free reign to the shock generator, but subjects did not avail themselves of this opportunity (see Experiments 12, 13, 14, and 15). Milgram's position, then, is clear:

> The act of shocking the victim does not stem from destructive urges but from the fact that subjects have become integrated into a social structure and are unable to get out of it. . . . Now and then a subject did come along who seemed to relish the task of making the victim scream. But he was the rare exception, and clearly appeared as the queer duck among our subjects. (Pp. 166-67)

Milgram's theoretical position is a lesson in eclecticism, a fusion of perspectives from sociology, developmental psychology, social cognition, attribution processes, and self-theory, with psychoanalytic and systems-theory principles added for good measure. This represents a rather sweeping transition in his own thinking, if one compares this (1974) analysis with the relatively austere approach to his first (1963) published article. The title of that article—"Behavioral study of obedience"—quite accurately, I think, reflected Milgram's primary orientation, that of an empiricist who was more interested in the investigation of obedience than in constructing an imposing theoretical superstructure. In this respect his approach was virtually identical to that of his mentor, Solomon Asch.

The present formulation is considerably different. Aside from the diversity of perspectives, his treatment is extremely *cognitive*. His central concept, the agentic state, is a relatively pure cognitive construct, as shown in this definition:

> Is the agentic state just another word for obedience? No, it is that state of mental organization which enhances the likelihood of obedience. Obedience is the behavioral aspect of the state. A person may be in an agentic state—that is, in a state of openness to regulation from an authority—without ever being given a command and thus never having to obey. (P. 148)

There are at least two reasons for Milgram's having adopted this particular theoretical approach. One concerns his general background and orientation. He had majored initially in political science as an undergraduate and pursued graduate work in the uniquely interdisciplinary setting of the Department of Social Relations at Harvard. Throughout his research career, including his influential contributions in the psychology of urban life and in cognitive mapping, Milgram's mode of conceptualizing problems reflected his basically diverse, multidisciplinary point of view. It is true that in working with Asch he was exposed to a far more conservative scientific approach, but his own background was, from the start, broadly based. His theoretical approach may also reflect the feedback he received in giving numerous lectures to an extremely diverse array of audiences. In the course of speaking frequently about the experiments and answering thousands of questions about them, Milgram had the opportunity to sharpen his conceptualization, to add or delete various ideas or points of emphasis.

Another force that may have shaped his 1974 analysis was the mounting cognitive emphasis in the discipline of social psychology. His book appeared at a time of explosive interest in processes of social perception, attribution theory, and perspectives on the self. Milgram's theory reflects considerably all of these developments.

EMPIRICAL EVIDENCE

In contrast to the voluminous data from the obedience paradigm itself, reviewed in earlier chapters, there is relatively sparse evidence bearing specifically on Milgram's theory. The most important component of his theory is the agentic state, in particular his assertion that subjects who have engaged in the agentic shift are disposed to attribute responsibility for their acts to a higher authority. There are two sets of data relevant to this issue.

Milgram (1974)

In Appendix 2, Milgram reports evidence obtained from subjects who participated in Experiments 1 through 4. These individuals were asked to assign responsibility for the act of shocking the learner against his will to each of three persons: The experimenter, the learner, and the subject himself. The 360 degrees of a "responsibility clock" were partitioned by movable rods rotating from the center of a large disk.

The results are shown in Table 8.1. Milgram emphasizes that the defiant subjects attributed more responsibility to themselves than to the experimenter, whereas obedient subjects attributed slightly less responsibility to themselves than to the experimenter. Obedient sub-

Table 8.1. Assignment of Responsibility by Defiant and Obedient Subjects

	n	Experimenter	Teacher	Learner
Defiant Subjects	61	38.8%	48.4%	12.8%
Obedient Subjects	57	38.4	36.3	25.3

Source: From Obedience to Authority: An Experimental View, by Stanley Milgram, Copyright © by Stanley Milgram. Reprinted by permission.

jects also attributed more responsibility to the learner, a kind of "blaming the victim" response. Milgram does not evaluate these judgments statistically. He recognizes that these perceptions were obtained after the subjects' participation and may not have existed in precisely the same form during the experiment itself—an issue endemic to all post-experimental judgments.

A less flattering interpretation of these data would emphasize the fact that both groups of subjects attributed virtually identical responsibility to the experimenter, whereas the agentic-shift hypothesis would predict far more responsibility to be assigned to the experimenter by obedient subjects than by defiant subjects. I would hesitate to view Milgram's evidence as a definitive test of the agentic-shift hypothesis. It was conducted during the original research program, predating by 10 years Milgram's published statements on the agentic state. There are also limitations regarding the methodology of this study. When subjects are asked to allocate responsibility to three sources so that the total equals 360 degree, it becomes difficult to assess the independence of these judgments. These findings are, nevertheless, relevant to the essential conceptualization of the agentic shift and can be viewed as at least partially supportive.

Mantell and Panzarella (1976)

In Chapter Four, a study by David Mantell (1971) was described, in which the obedience paradigm was conducted in Munich, West Germany. Mantell observed a high rate of obedience (85 percent) in his replication of Milgram's baseline experiment. In a variation in which subjects first observed a defiant subject (a confederate of the experimenter) challenging the experimenter's authority, obedience was reduced but still impressive (52 percent). In a final self-decision variation, similar to Milgram's Experiment 11, only 7 percent of the subjects pressed all 30 shock levers. These results were presented as a strong confirmation of Milgram's original findings.

In 1976, Mantell and Panzarella reported an additional analysis of the Mantell (1971) investigation. All subjects were interviewed during post-experimental debriefing and were asked this question, "Given 100 per cent responsibility in all, how much responsibility do you feel is yours and how much do you feel is ours?" (p. 241). Subjects were also asked to explain their answers.

The major finding, bearing on Milgram's theory of obedience, was that there was *no relationship* between the degree of obedience and the subject's assignment of responsibility. The hypothesis that the more subjects would comply with the orders, the less responsibility they would assign to themselves, was not supported. The investigators summarized their findings in this manner:

> What was most striking about the responsibility data was their variability. The mean for the responsibility variable was 36.72 per cent attributed to oneself with a standard deviation of 32.69 percent. In every condition there were subjects who accepted 100 percent of the responsibility and subjects who accepted none at all. There were both defiant and compliant subjects who accepted 100 per cent of the responsibility and who accepted none at all. Although the majority of subjects in a command situation like the baseline condition administer all of the shocks, they have not surrendered personal responsibility in becoming agents of the experimenter. Some have. But others continue to hold themselves responsible. A monolithic view of the obedient person as a purely passive agent who invariably relinquishes personal responsibility is a false view. (P. 242)

Mantell and Panzarella report that responsibility attributions were related to two factors, the age of the subject (older subjects assumed more responsibility) and the experimental conditions. The average attributed to oneself was 51 percent in the self-decision condition, 30 percent in the baseline, and 31 percent in the modeling-delegitimization condition. Thus, when the subject's *role* included more decision-making power, such as in the self-decision condition, subjects did assign themselves more responsibility. But *within* this condition, and in the other two, there were no significant correlations between how far the subject went in the shock series and his allocation of personal responsibility.

Why did subjects obey? Mantell and Panzarella note that in the interviews, subjects seemed intent on fulfilling their commitment, "they did not perceive themselves as loyal to the experimenter so much as loyal to their own commitment that they made a firm decision to carry out the experiment to the end" (P. 243). In the modeling-delegitimization condition, a number of subjects thought the model to have been irresponsible in failing to fulfill his role. However, there were individual differences here as well, as several participants did see the model as responsible and were influenced on this basis to follow his example and defy the experimenter.

Mantell and Panzarella conclude that the "particular theory of obedience as an agentic state in which personal responsibility is relinquished does not appear tenable" (p. 244). In their view, there are a variety of forces in the paradigm, all of which are potentially operative in inducing obedience—the voluntary nature of the subject's recruitment, the commitment factor, the payment to subjects, the desirability of contributing to scientific inquiry, etc. Thus, on the basis of the available evidence, the idea of an agentic shift as *the critical process* cannot be accepted.

Given their reservations concerning the agentic-shift formulation, Mantell and Panzarella are skeptical of the inferences which have been made from the obedience experiments. Noting that the celebrity of the experiments has derived from "their supposed relevance to the atrocities committed by ordinary men in wartime situations" (p. 244) —they refer to the Kelman and Lawrence (1972) survey in this context—the investigators are critical:

> Lt. Calley explicitly accepted full responsibility for his actions at My Lai. He claimed that he was acting under valid orders. Also at Nuremberg defendants explicitly accepted full responsibility for their roles in the Third Reich, although they disagreed in retrospect on whether their actions were justified or not. If one were to *presuppose* that obedience and responsibility are incompatible or that only one person in a command chain could be responsible for its outcomes, these would be inconsistent with defense claims. But such presuppositions are unwarranted. Responsibility is independent of obedience and may be attributed fully to more than one person. (P. 245)

For Mantell and Panzarella, the obedience experiments are provocative, but their precise meaning is unclear. They agree that "aggression" is to be ruled out—they accept Milgram's own evidence and rationale on this factor, but they also imply that the "obedience hypothesis" may be challenged. They suggest that given what is known to this point, "the definitions of the subjects' roles together with the circumstances under which they were accepted seem to offer more likely alternative explanations" (p. 245). Although not citing Orne and Holland, these researchers explicitly mention the possibility that subjects could have presumed that the learner's ultimate safety was assured.

Mantell and Panzarella's analysis is instructive. They are on strong ground in questioning the empirical support for the concept of the agentic shift. Their expression of caution regarding Milgram's treatment of this matter is very appropriate. It is too easy to stereotype the participants in bureaucratically administered genocide and claim that they *all* denied responsibility or that they all were following orders. Clearly the issue of "responsibility" is extremely complex and in need of clarification with respect to the obedience experiments.

I think, however, that Mantell and Panzarella are less convincing in other respects. They do not document their conclusion that the defendants at Nuremberg accepted full responsibility for their roles in the Third Reich. They do not seem to recognize the powerful situational influences in the obedience paradigm. Their alternative emphasis on the subjects' definition of their roles is vague in its reference and not empirically assessed. Their conclusion is in some respects surprising, given the basic objections to the precision of Milgram's theoretical analysis. Yet it demonstrates, I think, the impact the obedience experiments have had on many people. That is, even if it is not completely clear *why* people behaved as they did in these experiments, the potential implications are of immense significance:

> The compliance in harmful behaviour in the Milgram experiments is a clear and striking phenomenon and one with great social importance. Yet the precise meaning and relevance of these experiments remains obscure. Many variables are confounded in these experiments. They need to be unraveled through further research. (P. 245)

Empirical support for the concept of an agentic state remains unclear. The data from Milgram (1974) and Mantell and Panzarella (1976) are, at best, only partially supportive. In terms of Milgram's original research program, the hypothesis would be that each experimental variation would be more or less likely to induce an agentic shift in the subjects, who, in turn, would manifest more or less obedience. Mantell and Panzarella noted that their responsibility data reflect this kind of situational specificity. Milgram did not, however, present data relevant to situational variations in the responsibility judgments of his subjects.

My impression is that the agentic-state hypothesis has considerable potential value. Milgram's articulation of the concept is convincing. The quotations I present on the opening page of this chapter are, I think, relevant. Haig's comment is indicative of the agentic state, or at least a verbal statement pertinent to Milgram's conceptualization of the agentic state. Elie Wiesel's remarks to President Reagan illustrate the *opposite* of the agentic state, what Milgram terms "autonomy."[2] But these are, of course, only suggestive. The issue of whether or not a person is actually in a state of relative autonomy or agency is important enough to require an empirical verification of its role in the obedience phenomenon.

THE ROLE OF INDIVIDUAL DIFFERENCES

The importance of individual differences or personality factors in the obedience paradigm has been noted periodically in previous chapters. We have seen that there is a tendency for many people to think that the personality of the person in the role of "teacher" is *the primary determinant* of whether or not this person will obey the experimenter. I trust that this perspective will have been seriously weakened by this point. However, as has been acknowledged, there are patterns of variation in the experimental results—not all subjects obey to the same degree. Several investigations have examined this issue. Although it may not be quite appropriate to include this evidence in a chapter devoted primarily to Milgram's theoretical interpretation, it is an issue that must be considered nonetheless. Milgram himself addressed the issue in an appendix, immediately following his theoretical analysis.

Elms and Milgram (1966)

Elms and Milgram recruited 40 subjects who had participated in the "proximity variations" (Experiments 1 through 4) to return to the laboratory for a two-hour interview concerning their opinions and reactions. Twenty had been fully obedient, and 20 had defied the experimenter. Each subject was seen individually and paid $6.00 for this part of the study.

These subjects were administered a large variety of psychological tests: attitude scales, opinion items, etc. The interest was the degree to which a subject's responses to these assessment instruments would relate significantly to whether or not he had obeyed the experimenter. The battery of tests and questionnaire items included: A short form of the MMPI, the California F-Scale[3] (a measure of the subject's authoritarianism), semantic-differential ratings of such items as Father, Yale University, Conscience, Boss, Myself, Adolf Eichmann, Obedience, Mother, etc., attitude items concerning the subject's parents, descriptions of the experimenter and learner, and the subject's self-concept.

Obedient subjects scored significantly higher on the measure of authoritarianism. Other significant differences included attitudes toward: own father, experimenter, confederate, Yale, and willingness to shoot at men in wartime. There were no significant differences in terms of the basic personality structure or indices of psychopathology in the two groups. Elms and Milgram noted that there were many exceptions to any generalized profile of the obedient subject as an authoritarian or of the defiant subject as a warm humanitarian:

> The results of this study suggest certain broad personality differences which relate to obedience or defiance in the experimental obedience situation; but they do not reveal a single personality pattern which is inevitably expressed in one behavior or the other. (P. 288)

Expanding on these results in his 1974 text, Milgram noted that the data, often suggestive rather than statistically powerful, indicated that Catholics were more obedient than Jews or Protestants, the better-educated were more defiant than the less-educated, obedience was positively related to length of military service, with the exception that officers were more defiant than enlisted men. He reports, however, that many of these differences were not apparent when data from subjects other than the proximity variations were included. Milgram concluded that:

> My over-all reaction was to wonder at how few correlates there were of obedience and disobedience and how weakly they are related to the observed behavior. I am certain that there is a complex personality basis to obedience and disobedience. But I know we have not found it. (1974, p. 205).

Kohlberg (1969)

Lawrence Kohlberg, one of the major theorists of moral development, was a colleague of Milgram at Yale University. His theory presumes essentially that people pass through a number of increasingly more complex and sophisticated stages of moral development as they mature. His scale, perhaps the most influential instrument yet devised to assess moral development, was given to a number of undergraduates who had participated as pilot subjects in Milgram's initial work with the obedience paradigm. Kohlberg's findings and interpretation are contained in the following brief note:

> In this study, only the Stage 6 subjects would be expected to question the authority's moral right to ask them to inflict pain on another. Stage

5, "social contract" subjects, would tend to feel the victim's voluntary participation with foreknowledge released them from responsibility to him while their agreement to participate committed them to comply. As expected, 75 percent of a small group (6) of Stage 6 subjects quit as compared to only 13 percent of the remaining 24 subjects at lower moral stages. (1969, p. 395)

Kohlberg's interpretation is that a person's level of moral judgment can be a potentially significant *predictor* of action in moral conflict situations, particularly where the individual's moral decisions involve an interpretation of human rights or obligations in settings that are ambiguous. In Kohlberg's view, it is not that a Stage 6 (high moral development) individual *feels* more anguish or sympathy for the learner, but rather that he or she interprets or defines the situation differently.

It is interesting to note that Kohlberg's findings, linking moral development to the obedience paradigm, have been cited in an extraordinary number of sources. They are, without question, the most frequently cited data dealing specifically with the individual-difference issue. Yet they are among the least well-described experimental findings I have ever seen, certainly in terms of the obedience literature. The sample size itself would seem to impose severe limitations on its generality. Milgram, for example, was cautious, noting that "the findings are suggestive, though not very strong" (1974, p. 205). Yet, Thomas Lickona, in an anthology on moral development, made the following comment on Kohlberg's results:

Kohlberg's Stage 5, for example, would not rule out shocking the "learner" in Milgram's (1963) experiments (in order to keep the social contract with the experimenter) or preclude dropping the atomic bomb on Hiroshima and Nagasaki (to end the war sooner and "save a million lives"); Stage 6 would. (1976, p. 5)

Lickona's interpretation is quite reflective of many citations of Kohlberg's findings. Miale and Selzer, whose position was examined in Chapter Seven, were understandably ecstatic regarding the implications of Kohlberg's findings (1975, p. 12). That subjects are able to defy the experimenter *because* they are operating at a higher level of moral thinking is extremely congruent with any version of what I have termed the "pathology thesis."

Further Research on Individual Differences

David Rosenhan (Rosenhan, Moore, and Underwood, 1976) reports an unpublished study in which a number of personality variables likely to be associated with obedience—such as aggressiveness, anxiety, submission to authority—were unassociated with obedience as observed in a replication of the Milgram paradigm. He reported that although these specific traits, measured by traditional scales, were not related to behavioral obedience, "the tendency to be a 'nay-sayer,' that is, to be rather critical-minded and to possess high cognitive energy, was related to the capacity to defy authority and to disobey" (p. 243).

Kurt Haas (1966) investigated a type of obedience to destructive commands at a management workshop. Forty-four participants were informed at the last session that the highest company officials had determined that "something radical needed to be done with the men superior to the managers" (p. 33), that is, men higher than the participants themselves in their (actual) corporate structures. Each participant was asked to evaluate critically 23 of their own superiors and to indicate which of these should be dismissed. A variety of deceptions were employed to make this seem completely genuine. Anonymity was used to increase candor, and participants were told that their recommendations would constitute the "*final basis for action*" (p. 33). After the recommendations had been obtained, Haas administered the Siegel Manifest Hostility Test to the participants.

Haas categorized the recommendations in terms of six categories of increasing severity, ranging from 0 (refuse to participate) to 5 (dismissal of superior). The results were interpreted as indicating relatively low obedience—only 13 percent of the participants recommended that some of their superiors be fired. Approximately half of the participants recommended punitive actions short of dismissal, such as pay cuts, demotion, and discipline.[4]

The correlation between hostility scores and degree of obedience was .52, a highly significant correlation. Haas reported that interviews with the participants suggested "how seriously all participants viewed the situation" (p. 34). Haas concluded that unlike the high obedience figure demonstrated by Milgram, his findings indicated far less destructive obedience, suggesting that the generality of Milgram's results are open to question. He viewed his "managerial workshop" setting as a more realistic obedience scenario. He further questioned the significance of Milgram's interpretation by noting that the few subjects who were obedient, by his definition, "seemed to be exceedingly hostile so that it is difficult to ascertain whether they were exercising needs for obedience or hostility" (p. 34).

The research concerning personality factors as determinants of destructive obedience is, in my view, unconvincing. Certainly there are suggestive relationships. An individual categorized as low in authoritarianism, low in hostility, and high in moral development would perhaps be less likely to obey the experimenter than would an individual with a different profile on these personality variables.[5] What is lacking, however, is a research *program* on this issue.[6] The research reports reviewed here have a "one-shot" quality to them. There is no *paradigm*, no systematic large-scaled effort to develop the kind of extensive data base that would be required to analyze this issue. I should add that what I am suggesting here would be difficult logistically. Not only would it require a replication of the major variations in Milgram's paradigm, but the initial sample of potential research subjects would have to be sufficiently large in order to assure that appropriate "types" of individuals would be available for participation.

Another difficulty is more conceptual. Successful prediction in linking personality to social behavior is difficult because there are many factors which reduce the likelihood that a one-to-one relationship will inevitably be observed *even if there is an actual causal relationship*. Thus, what is required is a theory that conceptualizes under what conditions specified personality variables should be useful in predicting destructive obedience. Given the realistic obstacles to performing research of this nature, the prospects for a dramatic "assault" on the personality-obedience problem are not promising. I would reiterate the point, however, that this is an issue that is not going to disappear. Milgram's conception of the agentic state is actually very "individualistic" in its focus. Until we are able to explain why it is that behavior varies within specified obedience contexts—why, for example, 26 subjects in Experiment 1 went to 450-volts whereas 14 subjects *did not*—there will be a serious gap in our understanding of the problem Milgram introduced.[7]

CRITICAL APPRAISALS OF MILGRAM'S THEORY

We considered in Chapters Five and Six the extensive ethical and methodological controversies which have long been associated with the obedience experiments. Many of the arguments voiced in these discussions are relevant to Milgram's theoretical viewpoint, that is, to his interpretation of what his research achieved and why his research participants behaved as they did. It is appropriate, however, after reviewing Milgram's 1974 theoretical statement, to examine a number of reactions to this conceptualization. We will first consider positions that are critical of Milgram's theoretical contribution.

Marcus (1974)

Steven Marcus, a professor of English at Columbia University, reviewed Milgram's text in the *New York Times Book Review* (1974). We have noted his ethical objections in Chapter Five. On this matter, I should not omit reference to the imaginative artistic sketch of the obedience laboratory accompanying Marcus's review (on the lead page of the *Book Review*). "Torture" would be my choice for a caption to such a drawing.

Marcus is unequivocal in his disregard for Milgram's interpretation:

> The second question of interest that arises from this work has to do with how Milgram handles his data, what he does with it, what meanings he discovers, what theoretical schemes and explanations he enlists and arrives at, what conclusions he is led to draw. At this point, it has to be said, general disaster sets in. It is hard to know where, in this woeful and lamentable performance, to begin, and I shall have to limit myself to discussing only a few of the intellectual calamities that make up so much of this book. (P. 2)

Marcus presents a litany of what he views to be deficiencies. He is critical of the systems model and the agentic-state concept. He finds Milgram's reasoning to be overly subjective. He criticizes Milgram's writing style, objecting to his use of phrases such as "autonomous man" or "malevolent authority." Marcus contends that Milgram, unjustifiably, views these as real entities. He extends his coverage to social science in general, contending that it is perhaps rich in data but relatively thin in convincing theory. He contrasts this circumstance with older theories, those of Freud, Marx, Hegel, Durkheim, which were far more impressive in terms of their conceptual structure and scope, though admittedly weak in terms of relevant empirical evidence.

Marcus is not totally negative, however. He praises the experiments themselves, noting that they "Were devilishly ingenious, cleverly thought out, and—whatever one thinks of them—extremely provocative and probably important" (p. 2). Reflecting his great admiration for Freud, Marcus acknowledges the importance of understanding destructive obedience, that it reflects not the "id" but rather the "superego . . . enlisted in the active service of the very highest causes" (p. 3)—a position that Milgram might well endorse.

Marcus's review is not easily characterized. Much in it is critical. The style of his writing is almost punitive. Consider this sentence: "All the theoretical and explanatory parts of the book exist at this abysmal pitch of discourse" (p. 2). Yet he also endorses several important concepts, for example the ideas of "overarching ideologies," and sanctioned destructiveness. A number of Marcus's observations are insightful. However, I question his professional background and expertise in terms of evaluating the scientific merits of Milgram's theory. I suspect that his psychoanalytic perspective may have biased his evaluation of Milgram's theoretical orientation. Marcus has every right to his own perspective, but it is an issue that he should acknowledge more explicitly given the extraordinarily harsh accusations comprising much of his review.

Wrightsman (1974)

Lawrence Wrightsman, a prominent social psychologist and the author of one of the most popular textbooks in this discipline, reviewed Milgram's book for *Contemporary Psychology*, the major review journal for psychologists. The title of his review is revealing in itself: "The most important social psychological research in this generation?"

Wrightsman opens with some minor criticisms, such as Milgram's lack of statistical comparisons between experimental variations, his not referring to other relevant research—that of Mixon for example, the possibility that in the experimenter-as-victim condition (Experiment 14), subjects may have viewed the procedure as unsafe or untested. His major criticism, however, is at the level of theory:

> While it explains the outcomes of several experimental variations, it does not clearly generate new constructs that are subject to operational demonstration or independent measurement. It does not seek to explain why 35% disobey when 65% obey. And it is entirely post hoc. (P. 804)

Wrightsman expresses astonishment at the facility with which Milgram generalizes from his data, for instance, his phrase pertaining to the "fatal flaw nature has designed into us." Acknowledging the abundance of undiminished praise which has been given to Milgram, Wrightsman remains unconvinced:

> When I consider that the initial study was a demonstration and not even an experiment, that the research program lacked any initial theory or tests of significance, and that many of its conclusions are subject to alternative explanations, I am saddened that it is the obedience study that will go down in history as reflecting the 1960s in social psychological research. (P. 804)

Wrightsman, like Marcus, acknowledges a number of positive features, such as the robustness of Milgram's findings, the effectiveness of the situational variations in modifying obedience, and its relevance to the events of My Lai and Watergate as illustrating the tragic effects of obedience in the real world. He expresses regret, however, that there has been virtually no research on "the strength of obedience in other major institutions of the real world, on the ways that . . . students, patients, or soldiers respond to obedience-laden situations" (p. 805).

Wenglinsky (1975)

Martin Wenglinsky reviewed Milgram's book for *Contemporary Sociology*. His focus is primarily methodological. His major thesis is an endorsement of the demand-characteristic criticism, although Orne and Holland are not cited by name:

> Whether those who administered pain believed they were doing so or not, every one of them knew that they were in the world of an illusion, even if they didn't know where illusion left off and reality began. Something else was going on. There had to be a hidden agenda. . . . You are playing according to the rules of the experimental game—which includes the idea that you can't really harm anyone . . . And then Milgram steps outside the frame to blame you for what you have done. (P. 614)

Given Wenglinsky's perspective, it is understandable why he does not concern himself with the specifics of Milgram's theoretical account, for to do so would imply a basic acceptance of the methodological viability of the paradigm. Not surprisingly, Wenglinsky challenges the generality of the research:

> The question about Hitler is how anyone who listened to what he said could possibly not know that there would be extermination camps. The question about the Milgram experiment is how could anyone be expected to think that they would be asked to do someone real harm. (Pp. 614-15). . . . All Milgram shows is that if you work hard enough you can lull people into evil by making the situation resemble a non-evil one in as many ways as possible. And the final irony is that the so-called administrators of pain were correct in trusting their usual judgments, in treating the situation as a scientific experiment. For that is all it was. No pain was administered. They were right, and Milgram is wrong in thinking they did evil. (P. 615)

Unlike Marcus or Wrightsman, Wenglinsky finds virtually nothing to admire in the obedience research. His criticisms are fueled by an ethical misgiving as well, it seems, for in several instances, he speaks of Milgram "cheating" by manipulating his subjects into performing what they have every right to believe are completely justifiable and innocent actions, and then stepping outside of the subjects' context and generalizing to acts of immorality and genocide.

Milburn (1976)

Thomas Milburn, a psychologist at Ohio State University, reviewed Milgram's book for *Society*, a major social science journal. Milburn's review is mixed. He is positive regarding Milgram's approach, that is, varying the situation and observing effects on obedience, and is impressed with the reliability of the phenomenon. He emphasizes the sheer importance of the problem Milgram is investigating, noting that Milgram is "extremely interested in generalizing the results of all that is done here to the unique example of the slaughter of Jews under Adolf Hitler or the killing of Vietnamese at My Lai and other places in Vietnam" (p. 98).

However, Milburn is also critical. He is not convinced by Milgram's general theoretical account—"His concept of agency as an explanation somehow is not completely satisfying. A greater emphasis on the Freudian explanation of attitudes toward authority or those of sociologists would seem to have done equally well" (p. 97). Milburn, himself, is uncertain to what extent the obedience experiments should be extrapolated to the world outside the laboratory. He expresses the need for more information on individual differences, field research, naturalistic observations, exploratory interviews—in essence, he wants the phenomenon of obedience to be examined by a diversity of methodologies and perspectives.

Morelli (1983)

Mario Morelli, a philosopher, analyzes the obedience research in an article entitled "Milgram's dilemma of obedience." Early in this article, Morelli claims that Milgram's conceptualization of the basic issues of obedience and authority is unclear. Morelli is uncertain as to the precise way in which subjects perceive the experimenter—for example the "command" or "expert" factors noted in Patten's critique (see Chapter Seven). He also suggests that Milgram has not adequately differentiated the concept of obedience from other processes, for example compliance, persuasion, intimidation, capitulation.

Morelli's main contention is that the act of obeying authority may itself be a moral imperative for some subjects, and that Milgram is underplaying the moral component involved in such behavior. Morelli implies that Milgram is biased toward viewing the subject's siding with the learner as the only morally defensible position. Obedience to authority thus may reflect a moral commitment of its own, not a moral weakness or an abandonment of moral decision making as implied in the concept of the agentic shift.

In a published response to Morelli, Milgram (1983) addresses several issues. He acknowledges that there are diverse components to the concept of authority, that in his paradigm the experimenter presented the features of both a person "in charge" as well as an "expert." He agrees with Morelli regarding a measure of terminological vagueness in the concept of "obedience." Milgram adds that one could also include the terms "conformity" and "cooperation" in Morelli's list. He suggests, however, that obedience is a reasonable designation for what is being studied.

Milgram agrees that there is a moral basis to the act of obedience, but he seems firm on taking the victim's side. To treat both moralities—to obey, and to not harm—as of equal weight strikes Milgram as absurd: "If a torturer in a Buenos Aires prison, flogging a helpless victim to death can be said, within Morelli's terms, to be acting morally because he feels it is duty to do so, than I am not much impressed with Morelli's way of thinking" (p. 191).

Helm and Morelli (1979)

Charles Helm, a political scientist, and Mario Morelli collaborated on a critique of the obedience experiments that appeared in the journal *Political Theory*. Their analysis is a lengthy scanning of a variety of features of the obedience paradigm that have been the object of criticism, for example by Orne and Holland, Mixon, Baumrind, and Harré. A number of points raised by Morelli (1983) are also stated in this paper.

Helm and Morelli accept the basic methodological soundness of the obedience paradigm, but are particularly doubtful regarding Milgram's conceptualization of the agentic state. They suggest that Milgram is, in effect, absolving the subject by claiming that he or she bears no responsibility, that he is therefore sanctioning the subject's obedience. Helm and Morelli disagree:

> Our legal system rests fundamentally on the idea that an individual could have decided otherwise in the performance of a culpable act. Milgram blurs the whole question of morality by seeing it solely as an instrumental adjustment where the individual shifts from attention to the victim into slavish dependence on the authority. (P. 342)

It appears, then, that Helm and Morelli are adopting at least an implicit version of the "pathology thesis" here. That is, they are reading Milgram's interpretation as a justification for the behavior of his subjects. One sees this in the following observation:

> What are we to say about the obedient subject of Milgram? On Milgram's theoretical account, obedience to authority, even when it involves inflicting severe pain on a helpless individual is normal—part of one's physiologically, psychologically, and socially structured response to a hierarchically organized society." (P. 342)

Helm and Morelli obviously do not accept the view that obedience is "normal," and it is this fundamental distinction which, I think, is the primary focus of their extensive critical analysis.

I think their analysis is extremely pertinent, because it raises, once again, the inevitable difficulty many people have in coming to terms with the "normality thesis." Without elaborating, I would refer the reader to the discussion of Sabini and Silver on "moral responsibility" in Chapter Seven. Helm and Morelli *may* be confusing the issues of intent and responsibility, as clarified in Sabini and Silver's analysis.

Helm and Morelli's specific reservations concerning the agentic state are appropriate to note in this context. They quote Milgram: "Once the person has moved into the agentic state, this evaluative mechanism is wholly absent" (p. 147 in Milgram, 1974, cited by Helm and Morelli, p. 337).

They then quote from a transcript of the agonized obedience of Fred Prozi (Milgram, 1974, pp. 73-76), a subject who obeys to 450 volts but with extraordinary hesitation, tentative refusals, and pleas for the learner's welfare. Helm and Morelli, cogently I think, are skeptical: "As an explanation of Fred Prozi's behavior, this account is not terribly illuminating. If there is a shift into the agentic state, there appears to be a shift as rapidly out of it (p. 337).

Fred Prozi is, by definition, a completely obedient subject, but Milgram's detailed account of Prozi's emotional despair strikes Helm and Morelli as seriously discrepant with the agentic state hypothesis.

ENDORSEMENTS OF MILGRAM'S THEORY

There are, of course, commentators who have expressed extremely favorable opinions of Milgram's 1974 book. As Milgram's book is an archive of empirical data as well as a theoretical statement, reviewers have expressed a variety of positive sentiments regarding the obedience experiments—their ethics, methodology, and social and political impli-cations—as well as Milgram's theoretical analysis.

Riecken (1974)

Henry Riecken, a social psychologist at the University of Pennsyl-vania, reviewed Milgram's book for the journal *Science*. His reaction is resolutely positive on all counts. He likes Milgram's writing style, the calm and measured reaction to his critics, and his ethical sensitiv-ity to the welfare of subjects. He provides perhaps the most complete synopsis of Milgram's theory of any reviewer, and is enthusiastic here as well:

> The analysis is convincing. The origins of obedience lie not in the per-sonal characteristics of the participants, nor in the institutional auspices, nor even, indeed, in something so dramatic as a hardly repressed feral streak of aggressiveness. The analysis is correspondingly disturbing be-cause it makes clear how banal the sociopsychological origins of obe-dience really are and, therefore, how chillingly commonplace obedience is likely to be in any even minimally stable society. (P. 669)

Riecken views Milgram's research as a model of scientific inquiry —meticulous, systematic, socially significant—and as a classic embodi-ment of the social psychological perspective: "the linkage of individual (internal) states of cognition, affect, and motive with (external) social structure." (p. 669).

Damico (1982)

Alfonso Damico, a political scientist, has discussed the obedience research in the journal *Political Theory*. His favorable regard for the obedience research is shown in the repeated contrasts he makes with the Kohlberg data described earlier in this chapter. In Damico's inter-pretation, the subjects in the obedience paradigm were *not* confused about issues of "right and wrong"—their anxiety and tension were evi-dence on this matter. Their difficulty was in failing to *act* on their awareness. Damico views Milgram's orientation as congruent with his own political perspective. He implies that Kohlberg's orientation is "too psychological," that it is in a sense naive:

> While Kohlberg locates the problem of obedience in the stages of indi-vidual moral development, one hears, in reading Milgram, the much more familiar sounds of politics: commands, grudging compliance, open resis-tance, and even the cries of a victim (P. 427)

He endorses Milgram's central interpretive theme, namely the power of social structure to override individual expressions of conscience:

> Paying particular attention to what Milgram's subjects are doing and undergoing, one is struck by how much the individual recedes into the background to be replaced by actors constrained by their roles, the different expectations attached to those roles, and the support or lack thereof for resistance to malevolent commands. (P. 410)

Damico views the obedience research as valuable in forcing people to abandon intuitive presumptions regarding the dominant importance of close relationships, such as friendships, family, and intimacy. In his analysis, the obedience experiments reflect the power of *impersonal* social encounters. They sensitize us to the fact that in many social contexts, particularly in organizational settings, people interact with others in terms of their role or position. A theory of moral behavior that presumes that the individual, by virtue of his or her moral development, can readily transcend this political fact of life is unrealistic.

Damico observes that Milgram's empirical data speak quite cogently to the prospects for *resistance* to authority. In this context, he is mildly critical. He states that Milgram's (1974) theory, with its emphasis on the survival value and inevitability of obedience, is perhaps overstating the case for the pervasiveness of obedience, that there may well be more effective resistance to authority in the world than would be thought possible after reading Milgram's theoretical position. Damico acknowleges the point raised by Helm and Morelli (1979) regarding the importance of the close surveillance and prodding of the experimenter—namely, that these features are often *not* characteristic of obedience in more common bureaucratic settings. However, Damico concludes that the implications of the obedience research are profound because, although people in organizational settings may not be under the direct, physical scrutiny of their authorities, they are hardly in a situation comparable to that of the subjects in Experiment 11:

> Individuals are rarely left to themselves. When one transfers the discussion of morality—for example, responsibility, fairness, rights, and so on —to actions occurring within an organizational context or a hierarchy of authority, the single individual as an individual recedes into the background to be replaced by a more social and political actor. (P. 424)

Brown (1974)

Roger Brown, a prominent social psychologist at Harvard, responded to Marcus' *New York Times* review. "Outrage" would be a fitting
caption to his remarks. Brown seems provoked by the style of Marcus's
criticisms—their harshness—as much as by their substance. Brown's
position is clear:

> I have known about the experiments since they began 10 years ago; I
> studied the book in page proofs and am quoted on the dust jacket as
> believing that this series of experiments (there are 18 major variations)
> probably constitutes the most important social psychological research
> done in this generation. I stand by that judgment and am honestly stun-
> ned that the book could have stimulated so murderous a review. (P. 42)

Brown emits a volley of undiluted criticisms of his own. He suggests that Marcus' views reflect the inability of the humanities to come
to terms with the viability of studying "the human mind and personal
relationships" by experimental techniques. He surmises that books
that speak more glowingly regarding human nature tend to receive
less scathing reviews—"namby-pamby psychological trash is usually
favorably reviewed in *The Times*" (p. 42).

Brown is a personal admirer of Milgram and feels that Marcus effectively smeared Milgram's personal reputation. He expresses particular admiration for Milgram's expressive talent, and is incredulous at
Marcus's criticism on this score. Brown includes a reference to his own
experience with the obedience paradigm:

> In 10 years of discussing Milgram's research with Harvard students I
> cannot recall a single discussion that did not intensely interest the stu-
> dents and deepen their understanding of moral reasoning. Even if the
> theory does not fully satisfy the reviewer, even if he is uncomfortable
> about the deceit employed in the experimental scenario, how could he
> be so abusive about research of such profound importance and original-
> ity, carried out and reported with such clarity and restraint. (P. 43).[8]

Zimbardo (1974)

Philip Zimbardo, a social psychologist at Stanford and a target for
intense ethical as well as methodological criticisms regarding his prison-
simulation investigation, comments on the obedience research in a brief
note in the *American Psychologist*. His perspective is virtually identical
to that of Milgram. He argues that the reason people can be manipu-

lated so readily in contexts such as the obedience paradigm is that they maintain an illusion of personal invulnerability and control. He endorses the "normality thesis," noting that Milgram's research as well as his own document that evil deeds are often the result of noble bureaucrats simply doing their job.

Zimbardo thinks attention has been misdirected with an exaggerated focus on ethical issues, subjects' conflicts, and methodological ambiguities, when the real issue concerns obedience to authority. We desperately need to be enlightened on this problem, because we are manifestly ignorant about its pervasive influence. Zimbardo makes an interesting, quite original observation regarding the behavior of the *defiant* subjects. Usually they are portrayed in rather heroic terms, yet Zimbardo is far from satisfied:

> Did they intervene, go to his aid,[9] denounce the researcher, protest to higher authorities, etc.? No, even their disobedience was within the framework of "acceptability"; they stayed in their seats, "in their assigned place," politely, psychologically demurred, and they waited to be dismissed by the authority." (P. 567)

From this perspective, Zimbardo sees obedience as "total" in Milgram's laboratory.

Zimbardo thinks Milgram's research is more than "probably important"—quoting from Marcus's review—and then, in a somewhat depressed tone, concludes his powerful endorsement with the following, somewhat cynical thought:

> It ought to give each of us pause as no other single bit of research has. But it will not, because the vital lessons about human conduct are really not influenced by research psychologists or heeded even when nicely expressed by English professors. The lessons reach the people through their momma and poppa, the homeroom teacher, the police, the priests, the politicians, the Ann Landers and Joyce Brothers, and all of the other "real" people of the world who set the rules and the consequences for breaking them. (P. 567)[10]

CONCLUSIONS

Milgram's theoretical position can, I think, be evaluated in terms of two perspectives. One concerns the general coherence of his interpretation—the inclusiveness of his account, the ease with which one can envision concrete instances of the abstract components of his formulation, and the basic logic or plausibility of the approach. The other perspective is concerned with what might be termed the "hard evidence." Are there data which confirm *explicitly* the processes presumed by Milgram to account for his findings? Is his theoretical model sufficiently precise to differentiate it from other accounts?

I find the 1974 version of Milgram's theory to be strong on the first issue, but relatively weaker on the second. The basic model of obedience—that is, the agentic state, antecedent conditions, binding factors, buffers, strain—is, in my view, an extremely interesting and sophisticated theoretical statement. It is simply derived, draws upon ideas from a variety of disciplines in the social sciences, and is focused in terms of one pivotal construct, the agentic state.

The model clearly has pedagogical value. After describing the wealth of empirical findings to students, I generally find that the theoretical model is helpful in providing a necessary integration of ideas. Milgram's discussion is particularly useful in stimulating students to think of obedience as it affects their own lives. One can think of experiences in one's childhood or adolescence and identify antecedents of one's own tendency to obey. Milgram's conceptualization of binding factors—the importance of face-saving, embarrassment, etiquette —is, I think, of special interest. It represents a subtle dynamic that would certainly be unrecognized in any intuitive account of obedience to authority.

The plausibility factor is also strong. The quotation of Alexander Haig, Jr., on the first page of this chapter, has remained in my memory as a classic instance of the agentic state from the moment I read it. The testimony of Colonel Hawkins, cited in this chapter, seems also to reflect Milgram's conceptualization of this cognitive state. I think it is a distinct strength for a theory to stimulate people to think about a phenomenon in new ways, to be analytical in their outlook, to be on the "lookout" for instances which seem to confirm or disconfirm the theory at issue. Milgram's approach is clearly useful in this regard. If one were to ask what the single most important lesson might be in studying the obedience experiments, I would be tempted to say that one should be more wary of authority, more "on guard," more *thoughtful* about one's obedience. I think this can be achieved through a serious reading of Milgram's theoretical position.

In terms of the empirical support for his theory, I find myself in basic agreement with the critics. The status of the agentic shift must certainly be regarded as "unproven." This is the crucial variable in his theory, and there is no evidence to substantiate its actual behavioral significance. I am speaking in this regard of the kind of data that would be obtained in measuring responsibility attributions of subjects and correlating these responses with their behavior in the paradigm. The Mantell and Panzarella (1976) investigation is the major study to date on this issue, and it does not support Milgram's position.

Thus, while I have (perhaps too readily) cited the verbal statements of Alexander Haig and Colonel Hawkins as illustrations of the agentic state, I must confess that in terms of their actual psychological functioning, I have no evidence with which to *prove* that they were in a state of mind in strict adherence to the criteria for the agentic state as outlined by Milgram. I think it is important to distinguish between "verbal statements" which, at least superficially, resemble the agentic-state formulation and the covert processes of perception and responsibility attribution that are the true psychological basis for the phenomenon as outlined by Milgram. The problem is not untestable, nor is there a wealth of data contradicting the notion of an agentic-state. Nevertheless, empirical confirmation of the agentic state formulation is yet to be achieved.

Several critics have mentioned the post-hoc aspect of the theory, that it was formulated *after* Milgram had performed the experiments. This may be true, although one can actually find several of the major ideas in Milgram's 1974 theory in a much earlier, relatively obscure publication (1967), and it is my own view that he had the essential outlines of his theory in mind at the time of the experimental inquiry itself. A close reading of his proposal (1961b) is a relevant indicator of this. However, I think Milgram's primary intent was not to develop a precise, testable (that is, falsifiable) theoretical structure. His contributions were essentially empirical. His talents in terms of thinking *paradigmatically* were extraordinary—almost no one denies the incredible ingenuity of the experiments themselves, their programmatic, painstaking features, their artistic, creative quality. Thus, while it is understandable that he should attempt the kind of integrated analysis published in his 1974 book, I do not think his goals were to mount a fresh scientific assault on the obedience phenomenon, but rather to "wrap things up" in a manner that was intellectually defensible and interesting.

There is actually another sense in which Milgram's "theory" of obedience might be examined. This pertains to the "normality thesis." This thesis, in itself, is a kind of theoretical perspective, for it defines a behavioral domain (obedience) and formulates a basic set of processes which are predictive of that behavior and help to illuminate its nature. Milgram's experimental variations, described in Chapter

Three, are certainly testimony to the validity of his theoretical position, that obedience is powerfully influenced by relevant situational contexts—that it is capable of being produced at an extremely high rate or reduced to a complete absence *without taking into account any personality factors in the individual research participants.* I think Milgram's evidence—and, crucially, the extensive supporting research literature reviewed not only in Chapter Four but in Chapters Five and Six as well—speak convincingly to the basic social-psychological conceptualization that Milgram advanced.

In this context, it is appropriate to note that he was dissatisfied with the manner in which the obedience experiments were traditionally presented to students as well as more general audiences. He commented on this matter in one of his last publications, the preface to the 1979 French edition of his book:

> The most pervasive form of distortion, in the dissemination of the experiment to the larger public, is hardly noticeable to those not familiar with the methods of experimental social psychology. Yet it is most significant from an intellectual standpoint. There are two major components to the structure of this experimental study. First, there is the basic paradigm of a person being instructed to give increasingly more severe shocks to a protesting victim. A second, and no less important aspect of the research, concerns the systematic changes introduced in each of the 18 experimental conditions. The degree of obedience varied sharply depending on the exact manner in which the variables of the experiment are arranged in an experimental condition . . . Yet, in the popular press, these variations are virtually ignored, or assumed to be of only minor importance. (Pp. 7-8)

I would only add that the extent of the distortion extends far beyond the "popular press." I hope that the nature of this distortion referred to by Milgram has been clarified, and that the contextual specificity of obedience has been illuminated in this book.

EPILOGUE

It would not be hyperbole, I think, to say that the obedience experiments have sent shock waves throughout the academic world and beyond, for things have never quite been the same in social research since the appearance of Milgram's 1963 article. Rarely does even the most imaginative research transcend its academic origins, yet the obedience experiments have received truly unprecedented attention within the behavioral sciences and humanities. Recent issues of the *Social Science Citation Index* document an impressive list of references to the obedience experiments, a phenomenon which has been true for almost 20 years, and which could justifiably be the envy of any researcher. The broad impact of Milgram's studies was hinted at as early as 1964, when he received the Socio-Psychological Prize from the American Association for the Advancement of Science. His election, in 1983, to the American Academy of Arts and Sciences was further testimony to the interdisciplinary scope of interest in his research.

The primary research literature cited in this book has, of course, been heavily geared to the discipline of social psychology. I have pointed to the significance of Milgram's apprenticeship with Solomon Asch, one of the most influential figures in the history of experimental social psychology. Milgram earned his doctorate in this specialization, and the obedience experiments are, in the most fundamental sense, a reflection of a social-psychological orientation. This backdrop for the research was, however, certainly no guarantee that the experiments would be to everyone's liking. Given the litany of criticisms, often unjustifiable in my view, directed at laboratory experiments—

their sterile, removed-from-real-life aspect, their preoccupation with control and manipulation at the expense of applied relevance—one might have expected the obedience experiments to receive the usual fate of laboratory work, some initial interest and a lasting repose. This, of course, did not happen.

In performing these studies, Milgram touched a nerve. Many have interpreted them as revealing something very illuminating about human nature. It was this kind of reaction that elevated the experiments from the usual confines of in-house academic deliberations. The obedience research has, in my view, become a part of the history of great ideas, not solely because of the observed findings of the experiments per se, but because of the reflection and intellectual ferment that was to be occasioned by them. "If X tells Y to hurt Z, under what conditions will Y carry out the command of X and under what conditions will he refuse?" Regardless of the answer, this was a question for our time. It was a simple question, but Milgram addressed it in a manner that was captivating, that made people think about the issue in a new way.

"Who is responsible?" may be the most pressing moral question of our age. The consequences of "inappropriate" obedience are more salient to our awareness than ever, whether the context be that of the nuclear threat, political corruption, atrocities in war, or disasters traced to bureaucratic mismanagement. The pursuit of Nazi war criminals at a feverish pitch in the mid-1980s is, I think, a reflection of a national consciousness sensitized to the issues of destructive obedience and responsibility. We have become more alert to the ease with which an individual may lose a sense of personal accountability when imbedded in a social hierarchy. When we hear the phrase, "I was following orders," we stop and think about it, somewhat more carefully, perhaps, than in previous times. The obedience experiments have unquestionably facilitated an instructive examination of this complex problem. Milgram has made the issues seem more pertinent to our lives.

There are, of course, diverse reasons for the dramatic impact of Milgram's work, and these have been traced throughout this book. Certainly the association of the obedience experiments with the Holocaust is of particular significance. The ethical and methodological controversies generated by the experiments would have established the landmark status of the research in their own right, but it was the connection with the Holocaust which, from the start, endowed the experiments with a special charisma, giving them a larger-than-life quality. I have no doubt that it was the prospect of the obedience research revealing one of the crucial secrets of the Holocaust that in fact induced scholars, of many persuasions, to take the research so seriously.

As we have seen, many would still question whether the behavior observed in Milgram's laboratory was of precisely the same genre as that found in non-laboratory manifestations of destructive obedience. Yet, the debates on this point are of undeniable value. Even among those who are not totally convinced of their validity, the obedience research must evoke a measure of skepticism regarding the human condition. The experiments cast a shadow. They warn against relegating the potential for Holocaust-like events to the past, to a time of unenlightenment, to an era of primitive passions. They have an unsettling, futuristic relevance. They signify that destructive obedience, in a variety of contexts, may be a disaster "waiting to happen." Milgram, himself, voiced such a perspective. He concluded his 1965 article in *Human Relations* with this sobering question:

> If in this study an anonymous experimenter could successfully command adults to subdue a fifty-year old man, and force on him painful electric shocks against his protests, one can only wonder what government, with its vastly greater authority and prestige, can command of its subjects. (P. 75)

I would point to the development of the experimental paradigm itself as Milgram's singularly most impressive achievement. This is not to minimize the creativity of the experimental variations or the insight of many of his interpretations. Yet, what was pivotal, in my opinion, was his initial decision to gain analytical control by essentially stripping the obedience problem from the complexities of dramatic historical or political events, and exposing the phenomenon, reduced to its barest essentials, to laboratory investigation. Concepts heavily laden with abstract philosophical overtones—authority, freedom, obedience—were translated into specific, observable events. While anyone could have an opinion about what an individual would or should do when given destructive orders from an authority, Milgram went beyond speculation. A choice point was created in his laboratory—a moral "fork in the road." He constructed a telling moment of truth. Whatever course of action a subject pursued was of great interest.

What are the major lessons of the obedience experiments? I would suggest four: First, people clearly have the capacity to *disobey* authority. Disobedience is, at first glance, perhaps the least memorable finding of Milgram's research, yet it was the major result in a number of the experimental variations. It is the context that often is crucial, and people could conceivably arrange their social environments to facilitate disobedience, should this be necessary. In his provocative analysis of "groupthink" and its resultant fiascos in group decision-making, Irving Janis (1982) has provided a number of instructive procedures for avoiding the pitfalls of a group being over-reliant upon a directive leader. This is not precisely the issue of defying evil orders, but it is a reasonably close approximation. Like Milgram, Janis emphasizes social structures and their modifiability, rather than the personal characteristics of the acting individuals, as the key explanatory constructs.

Second, as a bumper sticker on the truck of a colleague advises, we should "Question Authority." Notwithstanding the political or ideological flavor of such an assertion, I think it captures elegantly a major theme to the entire obedience story. Certainly Milgram's lesson is *not* that we should always say "no" to the dictates of authority. Rather, we should monitor the legitimacy of the orders we or others receive, recognizing our potential for behaving very badly if we can absolve ourselves of personal responsibility.

A third lesson concerns the use of the phrase "blind obedience" with regard to those who have participated in genocide or atrocities or in the obedience experiments themselves. I think the obedience experiments show something quite different. One of the most instructive results of the experiments is the torment experienced by many subjects, regardless of their ultimate obedience or defiance. Conflict was ubiquitous in Milgram's paradigm—conflict born out of intensely experienced thoughts and feelings. Obedience was not a reflexive, instinctive, non-thinking response to authority, but rather a decision, often painfully reached after considerable wrenching and vacillation. The indiscriminate use of the phrase "blind obedience" suggests that immoral or evil actions could be performed only by those who are in a mindless or "blind" psychological state. This is a naive view of the process, one that reflects both our tendency to personalize the negative actions of others and our ignorance about the processes of influence involved in obedience to authority.

Finally, there is the question of authority itself. The obedience experiments do not address the issue of authority per se—how one becomes an authority, and what disposes an authority to issue destructive commands. But it would clearly be an oversight to avoid commenting on the glaring *power* of authority as revealed in the obedience experiments. True, we have seen that circumstances will, on occasion, permit defiance to prevail. Yet, when such conditions are not operative, obedience is raised to an extremely high level of likelihood. In such cases, we will need heroes to defy unjust authority. The admonition "choose one's leaders wisely" would surely be consistent with the findings of the obedience experiments.

A note on the ethical controversy is warranted in these closing remarks. I have pointed to the initial development of the obedience paradigm as of primary significance. Among other reasons for engaging in the research, Milgram, and others, have known that people are very poor at forecasting the results of the obedience experiments. The research thus had to be performed to learn what people would actually do. This "ends justify the means" perspective is, as we have seen, not universally accepted. In fact, I would suggest that even by many of his most enthusiastic supporters, Milgram would be acknowledged to have at least approached the limits of ethical research practices in subjecting the obedience problem to an experimental paradigm.

Some, of course, believe, and will continue to believe, that he exceeded the limits on this score. My own position is that the knowledge gained was of inestimable value, and that the demonstrable costs were relatively negligible. It is difficult, furthermore, to envision that the diverse, intellectually stimulating commentaries and criticisms would have emanated from investigating the obedience problem in a less rigorous or controlled setting. Ethically, as well as methodologically, social science is decidedly better off for having contended with the obedience experiments. However, given what has transpired in terms of contemporary attitudes toward research with human subjects, it may well be that future social scientists will have to develop new methodologies to shed light on the unanswered questions about destructive obedience.

In conclusion, my purpose in writing this book has been to examine the impact of the obedience experiments. I think that the impact has been extraordinary. Reactions to the research have been extremely varied, and I have often been impressed with the erudition of many of the commentators and analysts who have attempted to grasp the essential nature or meaning of the obedience experiments. Particular mention should be made of those who, in addition to Milgram, have conducted empirical research on the obedience problem. It is not, as should be abundantly clear at this point, a simple problem to study. Milgram's contributions as a principal investigator were unusually prodigious, but we are also extremely fortunate to have had access to the vital data obtained by other researchers.

My own, highly favorable position has been evident throughout the book, perhaps more glaringly in these final pages. I felt that it would be ill-advised to be completely neutral on this matter. I have been intrigued with the obedience research for over fifteen years, and I surmised that this attitude would influence my writing even if I attempted to suppress my personal views.

I hope, nevertheless, that I have been reasonably successful in presenting all of the relevant arguments and points of view. It has, at times, been a difficult path. On the one hand, my own biases may have influenced me to give greater weight or expression to certain lines of argument or evidence. On the other, in an effort to be fair, I may have given too much credence to positions I genuinely do not endorse. Candidly, I must confess to moments of kaleidoscopic transition in my own thinking, wherein certain assumptions regarding the experiments which I had previously held unquestioningly suddenly would appear far more elusive. I sense that my own position on Milgram's research is far from being a closed matter. I would like to think that the reader, too, will find this book to be a stimulus for interesting discussion and still further thinking regarding the obedience experiments.

NOTES

CHAPTER ONE

1. Milgram's first submission to the *Journal of Abnormal and Social Psychology* was rejected, as was his subsequent request to the *Journal of Personality*. Several months later, the editor of the *Journal of Abnormal and Social Psychology* recalled the rejected paper and published it. (Milgram, personal communication, June, 1984).

2. Milgram had published one paper prior to the appearance of the 1963 article on obedience. This was a report of his doctoral research, a cross-cultural extension of the Asch conformity paradigm (1961a).

3. Milgram conducted extensive research in areas other than obedience. An illustration of the diversity of his interests may be found in his collection, *The Individual in a Social World* (1977a). However, it is clearly the obedience research which has been responsible for his ranking. The number of references to the obedience experiments in the *Science Citation Index* is in the thousands.

4. A footnote in the 1963 publication (p. 378) referred to a forthcoming article that would describe the research program more extensively. This was in reference to a paper published in 1965 in *Human Relations*.

5. The shock generator was approximately 30 inches long and 12 inches high, larger than might be inferred from simply reading about it. The electronics of the generator were clearly audible to subjects. The apparent authenticity of the generator was emphasized by Milgram as important in contributing to the perceived legitimacy of the research.

6. It would have been of interest to know precisely the number of subjects who required a specific number of prods. For example, how many subjects who received the fourth prod from the experimenter did in fact continue to 450 volts? To my knowledge, Milgram did not perform this analysis.

7. Research by Ross, Bierbrauer, and Hoffman (1976) has shown that confronting people with a challenge to their perception of physical reality (for example, line lengths, or tone durations as in Ross et al.) is hardly trivial, as might be implied in Milgram's account. Intense reactions of stress and tension are frequently reported in these studies. Milgram's observation that the task used by Asch lacked "face significance" is, however, reasonable.

CHAPTER TWO

1. A useful reference is R. A. Wicklund and J. W. Brehm, *Perspectives on Cognitive Dissonance* (1976).

2. Self-ratings by the questioner were not elevated, and ratings of the contestant (by the questioner as well as the contestant himself) were approximately at an "average" level.

3. The film "Obedience" has had, in itself, an extraordinary impact. Almost 60 minutes long and in black and white, the film vividly documents "live" episodes of the performance of several subjects. While the essential features of the paradigm are readily conveyed by articles and photographs, the film is unique in capturing the "sounds" that are so much a part of this research—the mounting anguish of the subject in the presence of the learner's apparent agony and the stern monotone of the experimenter's insistent orders. It is somewhat curious that the film opens by presenting the performances of three subjects who, at varying stages, defy the experimenter and refuse to continue. Although the film subsequently emphasizes situational variations in obedience, the initial focus is on individual differences, a factor de-emphasized in Milgram's account. Milgram has written a valuable instructor's guide to accompany the film. The film invariably evokes considerable reactions in observers and these are, in themselves, interesting to analyze. In this context, Dirsmith (1983) has written an illuminating account of the use of the obedience film in his undergraduate classes in auditing in the College of Business at Pennsylvania State University: "It is useful for highlighting a question that the profession, or perhaps more deeply, our culture, may not provide adequate models for disobedience, for being independent in mental attitude" (p. 49).

4. Bierbrauer does not provide details on the re-enactment, such as the feedback from the victim, tension in subjects, etc.

5. The effect of a subject's gender on obedience has been examined by Milgram, as well as other investigators, as indicated in research described in Chapters Three and Four.

6. The percentage of subjects (240) in the respective categories was: internal, 24 percent; internal-external, 21 percent; and external, 55 percent.

7. Kelley's (1973) influential model of the attribution process asserts that if everyone behaves similarly in a given situation—for example, if all viewers like the movie *Amadeus*—that behavior or response will be perceived in situational terms. That is, the movie itself will be attributed as the (situational) cause of the (near consensus) favorable response, as opposed to the unanimous response being viewed as a reflection of the similar interests or tastes of the viewers. Sabini and Silver's argument is similar to this perspective on situational causality.

8. The difference between "expected" and "obtained" results with respect to obedience is, in certain respects, similar to the distinction between attitudes and behavior, a classic conceptual problem in social psychology (see Brannon, 1976; Wicker, 1969).

CHAPTER THREE

1. We have referred to the ethical controversy occasioned by Baumrind's (1964) critique of the obedience experiments (see Chapter One). In the 1968

symposium, an extensive methodological criticism by Orne and Holland was published, which also was to have a very substantial impact. Milgram's response to Orne and Holland appeared in an anthology edited by Miller (1972a). Issues pertaining to the methodological controversy are examined in Chapter Six.

2. Milgram (1974, p. 170) has addressed the issue raised by some critics (such as Patten, 1977b) that his subjects, because of their volunteer status, were unusually docile and submissive.

3. The grant proposal to the National Science Foundation is an important document. Milgram outlined a number of issues which, though of considerable interest, he did not (to my knowledge) investigate. These included propaganda about the victim, the effect of the victim's having the opportunity to retaliate, and the use of groups of naive subjects as compared to several variations in which assistants or confederates of the experimenter acted the part of peers to the true subject (for example, variations 17 and 18). The likelihood of increased rebellion to unjustified authority by *groups* of subjects—in contrast to Milgram's paradigm in which the true subject was always a solitary individual—has been shown in a provocative field experiment by Gamson et al. (1982). There is also an indication that Milgram was interested in obtaining evidence regarding personality factors and determining their role in the behavior of subjects.

4. From an ethical point of view, variation 4—Touch Proximity—would seem to be particularly objectionable. That is, the idea of forcing a subject to have physical contact with a protesting individual seems qualitatively more stressful than the other variations. Yet, this particular variation has apparently never been singled out by critics.

5. A study by Bandura et al. (1975) is relevant. They stigmatized the recipients of shocks by labeling them (intentionally) within hearing of the subject. Subjects subsequently inflicted more intense shocks on those who had been stigmatized than on those who had not been labeled. However, this experiment was not a study of obedience per se. Subjects at all times had an opportunity to select their own preferred level of punishment to administer.

6. The effect of "obedient groups" was described in a journal publication (1965c), but not in Milgram's 1974 book.

7. "Group pressure and action against a person" was described in a journal article (1964a), but not in the 1974 book. It is, of course, a study of conformity as distinguished from obedience.

8. Only the "expected behavior" studies (for example, in Chapter 2, p. 21) involved obtaining data from subjects seen in groups.

9. Milgram (1974) devoted two chapters in his book to a relatively detailed account of the performance of ten individual subjects. Of particular interest are the verbal rationales given by these individuals regarding their behavior in the experiment, and Milgram's interpretation of these accounts.

CHAPTER FOUR

1. The subjects were male German citizens, between the ages of 19 and 49, recruited on a voluntary basis from governmental agencies and private industry.

2. Mantell did not elaborate on the significance of the modeling-delegitimization findings, other than to imply that this condition produced a higher rate of obedience than might be expected. He suggested that by subtracting the 15 percent of subjects who, on the basis of the baseline results, would have defied the experimenter without any modeling experience, the "pure defiance" rate for the modeling-delegitimization condition was only 33 percent.

3. An experiment by Powers and Geen (1972) has also shown that subjects are less likely to administer shock to a victim if they have first witnessed a defiant model. This study departed substantially from the obedience paradigm in that no "prods" were employed by the experimenter, and the major response was not obedience per se, but rather the degree of shock administered. The findings, however, are essentially consistent with Mantell and Milgram (Experiment 17) in showing the influence of defiant models. Rosenhan (1969) is also relevant on this issue.

4. The study by Mann (1973) is noted in Chapter Seven, in conjunction with research by Kelman and Lawrence (1972) on public opinion regarding the trial of Lieutenant Calley for the massacre at My Lai.

5. Additional studies are pertinent. Rogers (1973) used army recruits as well as college students in a replication of the obedience paradigm. No prods were employed, however, as the key independent variable was the presence or absence of the experimenter. Obedience was generally reduced—26 percent of the subjects were completely obedient. No effects were associated with subject population or experimenter presence on percentage of maximum obedience, although the average maximum shock intensity was significantly higher with authority present. A number of investigations discussed in Chapter Six with reference to their methodological implications are further evidence for the general reliability of the phenomenon of obedience in diverse research contexts, such as Meeus and Raaijmakers; Ring et al. (1970); Sheridan and King (1972).

CHAPTER FIVE

1. Baumrind has published several major papers dealing with ethical issues in research with human subjects (for example, 1975, 1979, 1985). Although there are minor differences in these analyses in terms of her stated perspective, the Milgram experiments are a major target in all of her work.

2. Milgram gave me a copy of this report during an interview held in June 1984.

3. Dannie Abse, the English dramatist and physician, has written an imaginative play based on the obedience research, *The Dogs of Pavlov* (1973). The essential theme is that it is the subject who is the true victim. The published version contains an informative exchange between Abse and Milgram regarding the ethics of the research and its implications. Abse is critical, although he has an insightful perspective on the complexities of the issues involved. Milgram's strategy, in responding to Abse's objection to the use of deception, is to draw an analogy between the dramatist's use of illusion and the experimentalist's use of deception: "The fact is that the audience accepts the necessity of illusion for the sake of entertainment, intellectual enrichment, and all of the other benefits of the theatrical

experience. And it is their acceptance of these procedures that gives you warrant for the contrivances you rely upon. So I will not say that you cheated, tricked, and defrauded your audience. But, I would hold the same for the experiment. Misinformation is employed in the experiment; illusion is used when necessary in order to set the stage for the revelation of certain difficult-to-get-at-truths, and the procedures are justified for one reason only: they are, in the end, accepted and endorsed by those who are exposed to them" (Milgram, in Abse, 1973, pp. 39-40).

4. Morton Hunt reviewed the problems raised by the use of deception in a detailed and balanced review in *The New York Times Magazine* (September 12, 1982). Repeated references are made to the obedience experiments. One prominent social psychologist is quoted as having become disenchanted with the use of deception, not for philosophical reasons but seemingly out of frustration in obtaining approval of review boards. Hunt quotes Edward E. Jones, of Princeton University: "You don't even consider experiments that would run into resistance. . . . Whole lines of research have been nipped in the bud" (p. 142). Hunt surmises that "obedience experiments like Milgram's are now quite beyond the pale; most helping experiments are considered unacceptably hard on some subjects; and so are research designs which would even briefly frighten or embarrass subjects or teach them unpleasant truths about themselves" (p. 142).

5. It is intriguing that the study by Ring et al. (1970) has been cited to show the harmful effects of the obedience paradigm (Patten, 1977a; Baumrind, 1985) as well as the lack of such effects (Crawford, 1972; West et al., 1975).

6. Schlenker and Forsyth also presented analogous depictions of another controversial experiment, that of West, Gunn, and Chernicky (1975). This was a field experiment in which subjects were tempted to participate in a Watergate-like burglary. Far more agreed to participate under certain conditions than had been anticipated, particularly by subjects who had estimated the behavior in a method similar to that used in studies of "predicted obedience." Cook (1975) published an important ethical analysis of the West et al. experiment. Schlenker and Forsyth reported that their subjects produced similar judgments in their reactions to various descriptions of the Milgram and the West et al. experiments.

7. Rubin has subsequently expressed a similar position (1983, 1985).

8. It is certainly conceivable that members of a research team can experience unexpressed misgivings about their work or about their research supervisor. I am reminded of the legacy of abuses suffered by members of the Chicago Symphony Orchestra under the late Fritz Reiner, and by orchestras under such reputed autocrats as Toscanini and Szell. The glorious performances may well have masked hidden resentments. Yet, unless there is evidence to suggest that this type of dynamic was operative, I find it unconvincing to argue that Milgram exerted coercive influence on his research assistants. Baumrind, interestingly, makes the identical accusation in her recent essay (1985, p. 171).

9. There are, of course, many investigations in social psychology which have prompted ethical scrutiny. Zimbardo et al. (1973) is a relevant example. Zimbardo's

prison simulation investigation (1973) differed from the obedience paradigm in many important respects—it was not a paradigm or research program, but rather a six-day event. Crucially, it did not involve deception. Yet, it was similar to the obedience research in dramatizing the power of the situation to influence people to commit acts of destructiveness—and it has become an extremely well-known investigation, one with important social implications. For an ethical debate concerning this particular research, see H. B. Savin (1973) and Zimbardo (1973).

10. For other positive ethical commentary, see Brown(1985),Eckman(1977), and Simon (1980). For thoughtful discussions on the ethics of the obedience experiments which do not take an explicitly favorable or unfavorable position, see Allen (1978) and Brigham and Wrightsman (1982).

11. Among numerous research projects in the social sciences which have produced considerable ethical controversy are the following:

Project Camelot. This was a government-sponsored project, involving primarily sociologists, political scientists, and anthropologists, designed to investigate factors promoting internal conflict and war in Latin America. This project was unique in becoming ethically controversial before it was actually enacted, and in fact it was ultimately cancelled. The literature on Project Camelot is extensive. The seminal analysis is an anthology edited by Horowitz, *The Rise and Fall of Project Camelot: Studies in the Relationship Between Social Science and Practical Politics* (1967). Further valuable discussion can be found in Sjoberg's *Ethics, Politics, and Social Research* (1967), and Bower and deGasparis' *Ethics in Social Research: Protecting the Interests of Human Subjects* (1978).

The Harvard Drug study. This research, conducted by Alpert and Leary, used Harvard students as subjects to investigate the influence of hallucinogenic drugs. An informative discussion of the controversy generated by this research, particularly within the academic community at Harvard, can be found in Benson and Smith's *The Harvard Drug Controversy: A Case Study of Subject Manipulation and Social Structure* (in Sjoberg, 1967).

The Wichita Jury Study. Initiated in 1954 by faculty in the social sciences and law school at the University of Chicago, this research involved the secret recording of jury deliberations in a series of ongoing trials. The purpose was to obtain objective empirical data to test a variety of assumptions and criticisms regarding the jury system in American law. A discussion of the ethical dimensions of this research is found in Vaughan's *Governmental Intervention in Social Research: Political and Ethical Dimensions in the Wichita Jury Recordings* (in Sjoberg, 1967).

CHAPTER SIX

1. Holland's dissertation is complex, and contains some impressive scholarship. I feel, however, that he overstates the demand-characteristic argument. His line of reasoning depends critically upon unverified assumptions about the likely motives of subjects, their sophistication, etc. Some of his data are clearly non-

supportive of his particular thesis. Yet, I think Holland's work is an imaginative methodological critique, particularly considering that it appeared at a time when there was relatively little sensitivity to the social psychological dynamics of research settings.

2. The authors do not refer to Milgram's point that the Bridgeport variation did not yield a significantly lower obedience rate than the base line (1974, p. 69).

3. Milgram referred to an experiment by Rosenhan which involved a replication of the obedience paradigm in order to establish a base line for further variations. According to Milgram, Rosenhan "established the interviewer as a person independent of the experiment who demands a detailed account of the subject's experience, and probes the issue of belief even to the point of asking, 'You really mean you didn't catch on to the experiment?' On the basis of highly stringent criteria of full acceptance, Rosenhan reports that . . . 68.9 percent of the subjects thoroughly accepted the authenticity of the experiment. Examining the performance of these subjects, he reports that 85 percent are fully obedient" (1972, p. 141). For discussion of Rosenhan's research, see Rosenhan (1969) and Rosenhan, et al. (1976).

4. Sheridan and King emphasized the higher rate of obedience in their female subjects. Although that they were aware of Milgram's Experiment 8, they did not cite the research of Ring et al. (1970). Both of these experiments also found high rates of obedience in female subjects.

5. The subjects were males and females, aged 18 to 55. Their minimal level of education was the Dutch equivalent of high school. They were recruited through an advertisement in newspapers.

6. On this point, the investigators viewed their experiment as similar to Milgram's Experiment 9—the victim's limited contract. That is, the subject initially witnessed an agreement on the part of the experimenter regarding the welfare of the victim, only to observe a subsequent violation of this assurance.

7. As will become evident, role playing is a designation of a category of techniques. Although all of these share in the procedure of informing subjects that what is about to transpire is, in a fundamental sense, not "real," there is a wide range of information which may or may not be revealed to subjects, such as the hypotheses or major predictions, and specifics of the methodology.

8. On this point, the extreme stress reported to have been experienced by some of the subjects in Zimbardo's prison-simulation study is relevant. The Zimbardo et al. (1973) study is frequently cited to show that role playing can be extraordinarily involving—to the degree that subjects totally lose sight of the simulated aspect to the research context—and that, for this reason, role playing is not above reproach on ethical grounds.

9. Banuazizi and Movahedi (1975) have provided an interesting methodological criticism of Zimbardo's prison-simulation study. Their analysis is, in many respects, analogous to the Orne and Holland critique of the obedience research, as noted in their conclusion: "We have offered an alternative interpretation of

the dramatic outcome of the Stanford Prison Experiment. In our view, the subjects responded to a number of demand characteristics in the experimental situation, acting out their stereotypic images of a prison guard and, to a lesser extent, of a prisoner. To the extent that such confounding variables were operative, the subjects' behavior cannot be explained as strategic, coping responses to an assymetrical power situation analogous to that of a real prison" (p. 159). For counter-arguments, see Doyle (1975), DeJong (1975), and Thayer and Saarni (1975), as well as Movahedi and Banuazizi's rebuttal (1975).

10. Adair, Dushenko, and Lindsay (1985) have written an informative review of the current status of research practices concerning such issues as deception, informed consent, and debriefing. They report a continued reliance on deception and a minimum of explicit reference to the use of informed consent and to providing subjects with the right to withdraw from participation. Reports of debriefing are still less than typical. Adair et al. emphasize, appropriately, the close interplay between ethical and methodological features of research, and recommend that researchers give increased attention to all relevant ethical factors in the reporting of their research in journals and other outlets.

CHAPTER SEVEN

1. It is clear that a number of perspectives are required in even attempting to "account for the Holocaust." A complex of historical, political, and economic events was involved. The Milgram experiments do not address these factors in any direct manner. Their focus is psychological, but it would perhaps be inaccurate to overemphasize the distinction between perspectives (political science, history, etc.), given that Milgram's orientation was uniquely multifaceted. This was evident in a statement on the first page of his 1974 book: "Obedience is the psychological mechanism that links individual action to political purpose. It is the dispositional cement that binds men to systems of authority" (p. 1).

2. My selection of commentary relating the obedience research to genocide, in particular to the Holocaust, is necessarily selective, for hundreds of theorists and scholars have commented on this issue. It should be mentioned that the cogency of the linkage between the obedience research and the Holocaust rests upon the plausibility and accuracy of the accounts of both domains, that is, the experiments and the Holocaust. There are profound disagreements regarding the nature of the Holocaust, and, as we have seen, the "truth" or factual nature of the obedience research is also a matter of some debate. For this discussion, however, a reasonable degree of agreement on the essential nature of the experiments as well as events and personalities of the Holocaust will be presumed.

3. A study by Mann (1973) examined attitudes toward the My Lai incident in an Australian population. The findings again suggested that in a military context, many people have a distinct tolerance for destructive obedience: "The American public's attitude to My Lai cannot be viewed as a uniquely American response reflecting uniquely American problems. The fact that an Australian sample showed

a similar pattern of responses which in many ways resembled variations among the American public suggests that the ideology of duty, obedience, and discipline extends beyond the U.S. and is probably a powerful theme in many Western countries" (p. 21).

4. Kelman has written a provocative analysis of the Watergate political scandal. Similar to his account of sanctioned massacres (1973) and his research on public reaction to the My Lai incident (Kelman and Lawrence, 1972), Kelman emphasizes the domination of authority once an individual is locked into a hierarchical social structure, particularly in the context of high-powered governmental functioning: "Many of the witnesses before the Senate Watergate Committee expressed an orientation to authority based on unquestioning obedience to superior orders . . . They too seemed to assume that superior orders override the moral considerations that might apply in other situations and free them of personal responsibility for their actions" (p. 307). For discussion of the relevance of Milgram's research for legal issues of responsibility, see Hamilton (1978a; 1978b) and Freeman (1979).

5. Miale and Selzer add to their "delegitimization" of Kelley's position, noting that: "It is possible that the nature of his own death may throw light on his idiosyncratic perception of the Nazi leaders. Goering, it will be recalled, had cheated the hangman by swallowing a cyanide capsule which had been smuggled into his cell—we still do not know by whom. A number of extra capsules were found on his body. Douglas Kelley committed suicide with one of these (*The New York Times*, Jan. 1, 1958)." (P. 14).

6. Patten recognizes Milgram's argument that volunteer subjects tend to score lower on the F-Scale. He counters with the (correct) view that Elms and Milgram (1966) tended to minimize the role of personality factors, including the significant correlations between the F-Scale and behavior in the obedience paradigm. He then denies the cogency of Milgram's using the data on the lower authoritarianism of volunteer subjects to argue that such individuals would be less likely to be obedient.

7. Patten distinguishes between two types of obedience. In one instance, obedience is essentially descriptive and pertains to a subject who goes to the end of the shock board upon the commands of the experimenter. However, in another instance, "one is obedient when one consistently responds to commands by performing acts which one has every reason to believe are immoral, merely because one is ordered to do so" (p. 427).

8. See Muson (1978) for a discussion of a symposium on obedience in the context of Watergate, including John Dean and Stanley Milgram.

CHAPTER EIGHT

1. Cultures may, of course, differ in the general emphasis placed on obedience, particularly in terms of the impact on child development. Albert Speer, a high ranking Nazi, commented on this factor in his autobiography, *Inside the Third*

Reich: "For although it may sound strange today, for us it was no empty slogan that 'the Fuehrer proposes and disposes' for all. We had been rendered susceptible to such ideas from our youth on. We had derived our principles from the Obrigkeitsstaat, the authoritarian though not totalitarian state of Imperial Germany. Moreover, we had learned those principles in wartime, when the state's authoritarian character had been further intensified. Perhaps the background had prepared us like soldiers for the kind of thinking we encountered once again in Hitler's system. Tight public order was in our blood; the liberalism of the Weimar Republic seemed to us by comparison lax, dubious, and in no way desirable" (1970, p. 33).

2. Wiesel's response to President Reagan was a moment fraught with tension. Wiesel had just received a medal from the President honoring him in conjunction with his role on the National Holocaust Commission. Wiesel was then given an opportunity to respond. He chose to focus his remarks on the President's planned trip to a cemetery in Bitburg, West Germany, where, it had been discovered, a number of SS officers had been buried. A national furor resulted, among Jews and World War II veterans and many others who felt that the President's appearance at the site of SS graves would be an immoral act of unconscionable reconciliation. Wiesel was polite and soft-spoken, as befitting a guest in the White House. Yet, he spoke to his conscience, and in front of the President and on national television, he defied the President by strongly and repeatedly urging him to change his mind and not go to the cemetery. The President did, however, go to Bitburg. on May 5, 1985.

3. Persons who score in the authoritarian direction on the F-Scale endorse items in a manner suggesting a strong identification with authority, a traditional (some might say old-fashioned) set of beliefs about sexuality, a denial of feelings, and cynicism.

4. The Haas study departs significantly from the obedience paradigm, yet it has considerable interest in terms of attempting to maintain the idea of destructive obedience in a context with more "mundane reality," to use a phrase of Aronson and Carlsmith (1968). There would, I suspect, be strong ethical criticisms were this kind of study proposed today. In certain respects, this investigation is similar to that of Meeus and Raaijmakers (1985), described in Chapter Six.

5. There are a number of studies which have examined the relationship between personality variables and aggressive behavior in the form of administering shock on a Milgram-type generator (e.g., Larsen et al., 1972; Lefcourt et al., 1966; Baron, 1977). These studies do not deal with obedience per se, however, and will not be considered here.

6. Several investigations, not reviewed here, have failed to show predicted effects linking personality to obedience. Bock and Warren (1972) did not observe a predicted relationship between measures of religiosity and obedience, and deFlorance (1972) did not replicate the findings of Elms and Milgram (1966) concerning the correlation between obedience and a measure of authoritarianism (F-Scale).

7. In an interesting analysis, Funder and Ozer (1983) calculated the correlation between physical proximity of the victim (Experiments 1 through 4) and the maximum shock administered by each subject in Milgram's research. This correlation was .42. A similar analysis involving the proximity of the experimenter—absent in Experiment 7, present in Experiment 5—and the subject's maximum shock level yielded a correlation of .36. Funder and Ozer argue that there are substantial individual differences in Milgram's data, and that the "power of the situation," expressed in correlational terms, is not as high as might traditionally be expected. Funder and Ozer argue, quite convincingly, for a renewed and more sophisticated approach to the assessment of personality and the relationship between personality and various social behaviors.

8. Marcus's rejoinder to Brown is almost an "about face." He praises Milgram's research, noting that he, too, was extremely influenced by the Holocaust, that he was never an enthusiast of the proposition that the Holocaust reflected a unique character flaw in the German people. He maintains, however, a number of his stated reservations regarding the stylistic presentation and coherence of Milgram's theoretical position.

9. Harvey Tilker (1970) performed an imaginative experiment on this issue. Subjects were assigned to observe an enactment of the obedience paradigm. They were, according to their particular experimental condition, given either no responsibility or total responsibility for the welfare of the student (actually a confederate) in the role of learner. The experimenter then left the room, and the other subject, in the role of teacher (also a confederate), proceeded to deliver increasingly severe shocks in the usual manner. The responsibility manipulation was clearly effective (as was another manipulated variable, namely feedback from the learner). Subjects who had been explicitly given responsibility for the learner's well-being and who received feedback indicating distress on the part of the learner were far more likely to protest and take physical action to terminate the experiment than subjects who had not been given responsibility or feedback from the victim. Tilker's study is thus about factors that influence the likelihood of helping victims of destructive obedience. Like obedience itself, helping another on the basis of perceiving oneself as responsible is remarkably influenced by situational conditions.

10. For other positions endorsing Milgram's conceptual analysis, see Allen (1978), Eckman (1977), Etzioni (1968), and Rosenzweig (1974).

BIBLIOGRAPHY

Abse, D. 1973. *The dogs of Pavlov*. London: Vallentine, Mitchell.

Adair, J. G., Dushenko, T. W., and Lindsey, R. C. 1985. Ethical regulations and their impact on research practice. *American Psychologist* 40:59-72.

Allen, B. P. 1978. *Social behavior: Fact and falsehood*. Chicago: Nelson Hall.

American Psychological Association 1981. Ethical principles of psychologists. *American Psychologist* 36:633-38.

Arendt, H. 1963. *Eichmann in Jerusalem: A report on the banality of evil*. New York: Viking Press.

Argyle, M. 1969. *Social interaction*. London: Methuen.

Aronson, E. 1984. *The social animal*. 4th ed. New York: W. H. Freeman.

Aronson, E., Brewer, M., and Carlsmith, J. M. 1985. Experimentation in social psychology. In *The handbook of social psychology*, edited by G. Lindzey and E. Aronson, 3rd ed., 441-86. New York: Random House.

Aronson, E., and Carlsmith, J. M. 1968. Experimentation in social psychology. In *The handbook of social psychology*, edited by G. Lindzey and E. Aronson, 2nd ed., 1-79. Reading, Mass.: Addison-Wesley.

Aronson, E., and Mills, J. 1959. The effects of severity of initiation on liking for a group. *Journal of Abnormal and Social Psychology* 59:177-81.

_____. 1946. Forming impressions of personality. *Journal of Abnormal and Social Psychology* 41:258-90.

Asch, S. E. 1956. Studies of independence and conformity: A minority of one against a unanimous majority. *Psychological Monographs* 70 (9).

_____. 1955. Opinions and social pressure. *Scientific American*, November, 31-35.

Askenasy, H. 1978. *Are we all Nazis?* Secaucus, N.J.: Lyle Stuart.

Bandura, A., Underwood, B., and Fromson, M. E. 1975. Disinhibition of aggression through diffusion of responsibility and dehumanization of victims. *Journal of Research in Personality* 9:253-69.

Banuazizi, A., and Movahedi, S. 1975. Interpersonal dynamics in a simulated prison: A methodological analysis. *American Psychologist* 30:152-60.

Barnes, J. A. 1979. *Who Should Know What? Social Science, Privacy and Ethics*. New York: Cambridge University Press.

Baron, R. A. 1977. *Human aggression*. New York: Plenum.

Baron, R. A., and Byrne, D. 1984. *Social psychology: Understanding human interaction*. 4th ed. Boston: Allyn and Bacon.

Baum, A., Fisher, J. D., and Singer, J. E. 1985. *Social Psychology*. New York: Random House.

Baumrind, D. 1985. Research using intentional deception: Ethical issues revisited. *American Psychologist* 40:165-74.

————. 1979. IRBs and social science research: The costs of deception. *IRB: A Review of Human Subjects Research* 1:1-4.

————. 1975. Metaethical and normative considerations governing the treatment of human subjects in the behavioral sciences. In *Human rights and psychological research: A debate on psychology and ethics*, edited by E. C. Kennedy, 37-68. New York: Thomas Y. Crowell.

————. 1971. Principles of ethical conduct in the treatment of subjects: Reaction to the draft report of the committee on ethical standards in psychological research. *American Psychologist* 26:887-96.

————. 1970. Further thoughts on ethics after reading Milgram's "A reply to Baumrind." Unpublished manuscript. University of California, Berkeley.

————. 1964. Some thoughts on ethics of research: After reading Milgram's "Behavioral study of obedience." *American Psychologist* 19:421-23.

Beaman, A. L., Cole, C. M., Preson, M., Klentz, B., and Steblay, N. M. 1983. Fifteen years of foot-in-the-door research: A meta-analysis. *Personality and Social Psychology Bulletin* 9:181-96.

Beauchamp, T. L., Faden, R. R., Wallace, R. J., Jr., and Walters, L., eds. 1982. *Ethical issues in social science research*. Baltimore: Johns Hopkins University Press.

Benson, J. K., and Smith, J. O. 1967. The Harvard drug controversy: A case study of subject manipulation and social structure. In *Ethics, politics, and social research*, edited by G. Sjoberg, 115-40. Cambridge, Mass.: Schenkman Publishing Company.

Berger, S. M. 1962. Conditioning through vicarious instigation. *Psychological Review* 69:450-66.

Berscheid, E., and Walster, E. H. 1974. Physical attractiveness. In *Advances in experimental social psychology*, edited by L. Berkowitz, Vol. 7, 158-216. New York: Academic Press.

Bickman, L., and Zarantonello, M. 1978. The effects of deception and level of obedience on subjects' rating of the Milgram study. *Personality and Social Psychology Bulletin* 4:81-85.

Bierbrauer, G. 1979. Why did he do it? Attribution of obedience and the phenomenon of dispositional bias. *European Journal of Social Psychology* 9: 67-84.

Bock, D. C., and Warren, N. C. 1972. Religious belief as a factor in obedience to destructive commands. *Review of Religious Research* 13:185-91.

Borofsky, G. L., and Brand, D. J. 1980. Personality organization and psychological functioning of the Nuremberg War Criminals: The Rorschach data. In *Survivors, victims, and perpetrators*: *Essays on the Nazi Holocaust*, edited by J. E. Dimsdale, 359-403. New York: Hemisphere.

Bower, R. T., and deGasparis, P. 1978. *Ethics in social research*: *Protecting the interest of human subjects*. New York: Praeger.

Brandt, L. W. 1978. Don't sweep the ethical problems under the rug! Totalitarian versus equalitarian ethics. *Canadian Psychological Review* 19:63-66.

Brannon, R. 1976. Attitudes and the prediction of behavior. In *Social psychology*, edited by B. Seidenberg and A. Snadowsky, 145-98. New York: The Free Press.

Brigham, J. C., and Wrightsman, L. S., eds. 1982. *Contemporary issues in social psychology*. 4th ed. Monterey, Calif.: Brooks/Cole.

Brown, R. 1974. Letters to the editor, *New York Times Book Review*, February 24, 42-43.

———. 1985. *Social psychology*, 2nd ed. New York: Free Press.

Charny, I. W. 1982. *Genocide*: *The human cancer*. New York: Hearst Books.

Cialdini, R. B. 1985. *Influence*: *Science and practice*. Glenview, Ill.: Scott, Foresman and Company.

Cockerham, W. C., and Cohen, L. E. 1980. Obedience to orders: Issues of morality and legality in combat among U.S. Army paratroopers. *Social Forces* 58: 1271-88.

Collins, F. L., Jr., Kuhn, I. F., Jr., and King, G. D. 1979. Variables affecting subjects' ethical ratings of proposed experiments. *Psychological Reports* 44:155-64.

Cook, S. W. 1975. A comment on the ethical issues involved in West, Gunn, and Chernicky's "Ubiquitous Watergate: An attributional analysis." *Journal of Personality and Social Psychology* 32:66-68.

Cooper, J. 1976. Deception and role playing: On telling the good guys from the bad guys. *American Psychologist* 31:605-10.

Coutts, L. M. 1977. A note on Mixon's critique of Milgram's obedience research. *Personality and Social Psychology Bulletin* 3:519-21.

Crawford, T. J. 1972. In defense of obedience research: An extension of the Kelman ethic. In *The social psychology of psychological research*, edited by A. G. Miller, 179-86. New York: The Free Press.

Damico, A. J. 1982. The sociology of justice: Kohlberg and Milgram. *Political Theory* ·10:409-34.

Deaux, K., and Wrightsman, L. S. 1984. *Social psychology in the eighties*. 4th ed. Monterey, Calif.: Brooks/Cole.

de Florance, A. S. 1972. The disobedient victim—An empathy hypothesis. Unpublished thesis for Degree of Bachelor of Arts (Honors), Department of Psychology, University of Sydney.

DeJong, W. 1975. Another look at Banuazizi and Movahedi's analysis of the Stanford prison experiment. *American Psychologist* 30:1013-15.

Diamond, S. S., and Morton, D. R. 1978. Empirical landmarks in social psychology. *Personality and Social Psychology Bulletin* 4:217-21.

Dicks, H. V. 1972. *Licensed mass murder: A socio-psychological study of some SS killers*. New York: Basic Books.

Diener, E., and Crandall, R. 1978. *Ethics in social and behavioral research*. Chicago: University of Chicago Press.

Dirsmith, M. W. 1983. 'Obedience' in the classroom. *Journal of Accounting Education* 1:41-50.

Doyle, C. 1975. Interpersonal dynamics in role playing. *American Psychologist* 30:1011-13.

Drekmeier, C. 1971. Knowledge as virtue, knowledge as power. In *Sanctions for evil*, edited by N. Sanford and C. Comstock, 192-243. San Francisco: Jossey-Bass.

Eckman, B. K. 1977. Stanley Milgram's "obedience" studies. *Et cetera* 3:88-99.

Eiser, J. R. 1980. *Cognitive social psychology*. London: McGraw-Hill Book Company (UK).

Eisner, M. S. 1977. Ethical problems in social psychological experimentation in the laboratory. *Canadian Psychological Review* 18:233-41.

Elms, A. C. 1982. Keeping deception honest: Justifying conditions for social scientific research strategems. In *Ethical issues in social science research*, edited by T. Beauchamp, R. R. Faden, R. J. Wallace, Jr., and L. Wallace, 232-45. Baltimore: Johns Hopkins University Press.

―――――. 1972. *Social Psychology and Social Relevance*. Boston: Little Brown.

Elms, A. C., and Milgram, S. 1966. Personality characteristics associated with obedience and defiance toward authoritative command. *Journal of Experimental Research in Personality* 1:282-89.

Epstein, Y. M., Suedfeld, P., and Silverstein, S. J. 1973. Subjects' expectations of and reactions to some behaviors of experimenters. *American Psychologist* 28:212-21.

Erickson, M. 1968. The inhumanity of ordinary people. *International Journal of Psychiatry* 6:278-79.

Errera, P. 1972. Statement based on interviews with forty "worst cases" in the Milgram obedience experiments. In *Experimentation with human beings: The authority of the investigator, subject, professions, and state in the human experimentation process*, edited by J. Katz, 400. New York: Russell Sage Foundation.

Etzioni, A. 1968. A model of significant research. *International Journal of Psychiatry* 6:279-80.

Evans, R. I. 1980. *The making of social psychology: Discussions with creative contributors*. New York: Gardner Press.

Fein, H. 1979. *Accounting for genocide: National responses and Jewish victimization during the Holocaust*. New York: The Free Press.

Feldman, R. S. 1985. *Social psychology: Theories, research, and applications*. New York: McGraw-Hill.

Festinger, L. 1980. *Retrospections on social psychology*. New York: Oxford University Press.

Ford, D. 1985. A reporter at large: U. S. Command and control—Part I. *New Yorker*, April 1, 43-91.

Forsyth, D. R., and Pope, W. R. 1984. Ethical ideology and judgments of social psychological research: Multidimensional analysis. *Journal of Personality and Social Psychology* 46:1365-75.

Forward, J., Canter, R., and Kirsch, N. 1976. Role-enactment and deception methodologies: Alternative paradigms? *American Psychologist* 31:595-604.

Frank, J. D. 1982. *Sanity and survival in the nuclear age: Psychological aspects of war and peace*. New York: Random House.

————. 1944. Experimental studies of personal pressure and resistance. *Journal of Genetic Psychology* 30:23-64.

Freedman, J. L. 1969. Role playing: Psychology by consensus. *Journal of Personality and Social Psychology* 13:107-14.

Freedman, J. L., and Fraser, S. C. 1966. Compliance without pressure: The foot-in-the-door technique. *Journal of Personality and Social Psychology* 4:195-202.

Freeman, M. D. A. 1979. Milgram's Obedience to authority—Some lessons for legal theory. *The Liverpool Law Review* 1:45-61.

French, J. R. P., Morrison, H. W., and Levinger, G. 1960. Coercive power and forces affecting conformity. *Journal of Abnormal and Social Psychology* 61:93-101.

French, J. R. P., and Raven, B. H. 1959. The bases of social power. In *Studies in social power*, edited by D. Cartwright, 150-67. Ann Arbor: University of Michigan Press.

Fromm, E. 1973. *The anatomy of human destructiveness*. Greenwich, Conn.: Fawcett Publications.

Funder, D. C., and Ozer, D. J. 1983. Behavior as a function of the situation. *Journal of Personality and Social Psychology* 44:107-12.

Gamson, W. A., Fireman, B., and Rytina, R. 1982. *Encounters with unjust authority*. Homewood, Ill.: Dorsey Press.

Geller, D. M. 1982. Alternatives to deception: Why, what, and how? In *The ethics of social research: Surveys and experiments*, edited by J. E. Sieber, 39-55. New York: Springer-Verlag.

————. 1978. Involvement in role-playing simulations: A demonstration with studies on obedience. *Journal of Personality and Social Psychology* 36:219-35.

Gergen, K. L. 1973. Codification of research ethics: View of a doubting Thomas. *American Psychologist* 28:907-12.

Gilbert, S. J. 1981. Another look at the Milgram obedience studies: The role of the gradated series of shocks. *Personality and Social Psychology Bulletin* 7: 690-95.

Haas, K. 1966. Obedience: Submission to destructive orders as related to hostility. *Psychological Reports* 19:32-34.

Hamilton, V. L. 1978a. Who is responsible? Toward a *social* psychology of responsibility attribution. *Social Psychology Quarterly* 41:316-27.

————. 1978b. Obedience and responsibility: A jury simulation. *Journal of Personality and Social Psychology* 36:126-46.

Hampden-Turner, C. 1971. *Radical man: The process of psycho-social development*. New York: Doubleday and Company.

Harré, R. 1979. *Social being: A theory for social psychology*. Oxford: Basil Blackwell.

Harrower, M. 1976a. Rorschach records of the Nazi war criminals: An experimental study after thirty years. *Journal of Personality Assessment* 40:341-51.

————. 1976b. Were Hitler's henchmen mad? *Psychology Today*, July, 76-80.

Helm, C., and Morelli, M. 1979. Stanley Milgram and the obedience experiment: Authority, legitimacy, and human action. *Political Theory* 7:321-45.

Hendrick, C., et al. 1977. Role playing as a methodology for social research: A symposium. *Personality and Social Psychology Bulletin* 3:454-522.

Hilberg, R. 1961. *The destruction of the European Jews*. Chicago: Quadrangle Books.

Hofling, C. K., Brotzman, E., Dalrymple, S., Graves, N., and Pierce, C. 1966. An experimental study of nurse-physician relations. *Journal of Nervous and Mental Disease* 143:171-80.

von Hoffman, N. 1970. Sociological snoopers. *The Washington Post*. January 30, B1; B9.

Holland, C. H. 1968. Sources of variance in the experimental investigation of behavioral obedience. Unpublished Ph.D. dissertation, University of Connecticut.

Horowitz, I. L., ed. 1967. *The Rise and Fall of Project Camelot: Studies in the Relationship Between Social Science and Practical Politics*. Cambridge, Mass.: The M.I.T. Press.

Humphreys, L. 1978. *Tearoom trade: Impersonal sex in public places*. Chicago: Aldine Publishing Co.

Hunt, M. 1982. Research through deception. *The New York Times Magazine*, September 12, 66-67; 138-43.

Janis, I. L. 1982. *Victims of groupthink*. Boston: Houghton Mifflin.

Jelalian, E., and Miller, A. G. 1984. The perseverance of beliefs: Conceptual perspectives and research developments. *Journal of Social and Clinical Psychology* 2:25-56.

Jellison, J. M., and Green, J. 1981. A self-presentation approach to the fundamental attribution error: The norm of internality. *Journal of Personality and Social Psychology* 40:643-49.

Jones, E. E. 1985. Major developments in social psychology during the past five decades. In *The Handbook of Social Psychology*, edited by G. Lindzey and E. Aronson, Vol. 1, 3rd ed., 47-107. New York: Random House.

————. 1979. The rocky road from acts to dispositions. *American Psychologist* 34:107-17.

Jones, E. E., and Nisbett, R. E. 1971. *The actor and the observer: Divergent perceptions of the causes of behavior*. New York: General Learning Press.

Kantowitz, B. H., and Roediger, H. L. III. 1984. *Experimental psychology: Understanding psychological research*. St. Paul, Minn.: West Publishing.

Katz, J. 1972. *Experimentation with human beings: The authority of the investigator, subject, professions, and state in the human experimentation process*. New York: Russell Sage Foundation.

Kaufmann, H. 1967. The price of obedience and the price of knowledge. *American Psychologist* 22:321-22.

Kelley, H. H. 1973. The processes of causal attribution. *American Psychologist* 28:107-28.

Kelman, H. C. 1976. Some reflections on authority, corruption, and punishment: The social-psychological context of Watergate. *Psychiatry* 39:303-17.

————. 1973. Violence without moral restraint: Reflections on the dehumanization of victims and victimizers. *Journal of Social Issues* 29:25-61.

————. 1967. Human use of human subjects: The problem of deception in social psychological experiments. *Psychological Bulletin* 67:1-11.

Kelman, H. C., and Lawrence, H. L. 1972. Assignment of responsibility in the case of Lieutenant Calley: Preliminary report on a national survey. *Journal of Social Issues* 28:177-212.

Kennedy, E. C., ed. 1975. *Human rights and psychological research: A debate on psychology and ethics.* New York: Thomas Y. Crowell.

Kilham, W., and Mann, L. 1974. Level of destructive obedience as a function of transmitter and executant roles in the Milgram obedience paradigm. *Journal of Personality and Social Psychology* 29:696-702.

Kohlberg, L. 1969. Stage and sequence: The cognitive-developmental approach to socialization. In *Handbook of socialization theory and research*, edited by D. A. Goslin, 347-480. Chicago: Rand McNally.

Kren, G. M., and Rappoport, L. 1980. *The Holocaust and the crisis of human behavior.* New York: Holmes and Meier.

Kudirka, N. K. 1965. Defiance of authority under peer influence. Unpublished Ph.D. dissertation, Yale University.

Larsen, K. S., Coleman, D., Forbes, J., and Johnson, R. 1972. Is the subject's personality or the experimental situation a better predictor of a subject's willingness to administer shock to a victim? *Journal of Personality and Social Psychology* 22:287-95.

Latané, B., and Darley, J. 1970. *The unresponsive bystander: Why doesn't he help?* Englewood Cliffs, N.J.: Prentice-Hall.

Lefcourt, H. M., Barnes, K., Parke, R., and Schwartz, F. 1966. Anticipated social censure and aggression-conflict as mediators of response to aggression induction. *Journal of Social Psychology* 70:251-63.

Lickona, T., ed. 1976. *Moral development and behavior: Theory, research, and social issues.* New York: Holt, Rinehart and Winston.

Lifton, R. J. 1985. What made this man? Mengele. *The New York Times Magazine*, July 21, 16-25.

————. 1967. *Death in life: Survivors of Hiroshima.* New York: Basic Books.

Lifton, R. J., and Falk, R. 1982. *Indefensible Weapons: The Political and Psychological Case Against Nuclearism.* New York: Basic Books.

Mann, L. 1973. Attitudes toward My Lai and obedience to orders: An Australian survey. *Australian Journal of Psychology* 25:11-21.

Mantell, D. M. 1971. The potential for violence in Germany. *Journal of Social Issues* 27:101-12.

Mantell, D. M., and Panzarella, R. 1976. Obedience and responsibility. *British Journal of Social and Clinical Psychology* 15:239-45.

Marcus, S. 1974. Obedience to authority. *The New York Times Book Review*, January 13, 1-3.

Martin, J., Lobb, B., Chapman, G. C., and Spillane, R. 1976. Obedience under conditions demanding self-immolation. *Human Relations* 29:345-56.

Masserman, J. 1968. Debatable conclusions. *International Journal of Psychiatry* 6:281-82.

McGuire, W. J. 1967. Some impending reorientations in social psychology: Some thoughts provoked by Kenneth Ring. *Journal of Experimental Social Psychology* 3:124-39.

Meeus, W. H. J., and Raaijmakers, Q. A. W. 1985. Administrative obedience: Carrying out orders to exert psychological-administrative violence. Unpublished manuscript, University of Utrecht, Netherlands.

Meyer, P. 1970. If Hitler asked you to electrocute a stranger, would you? *Esquire*, February, 73-132.

Miale, F. R., and Selzer, M. 1975. *The Nuremberg mind: The psychology of the Nazi leaders*. New York: Quadrangle.

Milburn, T. W. 1976. Obedience to authority: An experimental view. *Society* 13: 97-98.

Milgram, S. 1983. Reflections on Morelli's "Dilemma of Obedience." *Metaphilosophy* 14:190-94.

_____. 1979. Preface to French edition of *Obedience to authority: An experimental view*.

_____. 1977a. *The individual in a social world: Essays and experiments*. Reading, Mass.: Addison-Wesley.

_____. 1977b. Subject reaction: The neglected factor in the ethics of experimentation. *Hastings Center Report*, 19-23.

_____. 1974. *Obedience to authority: An experimental view*. New York: Harper and Row.

_____. 1973. The perils of obedience. *Harper's Magazine*, December, 61-67.

_____. 1972. Interpreting obedience: Error and evidence; A reply to Orne and Holland. In *The social psychology of psychological research*, edited by A. G. Miller, 138-54. New York: The Free Press.

Milgram, S. 1967. Obedience to criminal orders: The compulsion to do evil. *Patterns of Prejudice* 1:3-7.

————. 1965a. *Obedience* (a filmed experiment). Distributed by New York University Film Library.

————. 1965b. Some conditions of obedience and disobedience to authority. *Human Relations* 18:57-76.

————. 1965c. Liberating effects of group pressure. *Journal of Personality and Social Psychology* 1:127-34.

————. 1964a. Group pressure and action against a person. *Journal of Abnormal and Social Psychology* 69:137-43.

————. 1964b. Issues in the study of obedience: A reply to Baumrind. *American Psychologist* 19:848-52.

————. 1963. Behavioral study of obedience. *Journal of Abnormal and Social Psychology* 67:371-78.

————. 1961a. Nationality and conformity. *Scientific American*, December, 45-51.

————. 1961b. Dynamics of obedience: Experiments in social psychology. Mimeographed report, National Science Foundation, January 25, 1961.

Miller, A. G., ed. 1972a. *The social psychology of psychological research*. New York: The Free Press.

Miller, A. G. 1972b. Role playing: An alternative to deception? A review of the evidence. *American Psychologist* 27:623-36.

Miller, A. G., Gillen, B., Schenker, C., and Radlove, S. 1974. The prediction and perception of obedience to authority. *Journal of Personality* 42:23-42.

Miller, A. G., and Rorer, L. G. 1982. Toward an understanding of the fundamental attribution error: Essay diagnosticity in the attitude attribution paradigm. *Journal of Research in Personality* 16:41-59.

Mills, J. 1976. A procedure for explaining experiments involving deception. *Personality and Social Psychology Bulletin* 2:3-13.

Mixon, D. 1979. Understanding shocking and puzzling conduct. In *Emerging strategies in social psychological research*, edited by G. P. Ginsburg, 155-76. New York: John Wiley and Sons.

————. 1977. Why pretend to deceive? *Personality and Social Psychology Bulletin* 3:647-53.

————. 1976. Studying feignable behavior. *Representative Research in Social Psychology* 7:89-104.

————. 1972. Instead of deception. *Journal for the Theory of Social Behavior* 2:145-74.

Mook, D. G. 1983. In defense of external invalidity. *American Psychologist* 38: 379-87.

Moore, B., Jr. 1978. *Injustice: The social bases of obedience and revolt*. White Plains, N.Y.: M. E. Sharpe.

Morelli, M. 1983. Milgram's dilemma of obedience. *Metaphilosophy* 14:183-89.

Moscovici, S. 1985. Social influence and conformity. In *The Handbook of Social Psychology*, edited by E. Aronson, M. Brewer, and J. M. Carlsmith, 3rd ed., 347-412. New York: Random House.

Movahedi, S., and Banuazizi, A. 1975. Reply. *American Psychologist* 30:1016-18.

Musmanno, M. 1961. *The Eichmann kommandos*. Philadelphia: Macrae Smith.

Muson, H. 1978. Blind obedience: John Dean meets Milgram, Szaaz, and others. *Psychology Today*, January, 12;112.

Myers, D. G. 1983. *Social psychology*. New York: McGraw-Hill.

Nisbett, R., and Ross, L. 1980. *Human inference: Strategies and shortcomings of social judgment*. Englewood Cliffs, N.J.: Prentice-Hall.

O'Leary, C. J., Willis, F. N., and Tomich, E. 1970. Conformity under deceptive and non-deceptive techniques. *Sociological Quarterly* 11:87-93.

Orne, M. T. 1969. Demand characteristics and the concept of quasi-controls. In *Artifact in behavioral research*, edited by R. Rosenthal and R. L. Rosnow, 147-79. New York: Academic Press.

———. 1962. On the social psychology of the psychological experiment: With particular reference to demand characteristics and their implications. *American Psychologist* 17:776-83.

Orne, M. T., and Evans, F. J. 1965. Social control in the psychological experiment: Antisocial behavior and hypnosis. *Journal of Personality and Social Psychology* 1:189-200.

Orne, M. T., and Holland, C. H. 1968. On the ecological validity of laboratory deceptions. *International Journal of Psychiatry* 6:282-93.

Osherow, N. 1984. Making sense of the nonsensical: An analysis of Jonestown. In *Readings about the social animal*, edited by E. Aronson, 68-86. New York: W. H. Freeman.

Patten, S. 1977a. The case that Milgram makes. *Philosophical Review* 86:350-64.

———. 1977b. Milgram's shocking experiments. *Philosophy* 52:425-40.

Penner, L. 1978. *Social psychology: A contemporary approach*. New York: Oxford University Press.

Penner, L., Hawkins, H. L., Dertke, M. C., Spector, P., and Stone, A. 1973. Obedience as a function of experimenter competence. *Memory and Cognition* 1:241-45.

Penrod, S. 1983. *Social psychology*. Englewood Cliffs, N.J.: Prentice-Hall.

Perlman, D. 1984. Recent developments in personality and social psychology: A citation analysis. *Personality and Social Psychology Bulletin* 10:493-501.

_____. 1980. Who's who in psychology? *American Psychologist* 35:104-06.

Perlman, D., and Lipsey, M. W. 1978. Who's who in social psychology: A textbook definition. *Personality and Social Psychology Bulletin* 4:212-16.

Powers, P. C., and Geen, R. G. 1972. Effects of the behavior and the perceived arousal of a model on instrumental aggression. *Journal of personality and Social Psychology* 23:175-83.

Rank, S. G., and Jacobson, C. K. 1977. Hospital nurses' compliance with medication overdose orders: A failure to replicate. *Journal of Health and Social Behavior* 18:188-93.

Raven, B. H., and Rubin, J. Z. 1983. *Social psychology* 2nd ed. New York: John Wiley and Sons.

Riecken, H. W. 1974. Compliant subjects. *Science* May 10, 667-69.

_____. 1962. A program for research on experiments in social psychology. In *Decisions, values, and groups*, edited by N. F. Washburne, Vol. 2, 25-41. New York: Pergamon Press.

Ring, K. 1967. Experimental social psychology: Some sober questions about some frivolous values. *Journal of Experimental Social Psychology* 3:113-23.

Ring, K., Wallston, K., and Corey, M. 1970. Mode of debriefing as a factor affecting subjective reaction to a Milgram-type obedience experiment: An ethical inquiry. *Representative Research in Social Psychology* 1:67-88.

Rogers, R. W. 1973. Obedience to authority: Presence of authority and command strength. Paper delivered at the Meetings of the Southeastern Psychological Association.

Rosenbaum, M. 1983. Compliance. In *Compliant behavior: Beyond obedience to authority*, edited by M. Rosenbaum, pp. 25-49. New York: Human Sciences Press.

Rosenbaum, M., ed. 1983. *Compliant behavior: Beyond obedience to authority*. New York: Human Sciences Press.

Rosenhan, D. L. 1973. On being sane in insane places. *Science* 179:250-58.

_____. 1969. Some origins of concern for others. In *Trends and issues in developmental psychology*, edited by P. Mussen, J. Langer, and M. Covington, 132-53. New York: Holt, Rinehart and Winston.

Rosenhan, D. L., Moore, B. S., and Underwood, B. 1976. The social psychology of moral behavior. In *Moral development and behavior: Theory, research, and social issues*, edited by T. Lickona, 241-52. New York: Holt, Rinehart, and Winston.

Rosenthal, R., and Rosnow, R. L., eds. 1969. *Artifact in behavioral research*. New York: Academic Press.

Rosenzweig, S. 1974. Letters to the Editor, *The New York Times Book Review*, February 24, 42-43.

Ross, L. 1977. The intuitive psychologist and his shortcomings: Distortion in the attribution process. In *Advances in experimental social psychology*, edited by L. Berkowitz, Vol. 10, 173-220. New York: Academic Press.

Ross, L., Amabile, T., and Steinmetz, J. L. 1977. Social roles, social control, and biases in social-perceptual processes. *Journal of Personality and Social Psychology* 35:484-94.

Ross, L., and Anderson, C. A. 1982. Shortcomings in the attribution process: On the Origins and Maintenance of Erroneous Social Assessments. In *Judgment under uncertainty: Heuristics and biases*, edited by D. Kahneman, P. Slovic, and A. Tversky, 129-52. New York: Cambridge University Press.

Ross, L., Bierbrauer, G., and Hoffman, S. 1976. The role of attribution processes in conformity and dissent: Revisiting the Asch situation. *American Psychologist* 31:148-57.

Rubin, Z. 1985. Deceiving ourselves about deception: Comment on Smith and Richardson's "Amelioration of deception and harm in psychological research." *Journal of Personality and Social Psychology* 48:252-53.

―――――. 1983. Taking deception for granted. *Psychology Today*, March, 74-75.

―――――. 1970. Jokers wild in the lab. *Psychology Today*, December, 18-24.

Rubinstein, R. L. 1976. Review of Miale and Selzer, *The Nuremberg mind: The psychology of the Nazi leaders*. *Psychology Today*, July, 83-84.

Rychlak, J. F. 1977. The flight of an albatross. *Contemporary Psychology* 22: 710.

Sabini, J. P., and Silver, M. 1983. Dispositional versus situational interpretations of Milgram's obedience experiments: "The fundamental attribution error." *Journal for the Theory of Social Behavior* 13:147-54.

―――――. 1980. Destroying the innocent with a clear conscience: A sociophychology of the Holocaust. In *Survivors, victims, and perpetrators: Essays on the Nazi Holocaust*, edited by J. E. Dimsdale, 329-58. New York: Hemisphere.

Safer, M. A. 1980. Attributing evil to the subject, not the situation: Student reaction to Milgram's film on obedience. *Personality and Social Psychology Bulletin* 6:205-09.

Sanford, N., and Comstock, C., eds. 1971. *Sanctions for evil*. San Francisco: Jossey-Bass.

Savin, H. B. 1973. Professors and psychological researchers: Confliciting values in conflicting roles. *Cognition* 2:147-49.

Schachter, S. 1959. *The psychology of affiliation*. Stanford, Calif.: Stanford University Press.

Schlenker, B. R., and Forsyth, D. R. 1977. On the ethics of psychological research. *Journal of Experimental Social Psychology* 13:369-96.

Schuler, H. 1982. *Ethical problems in psychological research*. (translated by M. S. Woodruff and R. A. Wicklund). New York: Academic Press.

Sears, D. O., Freedman, J. L., and Peplau, L. A. 1985. *Social psychology*. 5th ed. Englewood Cliffs, N.J.: Prentice-Hall.

Selltiz, C., Wrightsman, L. S., and Cook, S. W. 1976. *Research methods in social relations*. 3rd ed. New York: Holt, Rinehart and Winston.

Selzer, M. 1983. Compliance or self-fulfillment? The case of Albert Speer. In *Compliant behavior: Beyond obedience to authority*, edited by M. Rosenbaum, 213-28. New York: Human Sciences Press.

————. 1977. The murderous mind. *New York Times Magazine*, November 27, 35-40.

Shalala, S. R. 1974. A study of various communication settings which produce obedience by subordinates to unlawful superior orders. Unpublished Ph.D. Dissertation, University of Kansas.

Shanab, M. E., and Yahya, K. A. 1978. A cross-cultural study of obedience. *Bulletin of the Psychonomic Society* 11:267-69.

————. 1977. A behavioral study of obedience in children. *Journal of Personality and Social Psychology* 35:530-36.

Sheridan, C. L., and King, R. G. 1972. Obedience to authority with an authentic victim. *Proceedings of the American Psychological Association*, pp. 165-66.

Sherif, M. 1936. *The psychology of social norms*. New York: Harper and Row.

Sieber, J. E., ed. 1982a. *The ethics of social research*. New York: Springer-Verlag.

Sieber, J. E. 1982b. Ethical dilemmas in social research. In *The ethics of social research: Surveys and experiments*, edited by J. E. Sieber, 1-29. New York: Springer-Verlag.

Simon, H. A. 1980. The behavioral and social sciences. *Science* 209:72-78.

Sjoberg, G., ed. 1967. *Ethics, Politics, and Social Research*. Cambridge, Mass.: Schenkman Publishing Company, Inc.

Smith, C. P., and Berard, S. P. 1982. Why are human subjects less concerned about ethically problematic research than human subjects committees? *Journal of Applied Social Psychology* 12:209-21.

Smith, M. B. 1976. Some perspectives on ethical/political issues in social science research. *Personality and Social Psychology Bulletin* 2:445-53.

Smith, S. S., and Richardson, D. 1983. Amelioration of deception and harm in psychological research: The important role of debriefing. *Journal of Personality and Social Psychology* 44:1075-82.

Snyder, M., and Cunningham, M. R. 1975. To comply or not comply: Testing the self-perception explanation of the "foot-in-the-door" phenomenon. *Journal of Personality and Social Psychology* 31:64-67.

Speer, A. 1970. *Inside the Third Reich*. New York: Macmillan.

Steiner, J. F. 1967. *Treblinka*. New York: Simon and Schuster.

Steiner, J. M. 1980. The SS yesterday and today: A sociopsychological view. In *Survivors, victims, and perpetrators: Essays on the Nazi Holocaust*, edited by J. E. Dimsdale, 405-56. New York: Hemisphere.

Stollak, G. 1967. Obedience and deception research. *American Psychologist* 22: 678.

Tavris, C. 1974. The frozen world of the familiar stranger: An interview with Stanley Milgram. *Psychology Today*, June, 71-79.

Taylor, S. E., and Fiske, S. T. 1978. Salience, attention, and attribution: Top of the head phenomena. In *Advances in experimental social psychology*, edited by L. Berkowitz, Vol. 11, 250-88. New York: Academic Press.

Tedeschi, J. T., Lindskold, S., and Rosenfeld, P. 1985. *Introduction to social psychology*. St. Paul, Minn.: West Publishing.

Thayer, S., and Saarni, C. 1975. Demand characteristics are everywhere (anyway): A comment on the Stanford prison experiment. *American Psychologist* 30: 1015-16.

Tilker, H. A. 1970. Socially responsible behavior as a function of observer responsibility and victim feedback. *Journal of Personality and Social Psychology* 14:95-100.

Vaughan, T. R. 1967. Governmental Intervention in Social Research: Political and Ethical Dimensions in the Wichita Jury Recordings. In *Ethics, politics, and social research*, edited by G. Sjoberg, 50-77. Cambridge, Mass.: Schenkman Publishing Company.

Walster, E. 1966. Assignment of responsibility for an accident. *Journal of Personality and Social Psychology* 3:73-79.

Warwick, D. P. 1982. Types of harm in social research. In *Ethical issues in social science research*, edited by T. Beauchamp, R. Faden, R. J. Wallace, Jr., and L. Walters, 101-24. Baltimore: The Johns Hopkins University Press.

Wenglinsky, M. 1974. Review of *Obedience to authority*. *Contemporary Sociology* 4:613-17.

West, S. G., Gunn, S. P., and Chernicky, P. 1975. Ubiquitous Watergate: An attributional analysis. *Journal of Personality and Social Psychology* 32:55-65.

Wheeler, L., Deci, E. L., Reis, H. T., and Zuckerman, M. 1978. *Interpersonal influence*. 2nd ed. Boston: Allyn and Bacon.

Wicker, A. W. 1969. Attitudes versus actions: The relationship of verbal to overt behavioral responses to attitude objects. *Journal of Social Issues* 25:41-78.

Wicklund, R. A., and Brehm, J. W. 1976. *Perspectives on cognitive dissonance.* Hillsdale, N.J.: Erlbaum.

Worchel, S., and Cooper, J. 1983. *Understanding social psychology*. 3rd ed. Homewood, Ill.: The Dorsey Press.

Wrightsman, L. S. 1974. The most important social psychological research in this generation? *Contemporary Psychology* 19:803-5.

Zee, H. 1983. The Guyana incident: Some group dynamic considerations. In *Compliant behavior: Beyond obedience to authority*, edited by M. Rosenbaum, 229-42. New York: Human Sciences Press.

Zimbardo, P. G. 1974. On "obedience to authority." *American Psychologist* 29: 566-67.

————. 1973. On the ethics of intervention in human psychological research: With special reference to the Stanford prison experiment. *Cognition* 2:243-56.

Zimbardo, P. G., Haney, C., Banks, W. C., and Jaffe, D. 1973. The mind is a formidable jailer: A Pirandellian prison. *New York Times Magazine*, April 8, 38-60.

Zuckerman, M., Lazzaro, M. M., and Waldgeir, D. 1979. Undermining effects of the foot-in-the-door technique with extrinsic rewards. *Journal of Applied Social Psychology* 9:292-96.

INDEX

Journal of Abnormal and Social Psychology, 1, 3, 37
Journal of Personality and Social Psychology, 37

Kristallnacht, 186

learner, role of, 38, 40
learning, effects of punishment on, 5
legitimate authority, 56; expectation of, 225
Lewinian field-theory position, 45
Licensed Mass Murder: A Socio-Psychological Study of some S S Killers, 194
limited contract, victim's, 49-50

malevolent authority, 80
mass murder, humankind's capacity for, 179
Max Planck Institute, 69
Milgram paradigm, expectations of, 13
Milgram's experiments: Baumrind's criticisms of, 90-93; ethical ramifications of, 89
Milgram's theoretical interpretation, 13
Milgram's theory: critical appraisals of, 242-248; endorsements of, 248-252
Milgram's work, criticism by Orne and Holland, 142-146
modeling delegitimization condition, 68, 69, 235
modeling influence, of researcher, 102
moral decision making, 180
moral failure, 45, 46; obedience as, 121
moral judgment, level of as predictor of action, 240
moral relevance, of obedience experiments, 179
moral restraints, killing and, 196

moral responsibility: destruction of the innocent and, 187-189; vs. technical responsibility, 188
My Lai massacre, 98, 150, 181, 182, 196, 197, 213, 218, 245, 246

National Science Foundation (NSF), 40, 48, 93, 138
Nazi hierarchy, psychodiagnostic impression of, 191
Nazi Rorschach record, 211
New York Times, 251
New York Times Book Review, 243
New York Times Magazine, 208
negative emotion, 12, 82
non-malevolent authority, 80
normality thesis, 184, 185, 189, 190, 191, 192, 194, 195, 209, 212, 218, 248, 252, 254; vs. pathology thesis, 180
norm of internality, 23
North American Aerospace Defense Command (NORAD), 199
Nuremberg Mind: Psychology of the Nazi Leaders, The, 204
Nuremberg trials, 184, 191, 227

Obedience, 76
obedience: antecedents of, 233; to authority, 21-22; behavioral study of, 2-13; vs. conformity, 58; defined, 3; destructive, 61; experimental analysis of, role-playing methodology, 164; factors responsible for underestimation of, 35; as feature of human interaction, 3; harmful, 60, 67, 127, 140, 169; incidence of, 35; as learned social response, 75; overlearning of, 224; political or cultural factors relevant to, 68; potentially destructive effect of, 98; and psychological administrative violence, 160; social psychological context

ABOUT THE AUTHOR

Arthur G. Miller received his Ph.D. from Indiana University (1967). He is Professor of Psychology at Miami University (Oxford, Ohio), where he teaches courses in social psychology, prejudice, and social influence. He edited *The Social Psychology of Psychological Research* (Free Press, 1972), an anthology focusing upon methodological and ethical problems in research with human subjects. He also edited *In the Eye of the Beholder*: *Contemporary Issues in Stereotyping* (Praeger, 1982). His research interests include attributional biases, the perseverance of first impressions, and emotional and cognitive processes in stigma and victimization.

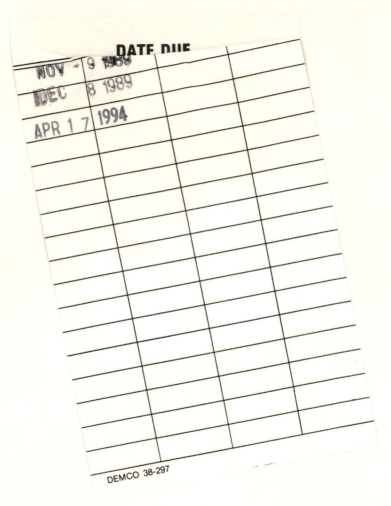